Dedicated to my teacher
and to all who seek to dive beneath the surface of life

The following account is a work of fiction based on my real-life experiences with my real-life teacher, Samvara, a Mystic SCUBA diving Buddhist monk.

These teachings of enlightenment, mysticism, and diving were all conveyed to me by Samvara. They are an offering to others who, whether they realize it yet or not, seek the exquisite, ecstatic truth of enlightenment. May you be relieved of your mental tensions, confusions, frustrations and depressions, and come to know this: Everything is perfect and you are completely free.

MYSTIC SCUBA

MY ADVENTURES DIVING INTO ENLIGHTENMENT

Vanessa Vitri

MY DIVE PLAN FOR LIFE

I've always loved the ocean. As a young girl, I would spend long sunburned summer days splashing in the waves on the beaches near my home in Northern California. The surf and tides and the marine animals and plants formed an exploratory haven, a continuous source of peace and happiness for me.

When I was eight, I joined the Amador Polar Bears swim team. I was shy and reluctant at first, so my mother had to bribe me into it by paying me $25 for the first season. Soon after I began, I fell in love with swimming. I spent the next seven years winning races at the weekly Saturday swim meets.

In my teens and early 20's, my love for the ocean often brought me to my family's small vacation home on one of Hawaii's outer islands. During my college years at Stanford and then in between internships working for NGOs in Africa, I would withdraw into my ocean refuge for extended retreats.

During my stays in Hawaii, I would often spend early mornings on the east side of the island. I had a favorite secluded cove where the sunrises were exquisite. I would step into the cool morning water just as the sun began to come up over the horizon. I would swim out and watch the sun rise up from the ocean, creating dazzling colors in the gentle morning waves.

Shortly after my 24th birthday, I had come back from Ethiopia where I was working with an NGO and an order of Mother Teresa's nuns to help disabled orphans and the poorest families in Addis Ababa. The extreme poverty and inequality that I had witnessed and the beautiful friendships I had made compelled me to take action.

I wanted to help the street kids and young mothers I had become close to by sending them money to start small businesses so they could support themselves. Since no aid organization I knew of would help them with this, I wanted to help. This, however, would require a big change in my professional life. I wanted to give myself enough time to consider the direction of my future, so I planned on staying on retreat in Hawaii for a full month.

My parents and their good friends Tim and Anne were already visiting our Hawaii house. They had been on vacation for a week when I arrived. I was excited about joining them after having been away for so long. Our reunion brought me welcome feelings of familiar comfort.

I spent the second week of their vacation with them in a similar fashion to many of our past vacations together. We would take long strolls through the lush botanical gardens. We would stay up late eating one of my mother's famous macadamia nut pies, talking about my recent travel adventures, my father's latest construction invention, Amador County politics, and the new litter of puppies my mother was raising. My father and I would often SCUBA dive at a popular site in the west. On their last day before returning home, we would always visit a scenic vista on one of the high volcanic mountains overlooking the sea.

As my parents and friends got in line at the airport, I hugged them and told them that I would see them in three weeks. I told them that I felt I might be making some big changes in that time. They wished me well in my deliberations over my future and were off.

Later that afternoon I stood at the volcanic shore with the waves leaping up at my feet. I watched as the beautiful Hawaiian sun began to set. The sky was a wondrous mixture of pink hues and darkening blues.

My mind was restless, burdened with a multitude of pressing concerns. *What am I doing with my life?* I thought. *Is it hopeless for me to try to make a difference? Is there really something I can do? Do I have what it takes to do it?*

I looked to the ocean and asked aloud, "What's next for me in life?" I stood in an unsettled silence, aching to know. Confused about my path, I watched as the glimmering waves rolled and crashed on the rocks and the sun slipped away.

DIVING DARSHAN

The next morning I decided to go SCUBA diving in my favorite spot on the west side of the island. As I approached the parking area, I could see that the seas were calm and clear. Since this was a popular location for snorkeling tourists, kayakers, and divers alike, finding parking required some extra time. Once I parked my car, I quickly donned my wet suit. I owned my own SCUBA gear and rented tanks at a dive shop about half an hour away from my house.

I had been SCUBA diving for a couple of years, thanks to a friend in San Francisco who fascinated me with stories of his diving experiences and compelled me to try it. I found a local dive shop and convinced my father to take the introductory SCUBA class with me. During the 2-week course we learned about using the equipment and how to safely SCUBA dive. Once I got past the initial awkwardness of wearing and operating all the gear, I fell in love with diving just as I'd fallen in love with swimming as a kid. Being able to spend an hour underwater observing marine life and the ocean world was wondrous to me. After becoming a certified SCUBA diver, I would dive several times per week with my father or friends when in Hawaii.

After turning on my air, buckling into my gear, and securing my camera's strap around my right wrist, I began to walk from my car over the sand and rocks to the water's edge. There were over a dozen tourists lying about in the sand. I had to adjust my walking path to avoid two children playing with a Frisbee.

At the water's edge, I applied anti-fog spray to my dive mask to ensure clear visibility during my dive. After rinsing my mask in the ocean waves, I put it on, and then I inhaled through my regulator to test the airway.

"Excuse me, Miss, what do you think you're doing?" I heard someone call from behind me. I looked over my shoulder and saw a darkly tanned man who looked like a local sitting cross-legged in a wetsuit. He was about 20 feet up the beach from me, sitting back from the water. There was a fair-skinned, younger man by his side and two sets of assembled SCUBA equipment next to them.

I was taken a little off guard and didn't answer. The man continued, "Diving alone is dangerous. If you don't mind sitting over there," he pointed to a large rock not far from me, "for 20 to 30 minutes, when I'm done with my student, I would be happy to supervise your dive."

The younger man looked surprised when his companion offered to supervise my dive, but then quickly gave me a reassuring and supportive smile.

A little embarrassed, I nodded in agreement and stepped back to the rock that he had pointed to. As I leaned back to rest my tank on the tall, wide rock, the man smiled at me and nodded. Then he turned around and began speaking to the younger man in a quiet voice. A moment later, they were both sitting completely still and quiet.

I immediately began to go over the incident in my head. *Did I do something really wrong?* I wondered. I knew that it is always a good idea to dive with a buddy, but I didn't have a buddy and I was so familiar with this dive site that I felt no danger. I had seen other divers dive here alone in the past, and I had done a few solo dives here before as well. *Why did that guy stop me? Was he a Divemaster?*

I looked over at the pair again. They were sitting in silence with their eyes closed and in unusually erect posture. Their hands were resting palms-down on their crossed legs. It looked like they were meditating. I had seen some other breath-hold divers meditate and do yoga prior to diving, so this sight wasn't unusual for me.

The local man had a neatly shaved head and looked like a suntanned Asian, as many Hawaiians do. He seemed bright and serene as he sat in meditation. The pale younger man looked like a mainlander. He, too, seemed to be deep in concentration as he meditated.

But why did he stop me? I wondered again. *It's not like it's that big of a deal to dive alone. He seems like he might just be a bossy, uptight, know-it-all. I wouldn't want to go diving with someone like that. It wouldn't be any fun,* I determined. *I don't have to listen to some guy on the beach anyway! I can just go in now while he's not looking. I have a good air consumption rate. I'll just stay under for as long as I can and he'll be gone by the time I'm back on land.*

I stood up from the rock, put on my fins and quietly entered the water. I kicked straight out toward the horizon till I was far from shore. I then halted, floating in the soothing sapphire waves to catch my breath. Before starting my descent, I looked back to shore where I could see the two men still sitting in meditation. I pressed the release button of my low-pressure inflator hose and descended beneath the blue seas. As I neared the coral bottom at 50 feet, I added air to my buoyancy control vest so that I could hover, neutrally buoyant.

I began looking around for my favorite local visitors to this site: dolphins. Unable to see any dolphins, I began swimming toward a group of large craggy coral heads. Several yellow tangs ambled around the finger corals. I floated for a couple of minutes watching a rainbow colored parrotfish pecking at algae-covered coral. I continued forward toward some larger eroding coral formations.

The water was cool and refreshing. The visibility was excellent; I was able to see over 100 feet in any direction. I watched as the many reef fish danced about the hard corals. Then something caught my eye below me. It was an unusual red fish. I descended down the sloping terrain to a huddled mass of large coral heads.

I was now at a depth of 70 feet. The red fish I saw was a rare Hawaiian lionfish floating quite still and low next to the coral. I had never seen one before and knew that not many divers are lucky enough to come across this unusual fish. Luckily, I had a camera.

I moved closer, under an eroded coral overhang, to get a better look. The lionfish was dark red with white stripes and poisonous spines like beautiful feathered wings. It sat there almost motionless, suspended in the water. I gazed in wonder at the rare and exquisite creature.

I moved in closer and lifted the camera just in front of my dive mask. Looking through the camera's viewfinder, I targeted the lionfish. Its white stripes glowed in a beautiful pattern. While holding a large volume of air in my lungs to steady myself for the shot, I kicked forward with my left fin slightly until the lionfish filled the frame.

Just then, the lionfish jetted forward toward me, turning out and extending its poisonous spines! A sting from a lionfish spine could be extremely painful and hurt for days. The lionfish's sudden movement surprised me. I reactively jerked, snapping a shot with my camera as the lionfish jolted at me. The flash from the camera darkened my vision. I sprang backwards, pushing off of the dead coral with my hands and kicking with my fins. I evaded the lionfish's spines, but immediately crashed into the coral overhang behind me.

The crash spun me to the left. As I turned, my regulator hose caught on the edge of the coral head and was pulled from my mouth. A second later when I stopped spinning, my regulator was free-flowing air bubbles behind my head and all around me. Dropping the camera, I desperately grabbed for my regulator, but could not reach it. I tried to spin around to see what it was stuck on, but my buoyancy control vest was also stuck on the coral overhang I had slammed into. I was stuck! I had no air! I kicked hard, trying to pull myself free from the coral, but didn't budge. I started really feeling the need for air. I began to panic. If I couldn't get free, I would inhale water, and drown! My one distinct thought was, *I can't die now. I haven't finished what I need to do in life!* I thrashed about in desperation, but my efforts were useless. I could not get free! I could not get my air!

Just then, I saw another regulator before my eyes. A hand quickly placed that regulator in my mouth and cleared it of water with a blast of air so that I could breathe. I inhaled deeply. I then saw that it was the hand of the man who had warned me about diving alone. He was geared up in his SCUBA equipment and I was breathing from his alternate air source.

He moved to my right and quickly dislodged my buoyancy control vest and regulator from the coral entrapment. He fiddled with my regulator to stop it from free flowing. He gave me the OK sign. I took a few more deep breaths on his regulator before giving the OK sign back.

He then gave me the ascent signal, raising his thumb, and we started up slowly. He watched his dive computer closely to keep a safe ascent rate. We continued buddy-breathing while safely ascending to the surface.

At the surface, he inflated my buoyancy control vest so that I could easily float.

"You're OK," the man said as a statement, not a question. I nodded, though I was very shaken up. "Did you inhale any water?" he asked.

"No," I answered, breathing heavily.

"Good," he said, observing me carefully, "and I can see that you're not coughing. Even a little ocean water in your lungs could cause damage to them."

The man and I slowly made our way back to shore. After exiting the water, we set down our SCUBA equipment and both sat in the sand. I was quite rattled. "Breathe deeply," the man said, gesturing calmly with his hands. I noticed that I was breathing very quickly. I took a moment to breathe more deeply and compose myself.

I was very grateful for his help. "Thank you so much! I would have drowned for sure if you hadn't popped out of nowhere."

"There's no need for thanks," he said. "It wasn't your karma to die."

Although that struck me as a peculiar statement, I went on to ask, "How did you know I was there?" With my breath more controlled now, I continued, "I mean, in the whole cove, how did you know to look for me in that exact spot?"

"The ocean told me where you were," he answered.

I looked at him quizzically, waiting to hear the punch line of his joke. He said, "Please, let me introduce myself. My name is Sam. I am a Buddhist monk." He pressed both of his hands together below his chin and bowed.

I giggled as if that was the punch line, but he seemed quite serious. I quickly gained my composure and said, "I'm Vanessa."

He smiled, adding, "Pleased to meet you."

"Are you really a Buddhist monk?"

"Yes, I am."

"And you're a SCUBA diver too?"

"Yes."

"That's funny, I've never heard of a SCUBA diving Buddhist monk before," I said.

"Many of the monks in my Buddhist school practice SCUBA diving as an integral part of our spiritual practice," he responded.

"Wow, that's…interesting," I said, somewhat bewildered.

We sat in silence for a moment. The monk, with a calm smile on his face, reminded me to breathe deeply. "Just breathe and relax for a while," he said. "Focus on your breath becoming deep and calm."

I did as Sam suggested. After a minute or so, my feelings of being rattled seemed to subside. Sam nodded to me, acknowledging my calm breathing. I started wondering about what Sam said to me earlier. I also felt a little uncomfortable sitting in silence, so I thought I'd ask a question.

"Did you say that the ocean told you where I was diving when I was in trouble?"

Sam answered plainly, "Yes." I nodded, but the idea completely puzzled me. Then Sam reminded me to focus on my breathing, saying "deeply and calmly," while gesturing slowly with his hands. Although I was clearly perplexed by Sam's answer, he simply remained silent, gesturing for me to breathe slowly with his hands from time to time.

After a couple more minutes of deep breathing, I became very relaxed. Though I had almost died 15 minutes ago, I now felt calm and peaceful as I sat attending to my breath. Sam ended his slow breathing hand gestures. It was now very warm. Sam unzipped his wetsuit, revealing a beautifully carved manta ray pendant. It was pearly gold in color and hung from a thin black leather necklace around his neck. I was getting hot in the tropical sun, so I unzipped my wetsuit too.

As we rested in the sand, I became curious about Sam. "What kind of Buddhism do you do? Zen or something?"

"I am an ordained monk of a Tibetan Vajrayana Buddhist lineage," Sam answered. "And I do incorporate some Zen observances in my practice as well."

Sam's English was eloquent and unaccented. "Are you from Tibet?" I asked.

"No," Sam answered, shaking his head, "I was born here in America."

I examined Sam's face. It exhibited the kindness and innocence that I'd imagine in a Buddhist monk, and his smile had a hint of whimsy. Though it was plain that Sam was my senior, it was difficult to guess his age. His skin was golden brown in color. His neatly shaved head was round and suntanned. He had dark, almond shaped eyes that flickered in the sunlight over his dimpled cheeks and round nose. His intermittent smile revealed a set of perfectly straight pearly teeth. He had no robes to be seen and looked quite comfortable in his wetsuit.

What Sam said about my karma began to stir my curiosity. "So, did you know that it was not my karma to die before I went into the water?" I asked.

"Of course!" he exclaimed. He leaned in slightly, "That's why I warned you not to go in alone, and helped you when you were in trouble."

"Well, I must have some really bad karma to get into this situation," I said.

"Not at all," Sam responded. "Actually your near-death experience on this dive was very good karma."

"How could that possibly be?"

"If you didn't get into this trouble, then we wouldn't have an opportunity to have this conversation. This conversation and meeting are the results of very good karma. It is what they call in India *darshan*, a meeting with enlightenment."

"Oh, I see," I said politely. "Then I suppose you're right." I was somewhat oblivious as to what Sam really meant, but nodded thoughtfully.

"You see," he continued, "karma is the universal law of cause and effect within your own mind. Your karma results in forming your awareness field, the screen through which you view all of life. The purity of your awareness field determines the possibilities of life that you are conscious of in any given moment. Karma results from your thoughts. Do you understand?"

"Sure," I said. I had heard about karma before from various people and books. I rattled off, "Karma is when you do something good for others and something good happens to you, or if you do something bad to others and something bad happens to you."

Sam shook his head, saying, "I'm not just repeating something that you already know. Your New Age definition of karma is so simplistic that it prevents you from understanding how karma works in the transformation of your awareness field and the evolution of your consciousness."

Sam continued, "If you gave away a million dollars to the poor, it doesn't mean that you have accrued good karma. Just as if you rob someone, it doesn't mean that you have received bad karma. It is quite common that what seems like a good action actually accrues bad karma. And it is possible that what seems like a bad action results in good karma. What determines your karma is the purity of your thoughts and the intentions that precede your thoughts."

What Sam said intrigued me. I thought about my plans to send money to the street kids and mothers I'd met in Ethiopia so that they could start small businesses. *That would be giving money to the poor*, I thought to myself. *That's "good", isn't it?*

I reflected on the subject some more. *It couldn't be possible to get bad karma for giving money to poor people. Could it?* I wondered. In light of the contradiction Sam had introduced, I found myself frustrated.

"Yes," Sam said nodding, as if he were reading my very thoughts, "I'm talking about your actual life here, not just philosophy."

Tightening my brow, I argued, "Well, how can robbing someone be good karma?"

"It's simple," Sam said, "if robbing someone serves the evolution of the spirit, then it is good karma."

I shook my head. Now the contradiction was no longer interesting; it was downright aggravating. "Stealing from another couldn't be spiritually evolving!" I protested. "I was robbed once in my first apartment in San Francisco. The robber took an aquamarine ring that my mother gave me. It was a family heirloom. The robber also took my stereo system, which was a graduation present, my computer with all of my college papers on it... not to mention my sense of security! I had to break my lease and move in with a girlfriend." I continued to shake my head in disagreement, "Anyone who takes what's not theirs from another is getting bad karma as far as I'm concerned."

Sam listened closely to my argument and then asked, "But what about Robin Hood? He robbed people. He took what was not his, but for noble reasons, right?"

I agreed, grudgingly. I was still frustrated, but he had a point.

Sam continued, "In a land where the rich oppressed the poor, Robin Hood employed thievery to right the wrongs of the time and bring balance to the country. He robbed a few so that he could help a great many. Though he did something that was against the law and generally considered to be bad, he did it for honorable and virtuous reasons. His robbing of others was spiritually evolving for him."

"Well, if you look at it that way, robbing a few oppressors to help many innocent people could be good," I said, agreeing.

"Exactly," Sam said, "if you look at it that way." He paused for a moment, raising his pointer finger, and then continued, "There are many ways to look at anything, but only one truth. Despite anyone's complex justifications and arguments of what is good and what is bad, the truth is always very simple. What really determines your karma is the purity of your thoughts. Good karma is the result of thoughts and intentions that reflect the *dharma*, the truth, that which is pure and serves life. Bad karma is the result of thoughts and intentions that obstruct truth and are impure, serving only the self."

"I get it," I said. "Things can be flipped around. What seems like it is bad could be good if your thoughts about it are pure and noble."

"Yes, that's it," Sam said. "In the same way, the person who robbed you could have had pure and noble intentions, thinking only of serving life while taking your valuable possessions."

"What?" I exclaimed. "The person who robbed me was no noble gentleman thief! He took my most valuable things, not just monetarily valuable but emotionally valuable. How can stealing a ring that means only a couple hundred dollars to him when he pawns it—and yet is priceless to me—be good karma?" I folded my arms and shook my head, thinking about how terrible being robbed made me feel. "How could the person who robbed me of my feeling of security in my own home be spiritually elevated by it?" I asked indignantly.

Sam responded, "I'm not saying that the person who robbed you was acting in accordance with the dharma. Generally people who bring themselves to carry out acts like these are filled with desire, greed, and tremendously selfish impurity."

I stopped shaking my head and continued to listen to Sam.

He went on, "But what if it's just as you said a moment ago, things can be flipped around. What seems like it is bad could be good if the robber's intentions were pure and life-serving."

I frowned.

"What if the money the robber got from hocking your family ring meant more to him than just a couple hundred dollars? What if it meant that he was able to buy three months of an expensive medication for his terminally ill mother that reduced her tremendous physical pain and extended her life? What if he was uneducated, poor, and unable to penetrate the medical bureaucracy to get any assistance for his mother? What if the only way he knew how to help her was to rob from you to lessen his mother's suffering?"

My frown relaxed. I began to explore new feelings of compassion for the robber that I had previously resented. "Surely if that were the case, things would be different," I speculated. "If I had met him and understood his situation, I'd have given him the ring, my stereo, computer, and even more to help him."

Sam continued, "The reason I'm talking about the person who robbed you is because it is very real to you. It was easy for you to say that things can be flipped around and what seems bad could be good before I mentioned a cause of suffering that is very personal to you. As I said before, I'm not just chitchatting about philosophical ideas with you. I'm talking about the reality of your life."

I nodded, paused for a moment, and then said, halfway jokingly, "Well, now I don't know whether I should be angry at the robber for stealing my things or happy that the robber was able to meet his noble needs by using my valuables."

"So you would be happy about it, if you found out that the robber really was using your valuables to buy lifesaving medications for his mother?" Sam asked.

"Sure."

"And you would be angry and resentful if the robber was just using your valuables to gamble or buy drugs and alcohol?"

"Yes, that would make me pretty upset," I answered. "It depends on whether the robber was doing something good or something bad."

"You're very stuck in a dualistic point of view," Sam remarked, laughing and shaking his head. "Life is incongruous, yet perfect. Life itself is the complete truth. Your obscured viewpoint incorrectly categorizes life into dual opposites, such as good and bad. Yet good and bad are only your transient interpretations of the complete truth of life. The truth is that there are good and bad in life. And that good and bad are the same truth."

Sam paused, stretched his open palm out toward the ocean, and continued, "Beyond your surface views of good and bad is the complete ecstatic truth of life. Instead of judging things as good or bad, look to the essence of life. See the extraordinary truth that pervades all dualistic circumstances such as good and bad, win and loss, life and death."

I raised my eyebrows, taking in the curiously remarkable ideas Sam had voiced.

"Besides," Sam went on, "it doesn't matter whether the robber's intentions and actions were noble or selfish; what really matters to your karma are your reactions to being robbed. If you get angry at the robber, then your thoughts become impure and selfish. Resentment draws your thoughts away from the dharma. Being upset at the robber only results in bad karma for you."

I paused for a moment, and then said, "I think I know what you mean, Sam. Two wrongs don't make a right."

"Again," Sam responded, "the saying you just quoted is dependent on judging things in duality as right or wrong. What I want you to see is that purity leads to a greater awareness of life. So instead of 'Two wrongs don't make a right,' I would say, 'Two impurities of thought don't make good karma.'

"Yet I'm really not saying anything is wrong or right, good or bad. I'm saying that there are things that evolve you and things that hinder your awareness of life. I'm telling you that these things are not things, but thoughts. The purity of one's thoughts creates a more enlightened outlook on life.

"The problem is that most people don't think with purity most of the time. Most people's thoughts and intentions are tremendously mixed with selfishness. If everybody thought pure thoughts that serve life, there would be peace, prosperity, and an enlightened society."

"This is very interesting," I said, "but on the other side, how can giving money to the poor be bad karma? That's not selfish or impure."

"Well, for example," Sam stated, "what if a rich country gave millions and millions of dollars to a poor country in order to boost future trade relations, but the leader of the poor country is a dictator who uses the money to oppress many innocent people? Then the great sum of money given to a poor country would not serve life."

"I agree," I said. This really rang true to me. I had felt for a long time that many of the dollars spent by my country to aid other countries were not spent to serve life, but to serve a political agenda.

Sam continued, "Also, when an individual or organization defines itself as 'the one' who gives money or aid, it may establish itself as the 'savior' of the community. It may thereby institute itself into the situation, adding hierarchy, bureaucracy, and aggravating problems. It may even stand in the way of aid when it does not enhance its personal ideals, or falls outside of its narrow views."

That's true, I thought. One of my frustrations working in Africa was that aid organizations sometimes imposed a bureaucratic barrier between outside aid and helping people.

I recalled a young woman I had met at a health clinic I was volunteering for. She was a mother with a young daughter from a small village on the outskirts of Addis Ababa. Her husband had left and they were on their own. She and her daughter would walk five miles each way to the city center to get food from an aid organization that distributed emergency rations every day.

Every time she picked up her food, she asked if instead she could have a small loan so that she could buy a goat. If she had a goat, she wouldn't have to walk into town everyday with her child and would be able to be productive in her village. The aid organization would not make her a loan, although they had fed her and her child every day for four years. Loans for village development were outside of their mandate and not in their policies.

It seemed to me that this woman was not being helped with her root problem, and instead her problems were being perpetuated. Seeing an obvious solution, I gave her $25. With the money, she bought a goat. No longer having to walk six miles in and out of town with her child everyday, she started working in her community's garden growing vegetables, traded goat's milk to neighbors for eggs, and was able to nourish and provide for her child.

"I see what you mean," I said.

We sat in silence for a moment. My thoughts then immediately turned to leaving. I figured that I'd better be getting home. I was getting hungry and wanted lunch. It was really awesome of Sam to rescue me and our conversation was strangely interesting as well, but I didn't feel like dragging it on.

I put my hand on my dive gear and was just about to tell Sam that it was nice meeting him and that I should be going when he interjected, "No. I don't think you see what I mean at all!"

He leaned forward and said, "What I mean is that every thought you've ever had brought you here today to dive. Every thought you've ever had led you to be stuck underwater to face death directly. It is because of your thoughts that you had the good karma to be rescued by me. There are no coincidences, there is no such thing as chance, and everything that happens to you is a direct result of your field of attention."

Growing irritated, I retorted, "OK, I guess I don't see what you mean! I'm not sure what karma is. I mean, I thought I understood what you were talking about for a while, but this is getting a little frustrating." I wanted to leave.

Sam pressed on, "Karma is that you were stuck on a coral reef with your regulator free-flowing behind you. Karma is that you panicked. Karma is that you were not aware that you could have reached your own alternate air source."

Sam's words struck me like a thunderbolt! *He's right*, I thought. *If I hadn't panicked after being unable to reach my regulator, I could have reached my alternate air source for sure.* My alternate air source was a second regulator affixed to the front center of my buoyancy vest for a buddy to use if they ran out of air. *Why didn't I think to use it?* My irritation vanished and I listened closely to Sam.

Sam continued, "Karma is that you were not aware that you could have unbuckled from your buoyancy vest, retrieved your regulator, and freed yourself from the coral. Karma is the result of your thoughts. Karma creates your field of awareness, the possibilities of life that you are conscious of in any given moment."

"So because of my karma, I was unable to apprehend as an option that I should try to get my alternate air source?" I asked.

"That's right," Sam said. "Every thought that you have ever had led you to a field of awareness where the karma results in that particular circumstance, your precise awareness of possibilities, and the exact outcome."

"But how do my thoughts create my field of awareness?" I asked.

"Your field of awareness can be said to be like your diving mask," Sam replied. "Just as you view the undersea world through your diving mask, you view the world and all of life through your field of awareness. Now, think of pure thoughts, thoughts that are selfless and positive, as having a cool and dry effect on your diving mask. Consider impure thoughts, thoughts that are selfish and negative, to have a warm and humid effect on your diving mask.

"The nature of your mask is to show you all of life. When your thoughts are pure, there is nothing to obstruct your view of life. When your thoughts are impure, the warmth and humidity begins to fog your mask and prevent you from seeing all of life. The foggier your mask gets, the less you can see the options of life. There are always unlimited opportunities for life, happiness, illumination, and enlightenment. Yet with impure thoughts and a fogged up mask you can't see them."

I was now really beginning to see what Sam was talking about. My understanding of karma was no longer just vague and high-level; it had become more personal, deep, and complex.

Sam continued, "Through thousands and thousands of pure and impure thoughts, you have conditioned your mind, your awareness field, in a particular way—the way you see the world. The way you see the world is flawed, obscured, and limited. Your panic and inability to remember your alternate air source are signs of your karma, a foggy mask."

"But it was also my karma to be saved by you?" I asked.

"Yes," Sam said. "You are a seeker. You seek greater awareness. From a place deep down inside you, a place you may not even be aware of yet, you sense a constriction, a tension. You met me for liberation from this tension. Your karma brought you to face and learn about death because only that would jolt you enough to pay attention to what I have to say."

I had to admit, the only reason I was listening to Sam was because he had just saved my life. Normally, I would never listen so deeply to the subject of spirituality, especially from someone I didn't really know. I grew up as an atheist and disliked some of the oppressive aspects and dogmas of organized religion. I also thought most Eastern spirituality seemed kind of spacey.

Sam continued, "Death is a powerful ally for a seeker of awareness. When you are more aware of death, you are more aware of life. This is why you love the ocean. This is why you love SCUBA diving. The ocean wields the power of death. When you enter the ocean you enter a power that can cause your death. You must always respect the ocean's power."

Sam went on, "Every time you SCUBA dive you enter a powerful mystery, beyond the capacity of human existence. When you SCUBA dive you put yourself in the imminent possibility of death. You dive into death so that you can experience more life. Your experience of almost drowning has brought your attention pointedly to death so that you can become aware of life more deeply, so that you can learn about the tension within you which almost caused your death."

"But I don't feel any tension," I said.

Sam replied, "Oh, but there is a deep tension within you. You are so conditioned by this tension that you think it's normal. You're like a fish who was born in a fish tank. You think that the small space in the tank is all there is. But deep down inside, you know that something is wrong. There is a conflict within you and you wish to be free from it. But you need help to release this tension and resolve the conflict. That is why we have met in this way. Our meeting is your good karma and affords you the opportunity to elevate your consciousness and explore the infinite seas beyond the constraints of your tension."

I looked at Sam, a little bewildered.

He continued, "If you were ill and had the good karma to have access to healthcare, you would find yourself with a doctor for healing. And if you wanted to improve your SCUBA diving skills, if you had the drive to learn and the wherewithal to afford it, you would find yourself with a

SCUBA instructor for guidance. It is the same way with spirituality. When you really want or need instruction for your spiritual health, advancement, and mastery, you will find yourself with an instructor one way or another.

"You see," Sam said, "the reason you almost died was because your mind is too tense. I can show you what I mean by helping you relieve some of the tension that has manifested as pain in your physical body."

"But I don't have any pain," I responded, though my shoulders and neck were a little stiff.

"You'll see a difference once this physical tension is released," Sam said. "Let me show you what I mean. Sit up comfortably for a couple of minutes and consider the colors of healing."

I wasn't quite sure what Sam meant, but I agreed to try. I sat up straight, squinting my eyes in the light of the bright sun. Sam began to explain, "There are specific sets of colors used for healing by practitioners skilled in Chinese medicine. The colors red, white, green, yellow, blue and black make up one of these sets. Simply envisioning these colors in the proper sequence will create a very beneficial healing effect. Close your eyes. Relax and envision these colors as I call them out."

I closed my eyes as Sam slowly spoke the colors, "Red…white…green… yellow…blue…black."

I tried to imagine the colors as Sam spoke. Rather than relaxing, I immediately noticed an extremely painful point of tension next to my left shoulder blade. My shoulders and neck were often a little tense, but this was much more vivid than what I was used to. The pain was so intense that I couldn't focus on anything else.

Noticing me wince, Sam asked, "What's hurting?" I explained the sharp pain in my shoulder blade. "Focus a little harder," Sam said. "Try to envision the colors as I say them." Sam continued slowly speaking the names of the colors.

I tried to imagine the colors, but the pain consumed my attention. Then suddenly, it was completely gone. My whole body unknotted itself and I became completely relaxed. I sat comfortably for another minute, until Sam said softly, "OK, that's enough for today. You did very well. How do you feel?"

"I feel relaxed," I said as I rotated my shoulders and neck. "That really loosened up my left side. I didn't even notice how tense it was before."

Sam nodded and said, "Come meet with me again tomorrow at the same time. I will teach you the art of Mystic SCUBA so that you can learn to release the deeper tensions of your mind."

I shrugged my shoulders and said OK with a half nod.

Sam smiled and said, "Now I have to be off. I must take my student to the airport." He pressed both his hands together under his chin and bowed, then departed.

I watched him walk over to an orange Jeep Wrangler. Sitting in the Jeep was the young man I had seen him with earlier. Before I could get my wetsuit off, Sam had disassembled his dive gear, loaded it into the Jeep and taken off.

THE UNSEEN-WORLD

Later that evening, as I repacked my SCUBA gear into my car in preparation for diving the next day with Sam, I sighed. I thought to myself, *I'm not sure if I really want to learn all this stuff Sam, the monk, is telling me about. He seems like a pretty interesting guy, and that stuff he told me about karma was thought-provoking, but I really came here to figure out if I should make a change in my professional life, so I could make enough money to help fund small businesses in Ethiopia. All this karma and spiritual SCUBA just seems to be a bit of a distraction from what I really want to do.*

I remembered a particular class discussion from the Community Organizing course I'd taken in college. The professor had written a number of activities on the board and asked us to respond with whether we thought they would improve the world. The list included opening a homeless shelter, authoring new healthcare policies, and, incongruously to me, meditating in a monastery for a year. When we got to the monastery line, only one student and the professor raised their hands to say that they believed meditating in a monastery would impact the world in a positive way. I was alongside the majority of students, thinking, *How the heck is meditation going to help the world? New healthcare policies definitely will help, but what does meditation have to do with social change and justice?*

Closing the trunk, I decided, *I'm not going to go back to the west side dive site to meet Sam tomorrow. I'm going to wake up early and swim out to watch the sunrise in my favorite cove. That's what I need—a quiet place to reflect, not a bunch of spiritual mumbo-jumbo.*

After a light dinner, I opened up my laptop and computer programming book for a serious study session. For the last month or so in Ethiopia, I'd been considering getting a job in technology once I came home. I knew programming paid well, and I'd taken a few classes when I was at Stanford and liked the challenging nature of coding. One of my good friends had majored in computer science, and loved her career working as a programmer for a Silicon Valley start-up. She'd offered to tutor me in the popular technologies that commanded high salaries. I'd brought the reference books and tutorials she recommended along with me to Hawaii.

I was motivated to change my career path from aid work to computer science because of an eye-opening experience. A few months earlier, I had interviewed dozens of women from the poorest families in Addis Ababa about how the NGO I was working with could better help them. Nearly all of the women were illiterate and were supporting their children, anywhere from two to eight kids, on the 50 cents a day they could earn carrying firewood down a mountain, crushing rocks to use to build the city streets, or washing richer families' clothes.

In spite of their lack of formal education, when I asked these women the open-ended question of what services they would like to receive, two-thirds of them instantly responded that they needed money to start their own businesses. Some of them had completely clear business plans that they explained to me in detail, telling me exactly how much money they would need as start up capital to fund their ideas. I was awed by their entrepreneurial spirit and completely humbled by the fact that $100 could transform an entire family's life.

I had read about microfinance as a strategy for true poverty alleviation when I was in college. Microfinance programs give loans to individuals who, because of their extreme poverty, would not qualify for credit in traditional financial institutions. Microfinance is often targeted at women in developing countries. The loan recipients are often organized into teams and are all responsible for making sure that the others in their group pay back their loans, which helps ensure everyone's success in business. Through my coursework I had learned on a theoretical level the way microfinance could change social structures. I knew that microfinance had the power to break cycles of poverty and directly address the social inequalities that bothered me so much.

When you empower mothers, you are helping their entire families and changing communities. Their children are able to go to school and also learn to be successful by watching their moms succeed. When I was interviewing the mothers in Addis Ababa, women who had befriended me during the months I was working for the NGO helping them, the need for microfinance became deeply personal to me. During every interview, I couldn't stop thinking that if I really wanted to help these women and their children, I should use the social situation I was born into as an American and Stanford graduate to earn as much money as I could, so that I could afford to give a loan to every woman I met who wanted one.

Although this logically seemed to be the thing I needed to do, I was still unsure if I wanted to go this route. I was accustomed to being immersed in the communities and organizations I was helping. I didn't want the disconnect of an eight-hour day job that had nothing to do with my goals but to fund them. I also had a good amount of self-doubt about whether I could really be successful doing something that was so different from what I majored in and the non-profit work I had been doing since graduation.

That night, I went to bed early. As I slept, I felt as relaxed and still as when my pain had subsided earlier while envisioning the healing colors. In my dreams I saw the colors that Sam the monk had conferred to me: red, white, green, yellow, blue, and black. The colors seemed to roll toward me like gentle waves and then flow through my body.

In the morning I awoke early, refreshed and calm. Looking from my window, I could see the blue dawn of the early morning, the moon still glowing over the papaya trees in my front yard. Putting on a pair of shorts and a t-shirt over my bikini, I grabbed a beach towel and departed for my favorite beach on the east side. When I arrived the sky was becoming bright with orange and blue morning hues, although the sun hadn't yet begun to come up over the horizon.

I plunged into the cool water and quickly swam out beyond the surging waves. As was my custom, I floated, bobbing in the water almost 100 yards out from shore watching the sun lift from the horizon. After the sun had completely emerged from the sea, I affixed my swimming goggles and began a one-mile swim. I swam from the north edge of the cove to the far southeast point and then back again.

I felt refreshed and awake. In a cheerful mood, I swam back to shore. Along the way, I stopped to admire a sea turtle as it ascended from the depths to have one of its first breaths of morning air.

As I reached the sandy shore and walked to the left to pick up my beach towel, I heard a voice call out, "Perfectly on time for our meeting."

I quickly glanced to the right from where the voice had originated. It was Sam the Buddhist monk! He was sitting in the sand cross-legged next to some coconut trees far off at the edge of the beach, with his dive gear assembled next to him. He was looking at the time on his dive computer and smiling.

"I'm sorry," I said quickly, "I was going to come meet you but…"

"But you have," Sam interjected, "and perfectly on time."

It dawned on me that it was about 8:30 am now and that was the approximate time that I had seen Sam the day before. I looked around to reconfirm that I was in my favorite, little-known beach on the east side of the island and not the dive site where we had met the day before on the west side of the island.

Did Sam not see me on the west side and then go around looking for me? I wondered. *No, that's impossible,* I concluded. If he didn't see me on the west side, it would take him two hours to drive to this side of the island. Sam started laughing. It must have been because I looked a little confused and lost.

"How did you know I'd be here?" I asked.

"Because it is the just-right dive site," Sam answered matter-of-factly.

"Wait a minute," I said, dismissing the idea that he could have somehow been following me. "Yesterday we were over two hours away on the west side. You asked me to meet you there again today at this time. And now you are here. Why?"

"Yes, yesterday we were on the west side of the island when we agreed to meet today," Sam answered. "However, yesterday, I did not state where we were to meet, only when to meet."

"But I didn't decide to come here until last night," I said.

"Mystics can see into the unseen-world to find the just-right dive site." Sam continued, "You're a mystic. I was sure you'd be here."

"I'm a mystic?" I asked. I fancied the title.

"Yes, you are," Sam responded frankly.

"How can you tell?"

"Because of your aura."

"My aura?"

"Yes," Sam said. "Your aura is the energy body that surrounds and encompasses your physical body. All beings have an aura, but only mystics have a double aura."

"Two energy bodies?" I asked.

"Not exactly," Sam said. "When I say that mystics have a double aura, I mean that their energy body exists in two places at once. A mystic's energy body exists in this world just like anyone else's, but it also exists in another world, an unseen-world. The unseen-world is the unlimited world, an ocean of magic. Anyone with a double aura is a mystic. Mystics operate energetically in the unseen-world. They have access to the unlimited side of life. They can swim in that sea of wonder. And they can learn to dive into enlightenment."

Sam's description of the unseen-world somehow reminded me of a feeling that I had from time to time, but was never able to describe. It was an incredibly uplifting feeling that seemed expansive and magical, yet ineffable. Sam's words transported me into this feeling. Sam looked at me peacefully and began nodding his head.

My awareness of this feeling was most intense during my childhood. I had even felt this magical feeling during very difficult times in my life, like when my dog Chloe died when I was 11. Chloe had passed away as I held her in my arms. I was very sad about her death, but when this magical feeling came over me like a saving grace, I somehow knew that everything was fine and Chloe would be OK.

Perhaps the double aura has something to do with this feeling, I thought.

After sitting quietly with Sam for a moment I asked, "Are you a mystic, too?"

"Yes, I am," Sam answered. "That's how I also knew to come to the just-right dive site to meet you this morning."

"What makes this place the just-right dive site?" I asked. "And how did I know it?"

"It's simple," Sam said. "This cove is a place of power. This place shines. The energy here is bright. Mystics are drawn to places that shine."

Sam continued, "Just like people, places have auras. This place has a luminous, powerful aura. This place has a strong energy that moves slowly up through the ground. The energy comes up over our heads. Then the energy flows to the south."

Sam gestured in exaggerated circular motions with his outstretched arms and then continued, "Here, the energy is bright and it vibrates quickly. The energy at this place will help you understand what you are learning from me."

I was unsure exactly what Sam meant by "energy," how I was drawn to it, and how it could help me learn about what he wanted to teach me.

Sam said, "Look, you can see it with your eyes." He pointed all around saying, "Places of power have tremendous visual clarity. We are 100 yards from that palm tree at the southern point. See how bright, clear, and in focus that palm tree is?"

Now that he had mentioned it, the palm tree was extremely clear. Sam continued, "Palm trees in town won't look so clear. Places of power always look beautiful and feel special. There's just something about the place that makes you feel good. Places of power have an expansive effect on your awareness field."

I nodded. I had always loved this cove. It was one of my favorite places in the world. It made me feel good and was very beautiful. It did always have an expansive effect on my outlook.

"This is why we met here today," Sam said. "In a place of power, where the energy is clear and expansive, your mind is clear and expansive. Here you can comprehend what we are doing together."

What are we doing together? I wondered. Sam's ideas were foreign to me, and yet they were somehow compelling.

Sam pointed over toward a patch of craggy lava rocks in front of the calm blue waters of the cove. "Please," Sam said, "just relax and look at those rocks. Just gaze in that direction with a soft focus. I will show you what you can see here."

I turned towards the black volcanic rocks about 20 feet away. I held my eyes in one place, softly focusing on the top point of one of the larger rocks. At first all I saw was rocks and water, nothing unusual.

Yet after a few more moments of gazing at the point on the rock, I noticed a white glow starting to rise from the rock towards the sky above it. The group of rocks came to have a distinct shiny four-inch border. As I further examined the border, it looked to be some kind of bright, blazing white light coming from the rocks.

Then the ocean behind the rocks began to glow with the same white light at its edge where the blue waters met the sky. I blinked a few times to make sure my eyes weren't playing tricks on me, but the glow coming from the rocks and the ocean persisted undeniably. This was not a phenomenon my mind could reason out and explain, yet it didn't feel strange or false to me.

"OK," Sam said, pointing the other way, "now please turn around and gaze over here, toward the center of the beach." I turned and looked to another formation of smaller lava rocks a little further inland. For a moment, they were just rocks like every other rock: solid and unmoving. A moment later I noticed that they were shifting—not literally changing positions, but it seemed like they were softly undulating. It was almost like the way air becomes visible rising from the asphalt on hot summer afternoons, yet this was somehow different. I knew it wasn't heat-related since it was still the early morning. I didn't really know what to make of it, but like the bright light glow of the larger rocks and the ocean, somehow it didn't seem unreal to me.

Remarkable! I thought. *So much for the idea of things being rock solid.*

After a few minutes of looking at the rocks, Sam said, "OK, very good."

"Wow!" I exclaimed. "Are these magic rocks somehow? Or do all rocks do that?"

"Yes," Sam said, "all rocks do that. All people do that. Everything does that. In Mystic SCUBA you learn to be aware of the energetic patterns of all things. You learn to see energy in places of power and to understand how the different vibrations and flows of energy affect your awareness. You learn the energetic makeup of your own being and how to keep your aura and physical body in good health. You learn to meditate, to still your mind, to relax, and to find peace. Most of all, you learn who you are by clearing your foggy diving mask and looking into the depths of the ocean of the self. In Mystic SCUBA you learn by exploring life under the sea and within your mind."

Despite my many doubtful thoughts, I found myself saying, "You know Sam, I think that's what I really need." I paused and then continued, "I need to look below the surface of my life and find out who I am and what I should do."

"In that case," Sam responded, "we must begin with the seen-world."

"What is the seen-world?"

"The seen-world is the world you can see with your eyes, hear with your ears, taste with your tongue, smell with your nose, and touch with your hands. The world that is solid, physical, and transient."

"You mean this world? The Earth?"

"Yes, but not just the Earth," Sam answered. "I mean the Earth, the sky, and the galaxy. I mean the economy, your job, and relationships. I mean the ground, your dive gear, and what you had for dinner last night."

I shook my head and said, "It sounds like you mean everything."

"Exactly! Everything!" Sam exclaimed. "The seen-world is everything you can talk about, touch, see, or even think about. Everything! It is vital to have a grounded attention in the seen-world when you wish to practice Mystic SCUBA."

"So you're saying that the seen-world is everything, and that I need to be grounded in the seen-world. OK, that's not obvious," I said a little sarcastically.

"Not at all," Sam responded, "because Mystic SCUBA is the study of the unseen-world."

"What is the unseen-world?"

"Everything else!" Sam exclaimed.

"But wait a minute," I said. "How could there be anything else if the seen-world is everything you can see, touch, or even think of? There is nothing else. If I can't think of it, it doesn't exist."

"Oh, but that's just looking at things with a foggy mask that can only see the seen-world." Sam responded. "There is much, much more that exists beyond what you can think of. Your thoughts define and limit your life's possibilities. In the absence of thought, life is limitless and all is possible."

"Well then, what is something that is real that I can't think of, touch, or see?" I asked.

"Love," Sam answered.

I thought about it for a moment. I couldn't touch love, though love could include touch. I couldn't see love, though I could tell with my eyes if two people loved each other. Oh, but I could do what I was doing at the very moment, think about love.

"You can't even think of love," Sam interjected just before I blurted out my determination.

"What do you mean? I was just thinking about love. We're talking about it right now. How could it be unseen?" I retorted.

"You're not thinking about it. You're thinking around it," Sam said. "Do you love your parents?"

"Yes, very much," I replied. My parents were very caring and had always directed me to foster my strengths. "I've always had a wonderful relationship with my parents."

"Good. Reflect on your love for your parents for a moment or two," Sam said.

I thought about my mother and father. I remembered my father's warm humor at dinner last week. I felt a strong sense of love for them and smiled.

"That's it," Sam said. "You have just entered the unseen-world."

"What do you mean?" I said. "I'm thinking about my parents and how much I love them. That is in the seen-world."

"Yes," Sam said, "and you are experiencing the direct awareness of your love. That is in the unseen-world."

"How so?"

"Can you describe your love in words, or hold your love in thoughts?"

I thought about it. I could say many things about my love for my parents, but couldn't capture what I actually felt in words. I could think of many thoughts that engendered my love, but couldn't hold the feeling of my love in any particular thoughts.

"That's odd," I said.

"No it's not," Sam disagreed. "Love is a power that exists in the unseen-world. Though you can talk about it and think about it as a concept, you can't know it in its actuality in the seen-world. The experience of love is an experience of the unseen-world."

"But everyone can feel love," I said. "It can't be that only mystics love."

Sam responded, "Every being is magical. The seen and unseen-worlds lay before all of us. There are, however, differences in awareness. Love is a destination in the unseen-world that all can get to, but there are magical places you feel that only mystics can be aware of."

Sam went on, "For example, what's one of your favorite songs? Can you hear it in your mind?"

I had recently become passionate about a dance song I had heard in a club in San Francisco. I thought about the song. I could hear it in my mind. I felt as if I were playing the song in my head. I felt like dancing and nodded my head to the rhythm of the song.

"Music is like magic," Sam said. "Like any true art form, it transports you from the seen-world to the unseen-world."

I did have a magical feeling. It reminded me of that unexplainably special feeling I get sometimes. I excitedly explained how the music made me feel to Sam. "Is that my double aura?"

"Yes," Sam replied. "You have a tendency to enter and experience the unseen-world in this particular way. It is magical, indescribable, and yet familiar. These feelings are the beginning of learning all about the unseen-world."

"Doesn't everyone have magical feelings like that?" I asked.

Sam shook his head, saying, "Destinations in the unseen-world are similar to destinations in the seen-world. Millions and millions of people come to Hawaii every year. The vast majority of them go to the beaches of Waikiki. Some come to the resorts of the outer islands, but few, almost none, come to this place of power. They don't have the eyes to see this place. Mystics, having an awareness of energy, see the magic of this place. With an awareness of energy, a mystic is able to use the power and information available in this place in ways that create beautiful, happy, and enlightening effects."

I understood what Sam was saying. I had brought a lot of friends to this special cove over the years, and most of them just thought it was a pretty boring place. They didn't think it was particularly beautiful, and it just seemed like any other beach to them. One of my best friends did see the magic here. She loved this place as much as I do. *Perhaps she's a mystic too*, I thought.

"So then," Sam said, "what you will learn in Mystic SCUBA is how to dive into many beautiful destinations of light and love in the unseen-world. There are ecstatic seas of light and oceans of awareness for you to explore. All this will come in time but first we must start with a grounded attention in the seen-world."

"OK," I said, "What do I need to do?"

"Learn to be a better diver."

"A better diver?" I asked, feeling a little deflated. "I'm already fully certified and very comfortable SCUBA diving. What's more to learn?"

"There's much more to learn," Sam said. "SCUBA diving holds endless lessons for life. How many dives do you have?"

"I'm not sure," I said. "I'd have to look in my dive logbook. Maybe around 40 or 45."

"What agency did you get your certification from?"

"PADI."

"And what is your certification level?"

"I'm an Open Water Diver."

"To do Mystic SCUBA," Sam said, "you should be an Advanced Open Water Diver."

In PADI, the Open Water Diver certification is the initial license to dive. It entitles you to rent tanks and equipment, and dive with almost any dive shop around the world. My first instructor told me that above Open Water Diver there were three additional nonprofessional certification levels: Advanced Open Water Diver, Rescue Diver, and Master SCUBA Diver. I was never that interested in continuing my diving education. I knew that higher certification levels taught useful SCUBA information, but I was just happy experiencing the undersea world.

"Mystic SCUBA requires that you are extremely competent with your diving skills," Sam explained. "It's impossible to focus on the mystical aspects of SCUBA diving if you are still struggling with your buoyancy, are unfamiliar with your equipment, and are uncomfortable underwater."

Sam went on, "In martial arts you don't really begin to learn the spirit of the art until you are a black belt. Musicians can't really connect with the magic of the music until they are skilled enough to play it perfectly. It's the same way in Mystic SCUBA. Your buoyancy must be perfectly controlled. You must be comfortable diving deep and navigating while underwater. You must know your equipment inside and out. You must drill your basic SCUBA skills over and over till you utilize them perfectly in the proper situations. When you are comfortable with the things in the seen-world of SCUBA, then you can extend your awareness through SCUBA to the magic of the unseen-world."

"OK," I said. "It'll take a few days, but I can get my advanced certification." I knew of a large five-star PADI dive shop on the west side of the island that had instructors teaching the Advanced Open Water Diver certification class everyday.

"It will take till the end of tomorrow if we begin right now," Sam said. "I'm a PADI instructor."

"You are?" I asked with great surprise.

Sam nodded as he reached into a waterproof pouch next to his dive gear and pulled out an instructor's manual.

"Fantastic!" I exclaimed.

Opening it to a bookmarked page, Sam said, "See, I love PADI. It was founded by Ocean Tribe. Here, let me read to you their philosophy for the Adventures in Diving program that leads to the advanced certification level that you shall take part in now."

Looking down at the binder-bound manual, Sam read aloud, "'The PADI Adventures in Diving program is based on the premise that diving is a means to explore other interests. Once comfortable with basic skills, divers want to conquer new tasks, see different creatures, journey into diverse environments and experience new adventures.'"

"Isn't that wonderful?" Sam asked, smiling. "SCUBA diving is philosophically the same as mysticism. You master an aspect or vehicle of the seen-world so that you can move forward to experience new adventures in the unseen-world."

"OK, that sounds great!" I was enthusiastic about getting my advanced certification and having adventures in Mystic SCUBA. I quickly retrieved my gear, which, thankfully, I had loaded into my car the night before.

SEEN-WORLD TRAINING

Sam conducted the Adventures in Diving course in much the same way any other instructor would, with no talk about karma, energy, or mysticism. He started by teaching me about buoyancy, navigation, and deep diving using the manual. After answering the Knowledge Review questions, we started our Adventure Dives in the cove.

The first Adventure Dive was Peak Performance Buoyancy, where I estimated and rigged my weight system. I did a buoyancy check, adjusting my weights to achieve neutral buoyancy at the surface. Then I made a controlled, slow descent to the bottom and adjusted my buoyancy control vest for neutral buoyancy. Sam then had me hover motionless in the water as well as swim horizontally while neutrally buoyant without touching the bottom. I then made small depth adjustments using breath control while demonstrating long, slow, gliding fin kicks. Finally we had some fun navigating an obstacle course of coral heads, and hovering upside down.

I became pretty good at hovering and discovered that I was habitually wearing too much weight. When we had reached land after the dive, Sam told me that my buoyancy skills had greatly improved.

After an hour-long surface interval during which Sam instructed me in how to use a wrist-mounted compass, we headed into the sea to start the Navigation Adventure Dive. During the dive I determined the average number of kick cycles and average amount of time required to cover 100 feet. I navigated to a predetermined location and returned to the starting point using a natural reference and then using the compass, estimating the distance with my kick cycles. Then I demonstrated the correct handling of a compass while swimming a square pattern underwater.

Though I actually have a good sense of direction on land, I had always been completely turned around underwater. As soon as I would enter the water for a dive, I was simply lost amongst the coral. I was never able to find the boat or the point where I had entered until I ascended to the surface. It always gave me a feeling of being lost, though I knew logically that I had not kicked far from my entry. Now that I had some navigational skills to use underwater, I felt much less anxious.

Sam seemed impressed with my underwater navigation skills. He told me that I had done a good job and gave me a high-five. I very much enjoyed his clear and supportive teaching style.

"The Navigation and Deep Adventure Dives are required for your Advanced Open Water Diver certification," Sam said. "We started with Peak Performance Buoyancy because I think it is extremely important, but you can choose the other two Adventure Dives yourself."

During our surface interval, I read about all of the possible elective Adventure Dives. Just as I realized that I wanted to do the Search and Recovery and Night Adventure Dives, I remembered that I had two papayas in my car. By now, much of the day had already passed, and I was getting hungry. I quickly fetched the papayas and offered one to Sam. "These papayas are from one of the trees in my front yard. Many of them are ripe now, and they're delicious," I said.

Sam thanked me and bowed. He took one of the papayas and began cutting it open with his titanium dive knife. "Delicious indeed," Sam said as he tasted the papaya. "I love Hawaiian papayas."

Looking at his knife, I said, "It's kind of funny that a Buddhist monk would carry a knife. Isn't that against your code of ethics or something?"

"Not at all," Sam answered. "Some Zen monks in Japan have even carried Samurai swords," he explained. "Through the art of the sword, they would perfect their Zen practice." I nodded, remembering a book a friend told me about called *Zen in the Art of Archery*, where Zen practitioners learned archery as part of their spiritual practice.

Sam continued, "We're like the Samurai of the sea. In Mystic SCUBA every piece of our equipment is essential for physical life and spiritual awareness. Incidentally, the dive knife is the most common rescue tool that I use. I used it to pry your regulator out of the coral head it was stuck in yesterday. This is why PADI requires divers to carry a dive knife as standard equipment."

I had a dive knife attached to my buoyancy control vest, but had never used it. Most of the time, I forgot that it was even there.

"When you are aware of your equipment's proper function and when to use it, SCUBA diving becomes very safe because you are utilizing all of your options for life," Sam said.

After finishing my papaya, Sam instructed me on the Search and Recovery and Night Adventure Dives skills. The sun was now low in the horizon and the sky started to turn a dusty orange and dark pink. I completed the Knowledge Reviews in the last light of the day.

As the sun set over the western mountains, Sam and I geared up. As it became dark, we began the Night Adventure Dive. During the dive we descended into the dark water using a reference line and communicated with hand signals and dive lights. Sam had me demonstrate the proper use of a personal dive light, submersible pressure gauge, compass, timing device and depth gauge. I navigated to a predetermined location using a compass and returned using the skills from the Navigation Adventure Dive. We maintained proper buddy procedures and ascended using a reference line. Sam was an attentive dive buddy. I felt safe and comfortable, knowing that he would be there if I needed anything.

After the dive, when we had returned to the sandy shore, Sam said, "Very good. I can tell you like diving at night." I smiled. I had been on a few night dives before. I found night dives to be fascinating because they were so different from daytime dives. At night there's a grand marine life shift change and a whole new cast of nocturnal characters appear on the reef. Marbled Shrimp, Swimming Crab, and camouflaged octopus become plentiful. You can find parrotfish slumbering in their self-made saliva cocoons. Most of all, at night, I love the contrast of the vibrant coral colors illuminated by my flashlight and the pitch black ocean.

As we began to disassemble and pack up our dive gear, Sam said, "Good, now you are only two Adventure Dives away from your advanced certification. You're doing just fine."

"That's fantastic," I said. "Hey Sam, how much should I pay you for the advanced certification class?" I knew that most shops would charge around $400 for this instruction.

"Good question," Sam responded. "How about you take care of the service and cost of fetching and refilling rental tanks, and I'll take care of the instruction?"

"But tank rentals are only $20 per day," I said.

"And perhaps throw in some of those delicious papayas," Sam added.

Unsure, I said, "It sounds like a great deal for me, but I don't get it. I mean, why are you spending all this time teaching me about Mystic SCUBA?"

Sam looked me in the eyes and answered, "It is my dharma to teach. One's dharma is their personal way of truth, their expression of enlightenment. I teach to share the Buddhist way with people who have a special purpose that would be aided by meditation and mysticism. You, like all who hear or read these mystical teachings, have a powerful dharma. In Buddhism we recognize that, like your darshan yesterday and our meeting today, there are no coincidences. Every encounter with spiritual teachings is regarded as a vital lesson on your pathway to enlightenment. Yet at the moment your potential is being limited by the mental tensions, confusions, and foggy diving mask that we've begun to address. I'm teaching you because there is something critically important you need to learn. I would no sooner walk away from teaching you Mystic SCUBA than let you drown, stuck on a reef."

I was quiet for a few moments, taking this all in. His genuineness and the simple power of his words struck me. Although learning Mystic SCUBA from a Buddhist monk was not something I ever could have imagined for my retreat in Hawaii, a deep part of me recognized the truth in Sam's words and the profound opportunity that lay before me.

Sam paused, laughed, and then added, "I was going to meditate and do Mystic SCUBA for the rest of my vacation anyway, and though it's hard work, I enjoy teaching."

Smiling, I said, "In that case, I'll do the tanks and the papaya payment plan."

Sam laughed again and then asked in a much more serious tone if I knew of a popular dive site on the northwest side of the island.

"Sure," I said, "I've been there several times."

"Are you positive that you know where it is?" Sam asked and then started describing directions to the parking area of the dive site from the main road.

"Yes, definitely," I said, "I know this dive site well. I love the steep sloping reef there."

"OK," Sam said. "I just wanted to make sure that you are aware of where we are to meet tomorrow at the same time we met today."

I laughed, a little embarrassed, and said, "I am aware of where to meet tomorrow. I'll be there."

Sam gave me a wry smile as he packed his dive gear into the back of his orange Jeep. Pressing his hands together below his chin, he bowed. Following his movements, a little awkwardly, I bowed back.

We pulled out of the parking lot at the same time. Sam took the road to the north. I turned the other way to the south for my short drive home.

The next morning I woke up early and made my way to the west side. I arrived well before Sam and assembled my gear. Just before 8:30 am he pulled up to the parking area. Sam saw me sitting in the sand by the dive site entrance and waved. Upon parking, he popped out of the Jeep, quickly donned his wetsuit, and assembled his dive gear. The next thing I knew Sam was on his way to me with his gear on and ready to dive.

"That was fast," I said, as I struggled into my buoyancy control vest.

"Not fast, but efficient," Sam responded. "With a clear mind you can do physical tasks such as assembling your dive gear with no wasted effort of action. The mystic's mind is an efficient mind." Sam said this as he checked the assembly of my equipment.

"What's the deepest dive you've ever done?" Sam asked.

"Around 70 feet."

"Very good," Sam said. "Do you feel OK about going to 110 feet today?"

"Sure," I answered, feeling a chill of nervous excitement. This dive would take me 40 feet deeper than I had ever been and within 20 feet of the maximum depth for recreational diving.

We buckled into our SCUBA gear and entered the sea. Before descending, Sam had me sign my name on an underwater writing slate. We followed the coral bottom to a depth of 110 feet. Sam pointed out a slight variation in our computers depth readings to show me that at greater depths, gauge accuracy may vary. Sam then had me sign my name again on the underwater writing slate to show me that pressure at great depth has an effect on manual dexterity. It took longer for me to sign my name and it was much messier than my first signature at the surface. We then made a slow ascent, carefully monitoring our computers. At 15 feet, we performed a three-minute safety stop.

I had an absolute blast on the dive! It was scary to go so deep, but it was great fun at the same time. Back on shore, I felt excited about the dive. Sam was very calm and quiet. He congratulated me on completing the Deep Adventure Dive. We unbuckled our SCUBA gear and sat quietly in the warm, pebbly sand.

After an hour-long surface interval, we geared up again and entered the sea. During the Search and Recovery Adventure Dive I demonstrated procedures for methodically searching a small area to find a submerged dive mask box that Sam planted. I demonstrated how to search a large area to find one of Sam's long fins that he had hidden behind a lava rock. Finally, I tied a lift bag to a 25-pound weight belt that Sam had brought down. I added air to the lift bag, and the weight belt floated to the surface.

When we reached the surface, Sam shook my hand and said, "Good job. You've completed all of the performance requirements for Search and Recovery."

I felt terrific.

Upon returning to shore and disassembling his dive gear, Sam filled out a temporary certification card and said, "Congratulations, you are now a certified Advanced Open Water Diver." He handed me a PADI envelope and instructed me to mail it in with a picture so that I would get my official certification card in the mail. I said that I would mail it in as soon as possible.

"So now can I learn Mystic SCUBA?" I asked. "I can go refill the tanks and come back in time for a dive."

"Yes, of course you can learn Mystic SCUBA now," Sam replied, "but we won't need any more tanks today. Before we get into the water and dive, you should be instructed in the foundation of Mystic SCUBA practice."

MEDITATION

Sam handed me a bottle of water and said, "Meditation is as refreshing and sustaining to the mind as water is to the body on a hot day. Meditation is the foundation of all practice—Buddhist practice and Mystic SCUBA. If you want to learn about Mystic SCUBA, you will have to practice meditation every day, at least for the period of time that I teach you. Are you willing to give that an earnest shot?"

"Sure," I answered, opening and drinking the bottle of water. I thought it was kind of funny that I was going to learn meditation, since it had never really interested me before. Yet in light of Mystic SCUBA, and the uncannily intriguing experiences I'd had with Sam the Buddhist monk, I was delighted to try it.

Sam closed his eyes. A moment later in a clear voice he began speaking, "Meditation is stopping thought. If you can stop thought, you can meditate. Meditation is silencing the seemingly endless chatter of the mind. It is moving beyond your everyday conditioned mind to the eternal unlimited essence of mind.

"When you stop thought, you stop the world. Your worries and concerns disappear. Your angers and depressions vanish. The tremendous burden of being you stops and you experience the peaceful condition of unbound reality.

"By practicing meditation your mind becomes clear; you become awake and alive to life. Meditation energizes and empowers you. Meditation awakens your intuition and many other subtle senses of awareness. It grounds you and heals you. Essentially, meditation makes you happy.

"Meditation is not running away from the hardships of life. It is balancing yourself within life so that you can handle any hardships. Many volumes have been written about the many methods and techniques of meditation in just the same way that many volumes have been written about how to SCUBA dive. Just as you learn what it is like to dive by diving, it is through experience that we learn what it is like to meditate. No words can explain these experiences of the unseen-world.

"Mystics experience meditation naturally from time to time. It usually occurs in nature. They may be alone on the beach, or walking through the woods, and then just feel complete peace. Many mystics who are SCUBA divers have had such experiences. Underwater, their thoughts subside and they become bright and ecstatic. In beautiful places of nature, and places of power, it is easier for mystics to be absorbed into the peace of unobscured awareness.

"Meditation is also a practice, a discipline. It is the period of time set aside every day, where one sits still and empty, mastering her mind and thoughts, defogging her diving mask so that she can see and be aware of life in its essence.

"The primary technique for meditation practice is focus. When your mind is strong enough to focus on one thing, one point, then your mind is strong enough to pierce through the wall of limitation.

"It's like this," Sam said as he detached the long thin metal stick he carried on his buoyancy control vest. Pressing it into the sand, Sam drew a small coconut-sized circle. "This is you, separate from the whole beach. You are aware only of what is within your circle of attention. Your circle of attention defines you as separate from the rest of the beach. Your circle of attention is also the wall of limitation that prevents you from perceiving anything outside of the circle.

"Your attention is carried off from moment to moment by thoughts. Your thoughts take you whizzing all around, bouncing off the wall of limitation." Sam illustrated this by moving the thin metal stick in curving strokes from side to side and up and down within the circle. As soon as the stick hit the circular borderline, it bounced off in a different trajectory.

"Thoughts are always moving your attention somewhere within the circle, but meditation is stopping the incessant hurriedness of your mind. When the mind holds many things, ideas, and thoughts, it is unable to muster the strength to break free. Meditation is holding your attention in one single point. It requires tremendous focus."

Sam held the metal stick at a slight angle against one side of the circle. "When you fix your attention undisturbed on one point, something miraculous happens. Your attention breaks through the wall of limitation, the wall of self."

Sam pushed the metal stick slightly forward and it crossed from the border of the circle to a few inches outside of the circle.

"Now your awareness has gone beyond conditioned habits. There is an opening in your mind. You have become aware of much more of the beach. You have gained a new view into a vast universe beyond anything you could have imagined before.

"Then with every meditation," Sam continued poking holes in the circle with the metal stick, "you gain greater and greater views of eternity."

"Finally," Sam said while wiping large sections of the circle away with his hand, "the self that was defined and separated by the circle is no longer." Wiping away the last of the circle, Sam said, "The sand that was within your circle of awareness is still right here, but you are not just here. Now your awareness includes what was within the circle and also stretches beyond, reaching everything outside of the circle. You are not any particular group of sand. You are the whole beach! This is enlightenment."

I paused for a moment, looking at the area in the sand where the circle had been. "So how do I fix my attention on one point?" I asked. "What do I focus on?"

"In mysticism we focus on energy centers in the aura," Sam answered.

"How do I focus on something that seems so vague?" I asked.

"It's not vague at all," Sam said. "Acupuncturists have used the aura in healing for thousands of years. They have studied the aura so completely that they have diagramed its subtle physical structure to a degree of pinpoint accuracy, if you pardon the pun.

"All people's auras have a similar structure the same way all people's physical bodies have a similar structure. Chinese medicine is the study of balancing energy in the aura so that physical-body effects occur. Acupuncturists have learned that the relationships between subtle physical structures and physical structures are real with repeatable results and have created a scientific medical study from it.

"If you had sprained your left ankle, an acupuncturist might stimulate an acupuncture point in your right shoulder with a needle so that the pain can be relieved. By stimulating different energetic meridians or energetic points within the aura, you are able to create healthy physical effects.

"At a very deep level of the aura there is a very spiritual dimension of your being. The structure of your energy body at this level consists of a single energetic pathway that corresponds to the area of the physical body running from the bottom of the spine to the top of the head. Along this meridian are seven energetic points that we call *chakras*. Chakras are just like acupuncture points, except when you stimulate them with the needle of a focused mind, the outcome is not physical health, but at this very deep spiritual dimension of your being, it is spiritual health, awareness, and illumination.

"In my Buddhist school we focus on three of the seven chakras in our meditation. Meditating this way gives us tremendous spiritual benefit. The first chakra that we focus on is the navel chakra. The navel center is located about two to three inches below the belly button. The navel center is the chakra of spiritual power. When you still your mind, calm your thoughts, and focus on the navel center, a spiritual dimension of your own being is unlocked. A doorway opens and a bright, comforting light fills you. It is the light of power…the power to overcome the difficulties and hardships of life, the power to evolve, the power to be happy. As we meditate upon the navel chakra, we cultivate, absorb, and store this spiritual power.

"The second chakra that we focus on in our meditation period is the heart chakra. The heart chakra is located directly in the center of the chest. Point to yourself as if to say 'me.' That's usually the perfect spot. The heart chakra is the center of love in your being. When you stop thought completely while focused on the heart, you are immersed in love. You experience love directly, unbound from a person, place, or thing. You experience and become love itself. It is in the direct and unobscured experience of love that your heart and compassion grow. As we meditate upon the heart chakra, we become filled with love for ourselves and all things.

"The third chakra that we focus on during our meditation period is the third eye. The third eye is located between the eyebrows and slightly above. The third eye is the chakra of wisdom, seeing, and dreaming. When you still the mind and silence thoughts while focusing single-mindedly on the third eye, you unlock your inherent wisdom. You are filled with a wise, ancient and intelligent light. In this light, you come to know the truths and secrets of life. In this light, you can see and discriminate between what is true and what is false. In this light your spirit is awakened. As we meditate upon the third eye, we come to see what is right for us, what is true.

"To really learn meditation you must practice twice a day. Constant earnest effort is required to learn this most noble discipline. It is better to meditate for a short time with your best effort than for a long time with a mediocre effort. In the beginning your meditation sessions may only be 10 to 15 minutes long. As you practice and strengthen your mind to become better at concentration and focus, you will naturally enjoy increasing your meditation session to about the period of one hour.

"It is beneficial to practice in the morning. Just as you rise from bed your mind is still. Take a shower, have some coffee or tea if you have to, and then meditate. It is also beneficial to practice in the evening. The time of the sunset is nice, or perhaps right before you go to bed. It is important that you do not meditate after eating a lot. When your stomach is full, your body uses a lot of its energy to digest food. Rather, you should wait until you have digested your food before you meditate. That way you won't feel tired and you'll have all of your body's energy at your disposal.

"So now, I'd like to meditate with you for just a few minutes. During meditation it is most important to sit up perfectly straight. It doesn't matter what position your legs are in. Sit in a way that is comfortable for you. It is just fine to sit in a chair. It also does not matter what position your hands are in. You may just want to rest them on your lap. Sit up straight as if there were a string attached to the very top center of your head pulling you up.

"During this meditation session I will direct you to focus on each of the three chakras. We will begin by focusing on the navel center. When it is time to bring the focus to the heart center I will say aloud 'heart'. When it is time to bring the focus to the third eye, I will say aloud 'third eye'. When we are done, I will say 'bow'. After completing a meditation session we always bow. This is a gesture of humility where we thank this whole ocean of consciousness, life, that we swim in.

"Close your eyes now. Bring your focus to the navel center. If you have difficulty focusing on any of the chakras touch the chakra lightly with your index finger. This will give you a stronger sense of where to bring your attention. After some time in practice, the area of the chakra will become distinct. You'll feel energy pulsing in the chakras as they are stimulated by your concentration.

"If thoughts arise as you focus on the chakra, simply let go of the thoughts and bring your attention back to the chakra. The practice is to— again and again—bring your focus back to the chakra.

"Let's begin. Hold your mind in the area of the navel center."

I had been listening closely to Sam's meditation instructions, and although I wasn't sure that I really understood what he meant by holding my mind two inches below my belly button, I was ready to try. I sat up as straight as I could. I closed my eyes and then lightly touched my stomach to find the navel center Sam had described. For a few seconds, my mind was quiet as I paid attention to my navel. Then I started noticing all kinds of random, trivial thoughts zipping around in my head. Although I tried to ignore them, I was pretty shocked by how many there were. I could easily visualize them ricocheting off the edges of the circle—me—that Sam had drawn in the sand.

Sam said aloud, "heart," and my focus became clear again. I lightly touched the area of my heart, and immediately felt something almost indescribable—a kind of clarity and purity that was similar yet more luminous than the special feeling I'd had from time to time since I was a kid. My thoughts stopped running around because I was absorbed in what was going on within my heart. It felt like the external boundary of my physical body wasn't really there any more. Instead, there was a soft, expansive, peaceful connection between me and an endless, beautiful golden light.

Minutes later Sam said softly, "third eye." I drew my focus up from my heart to the area just between and a little above my eyebrows. I felt a surge of energy rush to the middle of my head, and my concentration was sharp and distinct for a few seconds. Then my thoughts picked back up and I spent the next few minutes trying to ignore them.

Sam broke our silence by saying, "OK."

I opened my eyes. Sam pressed his hands together under his chin, saying, "And bow." We bowed deeply.

After bowing, I said, "I felt something nice during my meditation." Sam nodded knowingly. "I mean," I said, "for most of the meditation, my head was filled with the most mundane thoughts. But there was one moment when I felt a lot of brightness. While I was focusing on my heart chakra, it seemed somehow like there was a golden light that originated within me."

I paused, thinking about it and then said, "It's funny that I felt light and could even tell it was golden, but I didn't really see it. Maybe I was just imagining it. Maybe it was nothing."

"Don't dismiss the light so easily!" Sam said. "The light you felt was the luminosity of pure consciousness. As you reflect on your experience of that light, you'll recall that in the light you felt peace. Your experience of that light was illuminating and clarifying to your spirit. In that light, although it was for only a brief moment, you had no thoughts and no limitations."

I thought about it for a moment and then agreed. Sam was completely correct, but I felt I had only glimpsed the light and awareness he spoke of.

"In the beginning," Sam said, "the light in your meditation is like a trickling stream of luminosity. Yet as you explore that stream of peace through many meditations, you'll soon find that it leads to the ocean of enlightenment. When you dive into that ocean, you are free.

"In perfect meditation, called *Samadhi*, you are free from the binds of your disturbing thoughts, feelings, concepts, and definitions of life. In Samadhi you are free from the limited awareness of a separate self."

"Really?" I asked. "Can Samadhi free me from my confusion and existential tension?"

"Yes," Sam answered. "In Samadhi, the discord of your segregated attention is transcended, and your awareness is absorbed into unity with the universe. This ecstatic union is the illumination of the spirit's connection to all things. Samadhi is entered through absorption into the ocean of enlightenment. Experiencing Samadhi is diving into enlightenment."

Sam's description of Samadhi ignited a feeling of possibility within me. "I'd really like to experience Samadhi," I announced. "Do you think I can reach Samadhi if I work on it?"

"Without a doubt," Sam answered.

Sam paused for a moment and then continued, "It usually takes many years of practice and proper instruction to reach Samadhi. However, in mysticism there is a more efficient way. With my guidance and your earnest effort, you could experience Samadhi in a couple of weeks. But you must take the study seriously to prepare your mind for the experience."

"So, there's a shortcut to Samadhi?"

"No, there is no shortcut to Samadhi," Sam answered. "There are no shortcuts in life. You must move along the pathway to enlightenment one fin-kick at a time. Yet there are ways to do things with greater efficiency. There are ways to get to Samadhi more directly.

"For example, if a diver received instruction from an enlightened Divemaster that Samadhi was submerged somewhere along the steep sloping reef of this dive site, the diver would most pragmatically enter the water, descend, and fin along the reef until finding Samadhi.

"Yet if the enlightened Divemaster were inclined to aid the diver, the Divemaster could bring the diver directly to underwater Samadhi. If the Divemaster knew that the dive site had some significant current and that Samadhi was 130 feet deep, the Divemaster could maximize the diver's air supply by fighting the current at the surface, otherwise the diver might run too low on air kicking against the current underwater."

Pointing out to the ocean before us Sam said, "But remember, Samadhi is not a thing that can be located in the ocean." Bringing his pointer finger to his temple, he said, "It is a state of mind that you can experience through meditation and Mystic SCUBA."

I nodded.

Sam continued, "The reason that you have the opportunity to reach Samadhi more efficiently and directly is because I am an enlightened Divemaster. I know the exact location and conditions to bring you to Samadhi. But you must be prepared. I won't expose you to Samadhi unless you are ready for it. Just like in SCUBA diving, if you are not educated and lack the proper skills, what should be beautiful and transformative could be dangerous and unsettling."

"What do I have to do to prepare myself?" I asked.

"Meditation and Mystic SCUBA," Sam said. "But let's just start with making it through tomorrow's lessons. Now you better get home and get some rest."

The sun was now low in the horizon. Sam and I began disassembling our SCUBA equipment. As we loaded our gear into our cars, Sam said, "Tomorrow, let's meet at the dive site where we first met and at the same time as always." I agreed. Sam bowed in his usual fashion and we departed.

On my drive home I felt happy and light. Humming along with the melodious Hawaiian songs streaming from the car radio, I contemplated how different my day turned out to be from what I had planned. Just 24 hours ago I was ready to dismiss my encounter with the Buddhist monk, but now here I was, preparing to leap into Mystic SCUBA exercises. Spending the day with Sam, and the anticipation to learn more from him filled me with growing fascination. He was professional and knowledgeable in his role as a dive instructor, and at the same time, a gentle and kind Buddhist monk teaching me about meditation and mysticism. I found him to be mysterious and in all ways unlike anyone else I've ever met. Meditating with him was magical, and at the end of the day I felt a whole new world of possibility and wonder opening for me.

I was so inspired that evening I decided to meditate for a full hour. My meditation was tough. My mind, filled with an excitement about experiencing Samadhi in the beginning, quickly turned to thoughts of my confusion about work. After about 40 minutes of struggle, I just bowed and gave up. I had no feeling of light during the whole meditation. I was frustrated because I wanted to prepare myself for experiencing Samadhi as soon as possible.

THE FIRST RULE OF SCUBA

After a light dinner, I opened up my laptop and checked my email. I had a message from Genet, the woman I'd rented a room from in Addis Ababa. She was writing to say hello and to give me an update on the street kids who lived near our house whom I'd befriended. They were a group of ten boys, all between the ages of about 11 and 14, whose parents were either dead or couldn't afford to care for them anymore.

I had learned rudimentary Amharic and one of the boys, Haile, spoke a little English. With some occasional translating from Genet, we managed to communicate pretty well.

The boys had been living on the street for at least a few years. They had banded together as a group and always looked out for each other. They shared whatever money or food they got from begging or working small jobs when they could get them. They had constructed a house of sorts out of sticks and plastic tarps on a small side street about a quarter of a mile away from Genet's home.

The boys' resilience, kindness and complete loyalty to one another inspired me; they were a family. We'd grown very close over the time I was their neighbor, and before I'd left, we made an agreement that I would help them go to school starting in the fall. Their end of the deal was that they needed to stay completely focused on getting a good education during the school months and do really well in their classes. My end of the deal was that I would buy their uniforms and school supplies, rent a real room for them, pay for their daily food, and cover any medical costs if they got sick.

During the summer, I would give them some extra money so that they could start small businesses. With $100 to buy inventory and supplies, they could make a tidy profit selling gum, tissues, and snacks or shining shoes. I also planned to give them money to start larger businesses if they wanted to after completing their education.

Just before I left, we went shopping and they got an outfit and a pair of shoes each, a school uniform, and notebooks and pens. Their sheer delight at the prospect of finally getting to go to school and shape their own futures was incredible. Realizing that an education would lead him and his friends out of utter poverty, Haile said to me, "This day is the best day of my life!" In helping them to have this opportunity, it was the best day of my life as well.

Keeping up my end of the deal wasn't going to be easy though. As I'd figured, it would cost at least a couple thousand dollars a year. It wasn't a huge amount by American standards, but it certainly wasn't trivial either, considering my salary as a nonprofit aid worker.

After promising to send more money in my reply to Genet's email, I opened one of my programming books. *If I were a programmer,* I thought, *I would be able to help these boys even more, fund small businesses for the women I worked with, and help many other people in Ethiopia, other countries in Africa, and around the world.*

I started working through some of the sample programs. Although I was a little confused by some of the concepts, the material was interesting. Programming was kind of fun, more like solving fun puzzles than software engineering.

After coding for about an hour, I took a break and walked outside into my yard, into the quiet, fragrant Hawaiian night. A warm breeze caressed my skin. The stars in the sky twinkled. I noticed fallen plumeria blossoms illuminated by the moonlight, and suddenly, tears filled my eyes and started streaming down my cheeks. The contrast of where I was in this moment, halfway around the world, in so many ways, from where I'd been just a few weeks before, was overwhelming. The magnitude of the poverty I'd witnessed ripped at my heart.

Images from my time in Addis Ababa raced through my mind. I saw the sweet smile of an emaciated little girl who wrapped her arms around my waist at Mother Teresa's home for HIV-positive kids. I remembered lifting a crying baby from his dead mother's arms in a squalid barn where they slept amongst the cows. I remembered a disabled homeless widow on the street begging me for a couple of *birr* so that she could buy ingredients to make *enjera* to feed her children.

The weight of our extraordinarily unfair world crushed me. The kids I planned to help were just a few of the millions and millions of street kids in Africa. The mothers were just a few dozen of the hundreds of millions of people living in unbelievable poverty all over the world.

What does all of this mean? What do I do about it? I agonized over these questions, staring up at the starry sky.

I tossed and turned all night dreaming, waking, and thinking about Ethiopia and poverty and disease and street kids and inequality and death and America and social justice and computer programming and family and compassion and love.

In the morning I woke up late, feeling unrested and irritated. I quickly packed my SCUBA gear into the trunk of my car and rushed down the coast to meet Sam. I arrived 15 minutes late. This dive site, though one of my favorites, was far from my house. Sam was already there, sitting in the sand with his dive equipment prepared next to him.

"Sorry I'm late," I said, "I had a bit of a rough start this morning."

"No problem," Sam said with a warm, calm smile. I felt like Sam could see right through me, that he could tell how unsettled and confused I felt. He said nothing, continued smiling, and gestured for me to sit next to him.

I sat down and threw my SCUBA gear together.

"To begin your study," Sam said, "we will discuss the physical and mental health benefits achieved through Mystic SCUBA."

"OK," I said, with a small shrug.

Sam continued, "This is particularly important for you to pay attention to because your physical health was put in jeopardy when you almost died, the first day we met. It is proper for you to have a greater understanding and awareness of physical health.

"Most importantly," Sam stated, "learning about the health benefits of Mystic SCUBA will cure you of the mental tension that got you into the predicament which nearly took your life."

I felt my face flush. I was a little annoyed by Sam harping on my accident.

"Mystic SCUBA is a unique combination of meditation, deep breathing, and movement. It includes low-impact conditioning and light stretching. Mystic SCUBA strengthens the whole body, while maintaining a focus on physical relaxation. It improves overall health, while preventing and curing illness.

"Mystic SCUBA is more than just a physical activity. It is a meditative practice performed under the sea. Through concentration, physical attention, and awareness of the environment, Mystic SCUBA yields an expansion of spiritual awareness. Mystic SCUBA is not like sitting meditation. You don't close your eyes and sit still. It's more like walking meditation. You must be attentive and aware of your surroundings. You must control your buoyancy and watch your air consumption. Mystic SCUBA is like dancing. Dancing is filled with movement, balance, and complexity, yet in dancing you can disappear into the movement and become the dance itself.

"The relaxation, meditation, and deep breathing we exercise in Mystic SCUBA have proven to be beneficial to physical health through thousands of years of observances in comparable disciplines such as *Yoga*, *Chi Gung*, and *Tai Chi*. In addition, there are two other factors that make Mystic SCUBA diving unique and extremely beneficial. These are the healing nature of water and the partial pressure of oxygen."

My interest perked up a little. I always felt that water was very healing. Also, I had learned about the partial pressure of oxygen in my Open Water Diver certification course. It had something to do with how oxygen acts under the pressure of water, though I couldn't remember its significance and was unable to see how it would benefit my health in SCUBA diving.

Sam asked, "What is the first rule in SCUBA diving?" This was easy. When I took my initial SCUBA diving certification course, my instructor repeated over and over again that the first rule of SCUBA diving was to always breathe naturally. Holding your breath while SCUBA diving can cause a serious form of decompression illness.

Decompression illness is a potentially life threatening condition that can occur while SCUBA diving. It is caused by the decreased pressure on the body as you ascend during a dive. SCUBA divers can get one form of decompression illness by staying too deep too long or by ascending too quickly. The second form of decompression illness can happen to divers if they hold their breath at anytime underwater. This form of decompression illness can be avoided simply by continuously breathing.

"The first rule in SCUBA diving is just to breathe," I answered.

"That's right!" Sam exclaimed. "By learning the mystical aspects of the air and water elements, you will have the awareness of mind to never violate this rule again."

I tightly pressed my lips together. Sam's remark immediately aggravated me. It was just an accident. *A lionfish jolted at me, for heaven's sake! The same thing could have happened to anyone.* I could feel my face turning red. *Why is Sam rubbing it in?*

Adding to my chagrin, Sam said, "Let's begin by talking about the importance of breathing. You, more than anyone I've ever met, need to increase your awareness of this."

I scowled. I folded my arms and thought, *I don't have to sit here and take this abuse! Sam's insults and prodding are infuriating!* He really had a way of pushing my buttons. *Why does he irritate me so much?* I wondered. My breathing became shallow and fast. I frowned angrily at Sam.

Sam just smiled at me, apparently amused by my frustration. Then with what seemed like overly exaggerated concern he asked, "Are you OK? Are you breathing?"

I then became acutely aware of my shallow, choppy breathing. Sam smiling while scrutinizing my breathing irritated me further, making me very self-conscious. In fact, I became so irritated with Sam that I was having trouble breathing at all! I gasped for air.

Sam chuckled. I felt totally dejected. Sam was making fun of me for a diving accident that I had no control over. He had insulted me, aggravated me, and now he was laughing at me!

I indignantly turned away to my left to protest Sam's insulting laughter. As I quickly shifted, I banged my elbow into my SCUBA gear that was standing upright next to me. The collision caused my gear to fall to the ground and jolted my arm with a tingling pain.

"Ouch!" I exclaimed holding my arm. I had hit my funny bone and the pain inched its way up toward my hand.

"Don't worry," Sam said reassuringly, "you didn't break anything." I thought he was referring to my arm, but then saw that he was looking at my SCUBA gear, ignoring me completely.

The pain in my elbow quickly began to lessen, but my frustration with Sam grew. I'd had it. I made up my mind to leave. I threw my mask into my gear bag, picked up my fins, and practically yelled, "I don't know why you're giving me such a hard time!"

With an expressive hand gesture, Sam looked me in the eyes and said, "I'm teaching you how to save your own life." Sam's sudden genuineness halted my retreat. I put my fins down and listened. I wanted to know what he meant.

Sam continued, "You see, when darkness arises in the mind, it simultaneously creates ill effects in the physical body. Negative thoughts and feelings create physical tensions that start to constrict your respiration. Your breath loses its normal rhythm. You start breathing hard whenever negativity comes into your mind. This is easy to observe."

Sam pointed at me. Again I became aware that my breathing was rapid and shallow, although less so than a few moments earlier. Sam instructed, "Focusing on slow, calm breathing will calm your mind of negativity."

I began to calm myself by taking slow, deep breaths.

"Most people cannot perceive subtle defilements of the mind such as subtle fears, angers, or passions. If you watch, however, it is very easy to observe unhealthy respiratory changes, which are directly related to mental defilements. And it is easy to resolve the discord of negative thoughts and feelings through greater attention to your breathing."

Sam gestured to me with his hands to breathe slowly and deeply. I focused on breathing in deeply and exhaling fully. A moment later my physical body felt much more comfortable. My irritation with Sam had completely subsided as well.

Joining his fingers together, Sam continued, "This is an utterly integrated mental-physical phenomenon. When thoughts and emotions arise in the mind, muscle tension and respiration are immediately affected. Any mental negativity, thought or emotion will become noticeable in your breath in that moment. So by observing your breathing, you are actually observing your state of mind. Observation of your breath shows you the truth of your peace of mind both inwardly and outwardly."

Looking pleased that I was now breathing more calmly and deeply, Sam said, "But remember, it's impossible for you to calm your mind and relax your body if you break the first rule of SCUBA."

I noticed an immediate sensation of heat rush up my back to my head and felt my breath becoming fast and shallow again. I continued to focus on deep and slow breathing. My breath returned to a slower pace and no irritated thoughts seemed to emerge.

VITAL BREATH

Sam was watching me carefully. He began speaking in a formal manner: "Breathing is important. Breathing is essential in sustaining your life. Breathing is the way you provide your brain, nerves, and internal organs with oxygen, the body's most important nourishment. You can live without food for weeks and survive without water for days, but without oxygen, you cannot live longer than a few minutes."

"That's true, isn't it?" I realized. "Out of all the things we need for survival, air is the most urgent necessity."

"That's right," Sam said, "and did you know that your body gets most of its energy from air?"

"Really?" I asked.

"Yes," Sam said. "Scientists have shown that a chemical called adenosine triphosphate, ATP for short, is the chemical basis of energy production in the body. Oxygen is the most essential element for the production of ATP."

Sam paused, and then went on, "And you need air to eat."

"You mean, like how the body uses oxygen in digestion?" I questioned.

"Precisely," Sam answered. "The oxidation process supports converting carbohydrates, fats, and proteins into the energy your body requires. Without sufficient oxygen, nutrients would oxidize poorly.

"Oxygen nourishes every cell in your body. Oxygen repairs, rejuvenates, and recharges the whole body. Your brain is the largest consumer of this essential nutrient. If your brain is deprived of oxygen, you could have a stroke. If your heart is deprived of oxygen, you could have a heart attack. Insufficient oxygen may also cause normal body cells to become cancerous.

"Oxygen is essential for the health and vitality of every cell your the body. Therefore, increasing your consumption of oxygen is very beneficial. And to do that, all you have to do is breathe." Sam gestured with open hands, looking up into the vast Hawaiian sky and inhaling.

"You're like an air doctor!" I interjected. "How do you know all of this stuff about air and the health of the body?"

Sam went on, "Though all SCUBA instructors are well versed in the physiology of the respiratory system, I have conducted additional research on the matter in order to be able to teach the more mystical dimensions of our relationship to air.

"And, I studied our subtle-physical relationship with air even before I became a monk at the age of 19. Besides being a SCUBA instructor, I'm also an acupuncturist and have been studying Chinese medicine since I began practicing Tai Chi and Chi Gung at the age of 16. The subject of health and breath are deeply explored in these disciplines which I have studied extensively."

I began to take a greater interest in what Sam was teaching me. Ancient Asian observations of health in juxtaposition to SCUBA diving suddenly became fascinating to me. "It's interesting," I said, shifting my legs in the sand, "to learn so much about something that seems so simple."

"Exactly!" Sam exclaimed. "Breathing is simple. Breathing is the simplest thing we do. It's easy. We all know how to breathe. It's automatic. Yet with habitual mental and physical tensions, breathing can become restricted in ways that can cause ill effects in your physical, mental, and emotional health.

"As you've just seen in yourself a moment ago, there is a connection between your breathing and your mental state. A little while ago you were upset. Do you remember your breathing and physical posture then?"

I shook my head. I had been so riled up that I wasn't paying attention.

Sam explained, "You were leaning forward, restricting your diaphragm. You brought your arms together, closing your chest. You also raised your shoulders and bent your head down. Your posture greatly reduced your lung capacity."

I nodded, remembering that I had tightly folded my arms and lowered my head.

"As your mental tensions grew, your muscles constricted. The muscles in your arms, neck, and chest tightened. The muscles that control your thorax tensed up and restricted your breathing."

Gazing down the beach, I noticed a little boy crying. He had dropped a big scoop of bright red shaved ice from its cone. Somehow his tearful, grimacing face reminded me of my body tension when I was upset and reactive.

Sam continued, "Your breaths became short and rapid. After only a few seconds of this mental stress, your whole system became frozen and you had tremendous trouble doing the most simple of human actions: breathing."

I felt embarrassed, recalling how I had gasped for air when I was so upset.

Sam continued, "If you were to habitually hold negative thoughts and feelings in your mind, you would develop poorer and poorer breathing habits. Your physical vitality and quality of attention would decline because of the decreased availability of oxygen."

Raising his pointer finger, Sam continued, "On the other hand, when you are simply aware and focused, not agitated by any circumstances, your mind becomes concentrated in a way that beneficially affects breathing and health. When the mind becomes still and peaceful, through concentration, your breath becomes unrestricted and slow.

"It's like this." He pointed to the waves of the sea crashing nearby on the sand. "Count 10 individual waves. Mindfully note when they take form, when they reach their greatest height and when they crash. Watch closely. Miss none of these points as you observe the waves."

I looked over at the waves. I carefully observed the three points that Sam indicated. The first wave was large and wide. When it took form, I could see through its smooth face to view the green and yellow shapes of the hard corals just below and behind it. I noticed the wave's greatest height just before its white water crest began to fall. The wave's crash was an explosion of white mist which slowly settled and was pulled backward, drawn toward the next forming wave.

Somewhere halfway through the exercise, I became mesmerized by the shifting waters and lost count of what wave I was on. I continued my hypnotic wave watching. After a few more quiet moments, Sam said softly, "Very good." I drew my gaze away from the ocean and back to face Sam. It seemed as though the sand and palm trees were moving in a wavelike sway as my vision acclimated to the motionless land. Sam asked, "Now what about your thoughts and breathing? What do you notice about them?"

I observed my mind and breathing for a moment. I wasn't really thinking about anything, and my breathing was calm and slow.

"You see," Sam said, "this meditation stuff isn't so hard after all. I call this exercise the 'surfer's meditation.'" Smiling, he said, "Observing the waves moment by moment helps you to relax and become still both mentally and physically."

I felt quite satisfied with my experience. A moment later I began to recall my earlier troubles with breathing. I said, "I guess I am just exceptionally bad at doing what everyone else does with no problem."

Sam consoled me, "Actually your breathing habits are not uniquely poor. The way you breathe is very similar to the breathing habits of most people." Sam turned from facing the ocean and pointed up the beach to an area overrun by tourists. This section of the beach had fine white sand and was partially shaded by tall swaying palm trees. Dozens of people sunbathed, ate, and chatted there merrily.

"Most people," Sam continued, "have fast, restricted breathing. They don't take in enough oxygen and don't expel enough carbon dioxide. This leads to a reduction of vital energy and high susceptibility to disease."

I looked to the tourists and locals who lay about in the sand where Sam had pointed. I watched a hand-holding blond couple walk toward the ocean's waves. I observed a picnicking family as they laughed while eating sandwiches. They didn't seem to breathe any differently from me, and yet what Sam was telling me seemed to point out a bad habit that we all shared.

Sam went on, "In our society's couch-bound lifestyle, most people spend much more time watching TV than they do exercising. Most people use less than 20% of their lung capacity. As a result, almost everyone you see here is oxygen-starved, and their overall health deteriorates further as toxins build up and pollute their bodies."

"Why do we have such bad breathing habits?" I asked, looking over to two large middle-aged men sipping beers in beach chairs.

Sam responded, "Most people have restricted breathing because of tensions they carry. These tensions constrict their muscles and cause them to improperly exercise their lungs. They get sufficient air for survival, yet not enough for maximum health and vitality."

Sam turned back around to look out over the ocean. I shifted toward the crashing waves and continued listening to Sam. "Most people are oblivious to their breathing 99% of the time. Most people aren't even aware of how the breathing process works. Everyone can tell that when air comes in, it goes to the lungs, yet they are unaware of air traveling through their nostrils, down the nasal and oral parts of the pharynx, reaching the larynx and then the trachea and the lungs.

"Just as most people are wholly unaware that their breathing can be a significant factor for the improvement of their physical lives, emotional health, and mental state, they are wholly unaware of the physical aspects of breathing. Yet understanding and being aware of the breathing processes are very important in Mystic SCUBA, so let's review the anatomy of a breath."

I nodded, though my interest was waning. The word "anatomy" seemed to trigger an immediate decline in my attention.

Seeing my growing inattentiveness, Sam engaged me saying, "Let's start by you telling me what the elements are in breathing."

"Elements in breathing?" I repeated, uncertain what Sam meant.

"What is involved in breathing? What is breathing?" Sam asked plainly.

I questioned back, "Inhaling and exhaling?"

"You've got half of it, yet each normal breath actually consists of four distinct elements: inhalation, the natural turning of the breath between inhalation and exhalation, exhalation, and the natural turning of the breath between exhalation and inhalation. All four elements are involved in a complete breath."

Sam then went into great detail describing different kinds of breathing, breathing organs, processes, and forms of breath control.

BREATH-CHECK

After a thorough discourse on the anatomy of breathing, my attention had diminished. My gaze drifted away from Sam. I sat in the warm sun looking at the crashing waves of the sea. Sam clapped his hands and said excitedly, "Alright, now we're going to explore your breathing!"

Sam's outburst snapped me to attention. "How do I do that?"

"You're going to observe how you breathe by doing a breath-check," Sam said. "In a breath-check you examine the sensations and the qualities of your breath. You watch how you breathe. Don't correct your breathing, just observe it."

"Let's give it a try now," Sam said. "While performing a breath-check, there are four observances to attend to. I'll direct you to be aware of these considerations as you breathe now."

I nodded and shifted my legs in the sand to sit more comfortably.

"Close your eyes," Sam said, "focus on your breathing."

I closed my eyes and sat up straight.

"The first consideration," Sam said, "is where does your breath enter? Do you breathe from your nose or your mouth?"

My mouth was closed and I was breathing through my nose.

"Where does your breath go from there? Does it stop anywhere?" Sam asked.

My inhalations seemed to go right to my throat. Somehow in my throat I felt my breaths become constricted.

Sam paused, giving me a minute to observe my breath and then said, "The second consideration of the breath-check is, where do you breathe to? Which parts of your body move with inhalation and exhalation? Make the distinction between 'low,' 'middle,' and 'high' breathing. See where your body expands during inhalation: the upper chest, middle torso, or lower abdomen. Place your hand on your chest and diaphragm to feel the movement of your body as you breathe."

I placed my hands on my chest and diaphragm. My chest was moving out and in with every breath. My diaphragm was inactive.

Sam paused, giving me another minute to observe my breathing, and then said, "The third consideration of the breath-check is, how does your breath feel?"

I began to consider my feelings of breathing, but immediately became aware of how hot I was starting to feel sitting out in the open as the tropical sun rose higher in the sky.

"Is your breath short or long? Fast or slow? Irregular or even?" Sam asked.

I observed my breath closely. My breath was fast and kind of irregular.

"Is your breath jerky or smooth? Shallow or deep? Forced or effortless?"

My breath wasn't smooth and felt somehow obstructed in my throat.

"Is your breath anxious or peaceful? Narrow or broad? Obstructed or free-flowing?"

My breath was shallow and narrow. It was involuntary, yet a bit anxious.

"As the final consideration, we will consider your breathing rate," Sam said. "Use the clock on your dive computer to count how many breaths, a complete inhalation and exhalation, you have in one minute."

Looking at my dive computer, I timed my breathing rate. After a minute, I had taken 18 breaths. Sam told me that the average resting breathing rate for adults is 16 breaths per minute. In view of my difficulties earlier in the day, I was relieved that my breathing rate was about average.

Sam handed me an underwater writing slate and a pencil. The slate had all of the considerations of the breath-check listed on it.

"Note your observations," Sam said. "This will be helpful for comparison later."

I wrote down what I noticed about my breathing while I performed the breath-check.

DEEP BREATHING

Sam paused for a moment and then continued, "Now that you understand the general benefits of breathing and your habitual breathing, let's talk about the additional health benefits of deep breathing."

I was quite hot now. I took off my sunhat and began fanning myself.

Handing me a cold bottle of water, Sam said, "The high levels of stress that are endemic to our society have a strong effect on your body and your health. The stresses of daily life aggravate you, unbalance you, and ultimately make you tense up. This tension results in a very unhealthy condition: a condition of shallow breathing. Most Westerners are conditioned through these stresses to tighten their stomachs and hold in their gut. This is further exacerbated by the media messages telling us that a fat appearance is bad."

"Is that right?" I asked.

"Yes," Sam answered. "Just look around. Everyone is doing it."

I looked up the beach to where many tourists lay in the sun. I wasn't quite sure what Sam meant. I saw a muscular surfer sun tanning next to his surfboard on an oversized beach towel. I couldn't see any sign of unhealthiness in him. *That surfer looks as fit and healthy as anyone*, I thought.

"Through stress and social pressures you have unconsciously learned a habit of holding your tummy in. This unconscious tension cuts you off from the foundation of healthy breathing: deep breathing. Like most people, you breathe shallowly by opening and closing your chest. Unable to breathe to the abdomen, your restricted respiration contributes to ill health and mental stresses."

Sam directed me to observe his slow abdominal breathing, and then said, "I'd like you to consciously relax and extend your lower abdomen for a moment."

Sam gestured by extending his hand outward at the level of his belly button. I exhaled slightly and released the muscles in the area of my abdomen. To my surprise, I noticed an immediate letting go of a tension that I didn't even know was there. My stomach seemed to extend out and down by about two inches. My shoulders dropped about an inch. I felt relief and relaxation. I noticed that my breathing had lowered to my belly. Though I immediately felt markedly better, I also immediately noticed that I felt a little fatter.

"What a difference," I said, "I never knew how much I was holding my stomach in. Letting my tummy relax seems to take the tension out of my whole body."

Sam agreed, saying, "Yes, when you let go of holding in your tummy, it causes your whole body to relax. Practicing deep breathing with this consideration feels even better. And deep breathing actually strengthens and tones your stomach."

I looked back at the surfer. Though he was lying down on his back, I could now see that he was holding tension in his abdomen.

"During deep breathing," Sam said, "your abdomen expands and your respiration slows down. When you breathe deeply to your abdomen, your lung capacity increases because you fill the deepest parts of your lungs."

After giving me another moment to observe this feeling, Sam continued to explain, "In the Mystic SCUBA exercises, a lot of attention is paid to exhalation. Exhalation is the first concern of respiration. If you can exhale properly you will be able to inhale properly."

Gesturing to me, Sam said, "Try it. Exhale as much as you can and see what happens."

I exhaled completely, forcing the air out of my lungs till my shoulders hunched and my chest quivered. As soon as my exhalation was complete, my body automatically sucked a great volume of air back in.

"With shallow exhalations, you don't expel enough toxin-saturated air at the bottom of your lungs," Sam explained. "To do deeper exhalations, use the lower part of your diaphragm, the curved abdominal muscle that separates the chest from the abdominal cavity. It is the most important muscle in respiration.

"When you focus on exhaling from the bottom of your diaphragm, you improve your breathing overall. During exhalation, your diaphragm relaxes and moves naturally to a comfortable position after being pushed downward during inhalation. Then the diaphragm gently contracts to force more air out.

"After doing a deep exhalation, deep inhalation is automatic. The upper part of your diaphragm naturally expands as you take air in. During inhalation, your diaphragm will drop, pushing your abdomen out as your lungs fill with air.

"Would you like to give deep breathing a try now?" Sam asked.

"Alright," I said, refreshed as a cool breeze blew on us from the sea.

Sam began with his directions, "Consciously observe the four elements of breathing. Do four to six complete breath-cycles. Inhale to the area just below your belly button. We always begin respiration with inhalation, yet remember that in all the deep breathing exercises of Mystic SCUBA, your greater concern is your exhalation."

I sat up straight and began my inhalation. I let my abdomen relax as I had before. In the beginning of my inhalation, the air seemed to naturally go to my stomach. I focused on my breath going to the area just below my belly button. As my inhalation continued, I felt some resistance in my abdomen. It felt as if there was a balloon just below my belly button that I was filling. As I ended my inhalation, I felt that the balloon was filled to capacity.

I observed the turning of my breath and then started slowly breathing out. I allowed the air to calmly flow from me. At first it was effortless. Then as I reached the end of my exhalation, I pushed slightly with my diaphragm and expelled a lot more air than I knew was left in me.

As I inhaled after observing the turning of my breath, I found my inhalation to be more free and deep than I could have imagined. I was simply able to take in more air. My focus on exhalation automatically made my inhalation deep and full.

I continued breathing deeply for a few more complete respirations. I felt deeply calm and relaxed while I practiced. When I was done Sam said, "Congratulations, you have just taken your first deep breath."

I smiled, feeling some accomplishment.

"That was different from the way that I usually breathe. It felt better," I commented, "and it was actually easier."

Sam looked satisfied with my progress. "In Mystic SCUBA you exercise a more efficient way of breathing. Deep breathing conserves energy and relaxes your body."

I noticed that my breathing was now deeper. I felt my breaths going to my abdomen automatically.

"Now you know all you need to know to breathe well," Sam said with a bright smile. "All breathing in Mystic SCUBA is deep breathing. Now that you have experienced the benefits of deep breathing, it will start to become comfortable and habitual."

I was starting to see breathing in a whole new way. I realized that I had been completely unconscious of my breathing almost all of the time and that with a little awareness of this basic process, I could feel better. I felt more connected to my body. I felt more calm and relaxed.

"You've done very well today," Sam said. "Let's meet here again tomorrow at the same time. We'll have some more important information to cover."

"OK," I smiled, "I'll be on time tomorrow, I promise."

Sam bowed and was off in his orange Jeep.

I stayed at the cove and played in the cool water, snorkeling over the shallow reef. The ocean water was refreshing. From time to time I would rest, float in the waves, and practice Sam's breathing exercises.

Returning home in the late afternoon, I sat down at my desk to continue my programming studies, first checking my email. I had a message from Birhanu, my tour guide from Bahir Dar, a town in northern Ethiopia where I'd traveled with a group of friends to see the Blue Nile Falls. During our tour of the falls, there were kids who helped us on the muddy hike.

One of my friends, Rebecca, gave the little girl walking with her a tip of 200 *birr*, rather than a more customary tip of 2 *birr*. I remember talking that night with Rebecca about how 200 *birr*, about $25, was so much money in Ethiopia, and yet, only about what we'd spend on admission to a club in San Francisco on a Saturday night. We were curious to know what the little girl would do with her new wealth.

Birhanu was writing to tell me that he'd seen her and that she'd asked him to give her thanks to us. She'd used just a little bit of the money on a pair of new shoes, and then used the rest of it to buy a goat and some chickens for her family. They were now selling milk and eggs to other people in the village, and for the first time, they had enough money so that the girl didn't need to work for the tourists anymore. She was going to start school in a few weeks, something she'd only dreamed of before.

The possibilities that my friend's random act of kindness had opened for the girl and her family brought a tremendous brightness to my heart. At the same time I found myself saddened by the dramatic differences of opportunity. My mood turned back to my feelings of the previous evening. The idea that there was so much inequality in life for so many gnawed at me. My eyes started to fill with tears. I felt my throat become tight.

Suddenly, I realized that my breathing was starting to become constricted and shallow. Sam's lessons of the day burst into my mind. I began to practice deep breathing. After just a few respirations, my body relaxed and my breathing became deep and calm. I also noticed that my sadness had become distant and that with a light focus on deep breathing, I could maintain my equanimity.

I started working on my programming tutorials. I was able to make good progress in my studies. As I lay down to sleep, I settled myself in a relaxed posture, breathed deeply, and fell into a deep and peaceful slumber.

SUN

The next morning I met Sam right on time. After cheerfully greeting me, Sam said, "Now that you know all about breathing, let's shift our discussion to the next lesson." I smiled, feeling a positive sense of progression. Sam continued, "Let's talk about *sun*. Sun is an ancient Chinese term meaning relaxation. The disposition of the body, mind, and spirit in Mystic SCUBA is the disposition of sun.

"The Chinese art of sun is the practice of paying attention to relaxation. Relaxation doesn't mean being limp. It means using just enough effort and energy, with no additional force, strength, or tension."

Sam pointed to a fast growing wave taking form as it headed for the shore and said, "A wave is sun." The wave crashed forcefully on the sand.

Sam continued, "In paying attention to not being too hard, too strong, or too forceful, you learn a more subtle sensitivity—physically, energetically, and spiritually. When there is no excess force, action, and thought, you come into balance, a healthy condition of the body, mind, and spirit.

"During Mystic SCUBA exercises, relax your whole body. Loosen and open your joints. Consciously feel the loosening of your muscles. Release all tension. Tensions stop the flow of blood and constrict breathing.

"Your back should be long and open. Your shoulders should be relaxed. It's important to adjust your buoyancy control vest so that your back is not arching. Your elbows, knees, wrists, and fingers should all be slightly bent and relaxed. Your chest should feel open. Your abdomen should be free of tension, allowing your breath to become slow and deep."

"During SCUBA diving there is an area where I regularly feel a lot of tension," I said. "My ankles tend to feel stiff and painful after kicking for a while. I think my ankles are weak."

"Weakness is a strength in learning relaxation," Sam responded.

"What do you mean?"

"If your ankles were very strong, you would use the strength of your ankles when kicking. If you were able to overcompensate with your physical strength, you wouldn't see a reason to learn to relax. Many physically strong people have similar problems learning Tai Chi, where the movements are as relaxed and smooth as SCUBA diving kicks."

Sam continued, "Actually, there should be very little physical strength used by your ankles and feet while kicking in SCUBA diving. Principally the ankles should be relaxed and move like a wave. Your problem is that your fins are too stiff, causing you to exert physical strength at the beginning of downward kicks."

Sam paused and pointed to my SCUBA bag. "Didn't I see another pair of fins in there? Can you fetch them for me?" I did have an extra pair of fins. They were my backup pair. My backup fins were short and rubbery with a split down the middle of the fin and a closed heel. When I wore them, I would just slip them on my feet. I didn't like them very much because I couldn't move in the water as quickly as I could when wearing my longer fins, which were stiffer and had an open heel and an adjustable strap. On a couple of occasions the adjustable strap had broken, which is why I carried my backup pair with me.

I opened my SCUBA bag and retrieved the fins. I handed them to Sam. He examined them and said, "Use these fins for all dives with calm water conditions. With these, you will not be forced to use physical strength on your downward kicks because they are much less stiff. You will be able to kick, free of tension.

"With these fins you will move more slowly underwater, but speed and covering distance is never of much importance in Mystic SCUBA. However, there will be times where you will want to use your long fins. You should use your long fins on dives with a moderate or strong current. You may want to use them when you are shore diving and there is significant surge, or when you must make a long surface swim."

Handing me back my fins, Sam said, "With these fins you will be able to learn relaxation."

"Thanks," I said, "I'll give it a shot."

"You're welcome," Sam answered. "These fins will help you remain relaxed while diving."

With his calm smile, Sam looked at me and said, "The reason that you broke the first rule in SCUBA is that you were not relaxed. You need to relax. Without relaxation, you could find yourself breaking the first rule of SCUBA again."

I was immediately put off by Sam's words.

Raising his finger didactically, he said, "It's really quite simple. Relax your physical tension. Relax your mental tension. In order to prevent breaking the first rule of SCUBA again, all you have to do is relax."

I folded my arms. Sam was teasing me about my dive accident again. I felt my breath quicken and my brow strain. Sam continued, saying, "When you practice relaxation, it's easy to adhere to this vitally important rule."

I found myself heading right back to where I was yesterday: tense, short of breath, and very irritated at Sam. To thwart Sam's button-pushing insinuations, I said as calmly as I could, "Sam, it's not that I don't appreciate your help and instruction, but could you please just lay off the fact that I had a diving accident?"

Sam nodded in understanding and then continued, "When your mind lets go of its tensions, you will not be in jeopardy of breaking the first rule of SCUBA again."

Now I lost what reserve I had mustered. I looked at Sam with a sour frown. Sam continued calmly, "You see the first rule of SCUBA diving…"

"Again with the 'you broke the first rule of SCUBA'!" I yelled mockingly, putting my hands together under my chin as if bowing as Sam often does. I was tired of hearing this over and over from him. "Look! What is it with you always telling me to follow the first rule of SCUBA all the time! It was just an accident! It's not like I wanted to get stuck on a coral reef with my regulator free-flowing behind me! It's not like I was trying to drown myself! OK?!"

Sam calmly continued, "It is because of your tension that you got into the predicament. If you were relaxed, you would have seen more options for life in that moment. You would not have broken the first rule of SCUBA."

"OK, I've had it with this!" I yelled. "You're getting on my nerves!"

"Exactly," Sam said calmly. "So observe your mind."

I was about to yell at Sam again when he asked, "How is this inability to relax and stop anger now any different from your inability to relax and stop panic during your diving accident?"

Though I wanted to ignore it, somehow Sam's question took the steam out of my rant. I paused for a moment, considering the matter. I didn't have an answer.

Sam went on, "You are angry right now, yet there are infinite possibilities for happiness. You almost died during your accident when there were infinite possibilities for life."

My anger quickly subsided. I nodded, acknowledging the truth of Sam's words. *Why did I get so upset again?* I wondered. I logically knew I had no reason to get so angry at Sam.

I was about to apologize to him for my outburst when he continued, "This is the very tension that made you break the first rule of SCUBA. The tension in your outlook, the tension in your mind, is what caused you to see things incorrectly, lose your regulator, panic, and almost drown. Your accident was no accident. It was the outcome of your choices, mental conditioning, and karma. And they were all initiated by your tension.

"If you observe your mind in this moment, you can see this tension that causes you so much suffering. You can expose the crux of that which makes you so confused and dissatisfied with your life."

Sam's words deftly exposed a complicated feeling within me, a mixture of great fear and yet tremendous yearning.

"Can you do it?" Sam encouraged quietly. "Can you stop the stream of karma? Can you wake up to see that all of your tiring reactions just keep you running into a wall, a wall that vanishes as soon as you stop running into it? And all you have to do is stop, relax, breathe, and let go of the tension."

I felt a deep calm. My gripping feeling of fear and yearning started to subside. Sam asked in a near-whisper, "Can you clear your mask and see what has always been beyond the fog?"

For a moment, I felt as if a fog in my mind lifted. It was as if my consciousness had opened and I could see an infinity of formless possibilities beyond the world and self that I knew. I felt that I had gone to some beautiful, quiet place that was as expansive as the sea.

A moment later I realized that I was smiling. My awareness returned to my surroundings. I was sitting in the sand looking at Sam. I felt balanced and peaceful. The anger I had experienced just moments ago seemed impossibly distant now.

Observing me closely, Sam continued, "For now, you are up and down. In time you will be balanced. When you learn Mystic SCUBA, you will learn to free yourself of tensions and remain balanced so that you will never panic and break the first rule of SCUBA again."

"I just experienced something extraordinary. What just happened?"

"Yesterday I showed you the connection between your tension and your breath," Sam said. "Now you are starting to become aware of what this study is really all about. You have come to see and relinquish, for a moment, the root of the tensions of your being. This root tension at your spiritual core binds your awareness and holds you in limited states of consciousness due to self-oriented fear and ignorance. At the foundation of your being, this tension is the primary affliction preventing your happiness and peace of mind."

I sat quietly for a moment, taking all of this in.

BALANCING TENSIONS

"Next," Sam said, "to deepen your understanding of this tension, I will show you the connection between your tension and thoughts. Spiritual tension creates mental tension. Mental tension unbalances the way you comprehend life. Mental tension creates physical tension. Physical tension unbalances the way you interact with the physical world. For you, these tensions were so great that they almost caused your death."

Looking at me closely, Sam said, "Let me show you what I mean. If you would, please stand up. Stand on one leg, your strongest leg."

I stood and lifted my left knee, balancing on my right leg.

"Now pay attention to the sole of your foot," Sam said. "Feel the ground. You are connected with the ground."

I didn't know what Sam meant by "feel the ground." All I could feel was the pressure of my right foot on the ground.

"Now feel the ground from your knee. Push up and down slightly." Sam said, "And now from your hips. Push up and down from your hips. Feel the ground."

I did as Sam instructed. I started to feel that the ground was very solid and that I was supported in my movements by a strong foundation.

"Now move your shoulders from left to right and up and down. Feel the ground in your shoulders." Sam said, "Nod your head and feel the ground. Feel the ground from your whole body."

I followed Sam's directions. My body subtly rocked back and forth as I stood on one leg, my foot rolling slightly to maintain my balance. With each movement I became more aware of the ground holding me up. As I paid attention to the solid support the ground provided to my heel, to the ball of my foot, and to my toes, I felt as if the whole earth was holding me up. I could imagine a connecting line from my foot all the way to the center of the earth. I felt the whole earth beneath my feet!

"Very good," Sam said. "Now tighten your butt as tight as you can." I did. "See," Sam exclaimed pointing to my standing leg, "you just lost contact with the ground." With my muscles tightened as much as I could muster, all I noticed was my physical strain. I wasn't sure how I had lost contact with the ground.

Sam explained, "Now when you nod your head and move your shoulders, you cannot feel below the tightness of your waist."

My muscles started to tremble slightly. I rolled my head and rotated my shoulders. I was now able to see what Sam meant. My feelings of movement no longer stemmed from the earth. They felt somehow smaller and unsteady.

Sam continued, "Now tighten your shoulders as tight as you can." I hunched up my shoulders almost to my ears. My shoulders shook. The strain in my backside now started to hurt. Keeping my balance became increasingly difficult. "Whoa!" I blurted out as I fell to the right. I had to relax my shoulders and butt to extend my left leg to catch myself from falling over.

"That was a very good try," Sam said chuckling. "You almost lasted 10 seconds."

"I get it," I said breathing hard from straining my muscles. "You can't stay balanced when you are tense."

Sam agreed, and then said, "OK, back up. Continue to balance on one foot. This time relax your body."

I changed to balance on my left leg because my right leg had become tired. With my body relaxed, it was easy to stay balanced.

"I'm going to ask you some questions," Sam said, "and I'd like for you to answer them silently to yourself."

"OK," I said, still balancing easily.

Sam began, "What would your family say if they knew that you were doing this right now?"

They would probably think standing on one leg to learn Mystic SCUBA was ridiculous, I thought, laughing a little, *but they'd still be supportive and wish me well.*

Sam continued, "What was your most embarrassing moment?"

Well, there was the time in 6th grade where I walked out of the locker room to gym class and realized I forgot to put on my shorts. Then there was the time when I was waving to a guy I liked at the senior class dinner and I walked right into the marinara sauce on the buffet counter. The whole container completely emptied on me and covered my new white dress.

Thinking about this experience instantly transported me back to the feelings of humiliation I had that night. I started falling to the left. I had to snap out of my feelings to bring myself back into balance.

Sam continued, "Have you ever had a messy break up or other problems in an intimate relationship?"

Boy had I! The feelings I had about my last relationship started to flood my head. My balance became very unsteady. I couldn't seem to gain my stability. I was mired in the difficulties of my past.

Quickly Sam asked, "What is the thing that bothers you the most about your job?"

Street children, AIDS, poverty, injustice! These words and related images from Ethiopia flashed in my mind just before I became aware that I was falling to the ground! I caught myself just before collapsing.

"Tension creates imbalance, so in Mystic SCUBA we practice relaxation," Sam said. "You need to learn relaxation so that you can experience the blissful harmony of life. In the beginning of Mystic SCUBA there is a lot of attention paid to the physical body.

"Physical relaxation brings balance to the way you interact with the physical world. Physical relaxation alleviates mental tension. Mental relaxation balances the way you comprehend life. Mental relaxation alleviates spiritual tension. When you relinquish all of your tensions, you will have an awareness of life that is unlimited."

BASIC MYSTIC SCUBA EXERCISES

Sam said, "Now that you have an understanding of the health benefits of air and relaxation, you can start learning the basic Mystic SCUBA exercises. Mystic SCUBA exercises are meditative exercises. We will start by learning about buoyancy. Then we will work on two relaxation techniques and end with two deep breathing techniques.

"Being able to comfortably establish neutral buoyancy is essential in Mystic SCUBA exercises. It is very hard to practice deep, relaxed breathing if your attention is consumed with adjusting your buoyancy. Neutral buoyancy needs to be properly planned and intuitively realized."

Buoyancy? I wondered silently. *What's spiritual about buoyancy?* I had already learned all about buoyancy during my advanced certification.

"First of all, you have to understand something," Sam said. "When you dive, you don't swim, you fly. We use the physics of our SCUBA apparatus to fly in a denser atmosphere. Buoyancy is the art of flying underwater."

Sam pointed over to a nearby hibiscus bush where a hummingbird was feeding and said, "You can learn a lot about perfect buoyancy by watching a hummingbird fly."

I paid close attention to the hummingbird's body positions while it effortlessly hovered at a precise point in front of the flower's brilliant red petals. A moment later the hummingbird rapidly elevated to another high-standing outstretched flower.

As I continued to observe the hummingbird, Sam said, "Yep, flying underwater feels the same as when you fly in dreams."

Sam's statement instantly reminded me of a remarkable dream that I had not too long ago. In the dream I was flying through the sky, over the tall ohia trees of the Hawaiian mountains, to the white sand beaches of the west shore, and over the ocean. I nodded with a dawning recognition of what Sam meant; my feelings of flying in the dream reminded me of my feelings of neutral buoyancy while diving.

"There are two new utilities that I would like you to use," Sam said. "The first is one of these." Sam pointed to the 16-inch metal rod that was fastened to his buoyancy control vest by a 2-foot white plastic chain. He had used the metal rod several times during my Advanced Open Water Diver course. He used it to point at things, and banged it on his tank to get my attention.

"This is a diving wand," Sam said. "It is used as a buoyancy tool in the beginning and then as a communications tool later. Even advanced divers find themselves bumping into coral and bottoming-out on the sea floor from time to time. This is unacceptable as far as I'm concerned. You must master your buoyancy. Until your buoyancy is at its peak performance, the wand will help you control your damage to the reef. If you find yourself out of control and think that you are going to crash into the reef, extend your wand to an area of the reef that appears most barren and push off. This way, your whole arm or leg will not hit the reef and cause more damage."

Sam pulled an extra dive wand from his gear bag. Reaching over to my unassembled SCUBA gear, he attached it to my buoyancy control vest. He then pointed out something in the pocket of his buoyancy control vest that I hadn't seen before. It was a silver metal hook that looked like the top of a clothes hanger, but sturdier. The hook was tied to a thin six-foot rope which was clipped on to Sam's buoyancy control vest. Pulling an extra hook and rope from his gear bag, Sam clipped the tool onto my buoyancy control vest as well.

"The second tool that I'd like you to use is the reef-line," Sam said. "The reef-line can be carefully hooked onto a rock in an area that has been examined to make sure that there is no living creature. Alternatively, you may bring an extra weight belt to lay in the sand and hook on to, as we will today. Once hooked on, you may add air to your buoyancy control vest to become slightly positively buoyant. Then you will float up, but be held down by the weights or the rock at the end of the line. This allows you to practice meditative exercises with no worries of shooting up to the surface.

"We'll start by working on the relaxation exercises," Sam said. "For the first relaxation exercise, you'll rig your reef-line and become positively buoyant. Then just relax. Relax your eyes, relax your brow. Relax the crown of your head and relax your jaw. Consecutively focus on relaxing every single part of your body down to your toes. Relax each area, one at a time. Take your time. Work on relaxing underwater with your SCUBA kit on. When you have completed that exercise, sit up and we'll do the next relaxation exercise.

"For the second relaxation exercise, I'd like you to make yourself negatively buoyant. Try relaxing by lying in the sand. In this exercise, you'll focus only on the area of your body that is the most tense. Often in the first exercise, you'll expose areas of the body that are difficult to relax. Work on relaxing the one area that has the most tension. If you didn't find any particular areas of tension in the first exercise, you could focus on any area of your body where you commonly have tension or pain.

"Breathe into the tense area. Direct your attention to the area of tension as you inhale. Feel your breath filling the area of tension. Exhale to the tense area. Direct the tension out of the body as you exhale to the area. You may also tighten and release the area of tension if breathing alone does not alleviate it. To do this, as you inhale, strengthen the muscles around the tense area to a comfortable level. As you exhale, completely release the tension in the muscles."

When Sam was finished explaining, I was a little perplexed. He asked, "Do you have any questions?"

I didn't. I didn't really understand what he was talking about. I wasn't sure how I would breathe to my elbow where I felt some tension, but I had no question that wasn't extremely vague.

Seeing my confusion, Sam summarized the exercises again and then said, "Don't worry, you'll really learn it by doing it."

"OK," I said. I was tired of sitting in the hot sun and eager to get into the water.

Sam said, "We will do this dive in the open water at the southern reef here. During this dive, you will focus on buoyancy and practice both of the relaxation techniques. You'll do a breath-check just before we dive, floating in the water with SCUBA gear on."

We strapped our tanks into our buoyancy control vests and prepared to dive. Sam refreshed my memory of the hand signals and the important points of each exercise. Pausing to touch the water with his hand as we reached our entry point, Sam said, "OK, let's dive."

We waded into the gentle ocean waves. The water was cool and refreshing. We kicked off to the south reef on a surface swim. "Let's do your breath-check here," Sam said as he clipped his underwater writing slate on to my buoyancy vest.

As we bobbed on the surface, I performed a breath-check, finding that my breathing felt generally shallow, short and fast. I was only aware of breathing from my mouth and feeling the air touch the back of my throat. Placing my hands over my chest and abdomen, I could feel that my chest was moving. Using my dive computer to time myself, I found that I was breathing 17 breaths per minute.

After noting this information on the slate, I showed it to Sam. He smiled and said, "Remember now, you're flying."

"OK," I said.

Sam signaled for our descent. I expelled the air from my buoyancy control vest and cleared my ears. Submerging myself in the blue water, I quickly reached the top of the coral reef at a depth of 60 feet.

Sam, waving his arms up and down, signaled for me to focus on flying. I added air into my buoyancy control vest to become neutrally buoyant. After floating for a moment, we began to cross the reef toward some large mounds of hard corals. Imagining myself to be flying rather than swimming filled me with an exuberant joy as we glided forward, traversing the sea. Flying felt so different than swimming. This consideration in movement suddenly seemed revolutionary to me!

As I excitedly soared between the coral heads, Sam tapped his tank three times with his dive wand. I looked to Sam. He signaled me to do the first relaxation exercise. Sam had added two of his weights to an extra weight belt that he had brought for the reef-line exercise. He laid the weight belt down in a large sandy patch. Sam signaled me to hook the reef-line by making a hooking motion with his finger. I pulled the silver hook of the reef-line from my pocket and hooked it to the weight belt. I then added a little air to my buoyancy control vest and slowly floated up to the full length of the extended reef-line.

As I floated there suspended above the rock, I began to relax. I tried to sequentially relax my body from head to toe. *Sam told me to relax my eyes*, I thought to myself. I closed my eyes half way. *How do I relax my eyes?* I wondered. I wasn't sure if I relaxed them, but I figured I should move on.

Now, how do I relax my brow? It's kind of smashed under my dive mask. Well, maybe I should just move on to the crown of my head. I never really thought about the crown of my head before, what is it anyway?

My whole exercise continued this way. When I was done with my pinky toe, I was confused as to if I had done it right. I didn't feel more relaxed, but I finished anyway. I turned to Sam and shrugged my shoulders.

Sam applauded and signaled me to do the second relaxation exercise. I deflated my buoyancy vest and slowly fell into the sand. I pulled the reef-line hook from the extra weight belt and stuffed it back into my buoyancy control vest pocket.

I wasn't sure where I had felt tension during the first exercise. It seemed that I had been pretty tense all over. I remembered the tension that I had felt in my shoulder the first time Sam helped me relax after saving me from drowning. I began to breathe to my shoulder where I had felt that pain. I inhaled and exhaled over and over, but I didn't feel a difference. I wondered if I was doing it correctly. I was having trouble feeling that I was even breathing to my shoulder so I reached around to my shoulder and touched it to remind myself that my breath should be there.

Still, nothing seemed to happen. Either it wasn't working so well, or I was doing it poorly. I remembered that Sam said that if I was having trouble releasing tension that I should tense the muscle. I tensed up my neck and shoulder muscles as tightly as I could during a big inhale. I was glad I was on a reef-line because otherwise, I would have floated to the surface. As I exhaled, I tried to loosen my neck, but I felt a tight pinch as I did. I tried inhaling and tensing again. The pinch remained. My exhalation didn't help. After a while I stopped the exercise and looked over to Sam. Wiggling his pinky and thumb, he gave me the Hawaiian *shaka* sign and signaled me to ascend to the surface.

Sam grabbed the extra weight belt and we ascended. When we surfaced, Sam said, "You did well."

"But I couldn't even relax," I said. "And on the last exercise I think I hurt myself." I rotated my head trying to get the pinch out of my neck.

"I understand. You did well," Sam said again. "The first step in learning to be relaxed is to realize that you're not relaxed. With practice you'll loosen all your knots."

Looking at me as I massaged my neck, Sam said, "Perhaps you shouldn't tense the muscles in your neck for a while during this exercise. You tensed too strongly and didn't let go of the tension when you exhaled. So your end result was a greater tension than when you began."

Oh great! I thought, growing aggravated. I felt like I couldn't even do the most basic exercise right.

"Just practice breathing to the area of tension until you see some progress while doing this exercise," Sam said. "You'll find in time that this exercise is very helpful. Take a moment right now to relax your shoulders and breathe deeply. You will feel better with proper relaxation."

I relaxed my shoulders and focused on deep breathing. The pinch in my neck began to loosen. My inhalation made my neck feel somehow full. I then exhaled deeply. It seemed as though a kind of pressure had left my neck. I dropped my shoulders down a couple of inches and then inhaled to my neck again. I felt a greater and greater sense of unwinding as I breathed to and loosened my neck for a few more minutes.

Then we swam the short distance back to shore. Sam and I sat down in the sand. It was now afternoon and I was getting hungry. I fetched two bottles of water, a ham sandwich, and two papayas from a cooler in my car. I gave Sam one of the bottles of water and a papaya. Sam thanked me with a bow.

"Would you like half of my sandwich?" I asked.

"No thanks," Sam said, "I don't eat ham."

"Oh, of course not," I said, considering that Buddhist monks probably had strict dietary observances.

"I'm very content with the papaya," Sam said, smiling as he cut the papaya open with his dive knife.

After a short lunch, I left Sam and drove for a half hour to a small dive shop to refill our tanks with air. The dive shop was situated halfway up a steep hill. I pulled off the road into the driveway and parked under a large green awning next to the perpetually humming air compressor where my tanks would be refilled.

I looked for Michael, the shop owner and Divemaster, through the large open sliding doors in the main shop. I could see that he was not standing by the white cash register desk and that there were no customers near the dusty buoyancy vest, regulator, and wetsuit displays.

Michael's dive shop was run-down and slightly disheveled. Compared to a five- star PADI dive shop it was more like a dive shack. Actually I wondered how anyone found the place. It was far up a remote road in a lightly populated section of the island. I had only come across it myself after getting lost. However, I always came to this quirky dive shop since it was located near many of my favorite dive sites.

"Aloha, Vanessa!" I heard Michael call out as he emerged from the closet of the compressor room where the weights and weight belts were piled in the corner.

"Hi Michael," I waved.

Michael had a full head of silvery hair, pale wrinkle-free skin, and bright blue eyes. He manned the dive shop only in the afternoon since he lead morning boat and shore dives for tourists on most days. My father and I had been renting air tanks from Michael since we started diving in Hawaii. I always found him boring.

Michael always excitedly subjected me to droning ocean-fact lectures while he refilled or exchanged my tanks. Today he immediately launched into telling me trivial facts about SCUBA diving and the difference between yellowmargin moray eels and yellowhead moray eels.

"Yellowmargin morays not only have sharp teeth growing from the top and bottom of their jaws," Michael said, "but they also have teeth growing from the roof of their mouths. This helps them capture and stabilize their prey."

" Oh? That's interesting, Michael," I said, feigning interest.

I was always relieved to leave the dive shop as soon as my tanks were filled.

Sam waited for me on the beach. When I returned and brought the fresh tanks over to him, he smiled and invited me to sit next to him in the sand.

"On the next dive, you will work on two deep breathing exercises. The first exercise is called 'Holding the Ocean'. To perform this exercise, hold your arms in front of you in a rounded manner, as if you were hugging a beach ball. Your arms should be positioned low, at the level of the abdomen. Your palms should be facing towards the body."

Sam demonstrated the arm and hand positioning as he spoke. I followed his movements and asked, "Is this right?"

"Keep your shoulders relaxed," Sam said patting my left shoulder. "Keep your elbows, wrists, and fingers lose. Gently spread your fingers.

"You will be doing this exercise while neutrally buoyant. Begin by relaxing your body. Your eyes should be opened and relaxed, gazing ahead with a soft focus. Practice deep breathing. Once you've established deep slow breaths, bring your attention to your navel chakra. Breathe to your navel chakra, the power center. Focus on your inhalations filling your navel chakra with air and your exhalation emptying your navel chakra of air.

"There is no external focus. Bring your attention inward to your breath and navel chakra. Breathe smoothly and evenly. Practice Holding the Ocean using the principles of deep breathing.

"Practice for a period of time that is comfortable. There's no set amount of time for any Mystic SCUBA exercise. What determines the duration of the exercise is your comfort level. An exercise may take as little as 20 seconds or as long as 60 minutes, depending on the safety of your diving conditions and how you feel."

"OK," I said. I was glad that I was free to do the exercises for as long as I was comfortable. Even a simple exercise like this one could be quite stressful in conditions of heavy surge or poor visibility.

"When you are done with this exercise," Sam said, "give me the OK signal and we'll move on to the next breathing exercise. The second breathing exercise will be done while rigged to your reef-line. It is a powerful technique called the 'Orbit'."

"What's an Orbit?" I asked, intrigued by the name.

"The Orbit is a SCUBA diving adaptation of an advanced *Taoist* meditation for health and enlightenment," Sam answered. "This technique supercharges the body with vitality and clarifies the mind. It's called The Orbit because you are orbiting energy, in this case, around the midline of the body."

"How do I do the Orbit?" I asked.

Sam answered, "You begin this exercise by establishing deep breathing. Then focus your mind on your navel chakra. Once you've established an awareness of energy in the navel, you exhale and move the energy down your front to the very bottom point of your spine."

"Move my energy down my front?" I asked. "How do I do that?"

"You move the energy with your mind and breath," Sam answered. "Feel and focus your attention along your body as you breathe. Where you place the mind's attention, the energy will move. Your focused mind stimulates and energizes the breath. You will feel as if energy is being moved along your body as you focus and breathe.

"After you feel the energy reach your bottom point while exhaling, inhale and bring the energy up the spine. As you inhale, focus your mind inch-by-inch up the outside of your back to the top of your head. With the energy focused at the top of your head, again exhale and bring the energy from the top of the head down your front to your bottom point. Continue breathing in this way. Breathe slowly, moving the focus of your mind with the duration of your breath."

I listened carefully to Sam's instructions, intent on doing the exercise right.

Sam said, "During the dive, after you've completed your Orbit exercise, you will do another breath-check."

"Underwater?" I asked.

"Yes," Sam said, "you can do a breath-check on land or underwater. You can do a breath-check before and after any exercise to measure how the exercise has affected you."

"What do you mean?"

"Well, you know how you were breathing earlier from your breath-check on land. Now you can measure in breaths how these practices affect you. Write your new observations alongside the old notes."

"OK," I said, "kind of like a breath progress assessment."

"Yes," Sam said, "and now that you understand the relationship between breath and mind, this progress assessment yields even deeper insight."

Sam and I geared up into our SCUBA equipment. We checked the proper functioning of our gear and then entered the sea. We swam back out to where we did the first exercises. Sam looked down to check our positioning, then gave me the descend hand signal. I let all of the air out of my buoyancy control vest and dived down to 40 feet. The bottom was mostly sandy here with sparse lumpy coral heads. Sam and I sat on the sandy bottom. Sam signaled for me to begin Holding the Ocean.

I put some air into my buoyancy control vest so that I was hovering with my fins touching the sand. It took a moment to focus on buoyancy before I could concentrate on proper abdominal breathing. I held my arms out rounded in front of me as Sam had showed me and began deep breathing to my navel chakra.

This exercise was quite comfortable. Instantly, I felt calm and relaxed. After a few minutes of practice I felt a glowing warmth in the area of my navel. After a few minutes I turned back to Sam. He signaled me to do the Orbit.

I took a moment to position myself, reestablishing neutral buoyancy. I brought my attention to my navel center, and then focused on my breath. As I exhaled and inhaled, I imagined a flow of energy looping around my body with my breath. I enjoyed paying attention to my breath as I tried to feel the flow of energy around my body. I turned and floated upside down practicing the Orbit, smiling at the sight of my fins above my head and enjoying the freedom from gravity. The sunlight shining through the surface of the water had turned a deep and beautiful gold in the late afternoon.

I turned right-side up again, noticing a small shimmering school of fish approaching. As they came closer I could see that they were some kind of squid— they had an iridescent shine, distinctive fins encircling their bodies, long wiggly noses like elephants, and big eyes. They watched me. I continued hanging very still, watching them. The movements of their fins softly undulating around their bodies looked just like the Orbit exercise I was practicing. They were enchanting! There was something so beautiful and perfect about them. I gazed at them for several minutes until they swam away.

Sam gave me the OK sign. I unhooked my reef-line and secured it in my buoyancy vest pocket. Handing me his underwater writing slate, Sam signaled me to do another breath-check. Following the list on the slate I observed my breath in the four considerations of the breath-check. My breath was long, slow, and regular. My breath felt smooth, deep, and effortless. I felt peaceful as I took broad, free-flowing breaths.

I was breathing smoothly from my mouth. The air of my inhalation flowed over my tongue and filled my mouth. I felt the air rushing against my throat, then filling my lungs and abdomen. I placed my hands on my chest and diaphragm. My chest was moving slightly, but much to my surprise, my diaphragm was active, extending and contracting with each breath. Looking at my dive computer, I timed my breathing rate. After one minute, I had only eight deep breaths, fewer than half of what I had resting on land.

Excitedly, I gave Sam the OK sign when I was done. Sam returned my OK sign and then picked up the extra weight belt. Sam gave me the thumbs-up ascent signal. We made a slow ascent up to the gold sunlight at the water's surface and kicked to shore.

Upon reaching shore, I said, "My breathing was deep and smooth. And my abdomen was moving. My breathing rate was half of what it was earlier!"

"Good," Sam said. "You are already showing some improvement in your skills. You are starting to loosen the tensions of the body and breath. With more practice you will notice an equally dramatic effect in the tensions of your mind."

"Now I think I know what you're talking about!" I exclaimed, grasping a deeper dimension of what Sam had been teaching me.

"Yes, I think you're starting to see," Sam said, smiling.

We headed back to the shore and upon exiting the water, disassembled our SCUBA gear. It was now late in the afternoon, but still sunny and hot. With our equipment properly packed, we carried our gear bags to the cars.

"You did very well today," Sam said. "Tomorrow let's meet here again at the same time."

"I look forward to it," I responded.

"We will spend some more time practicing the exercises that you learned today," Sam said. I nodded. I stowed my gear in the trunk of my car. Sam bowed to me and we departed.

When I returned home the sun had just begun to set. I cooked a hearty dinner and reflected on all of the constructive experiences of the day. After dinner, I opened my laptop to continue my computer programming studies. As I worked through the exercises in the book, I noticed a big difference in my emotional disposition. I didn't have any extraneous thoughts about why I was studying or what it all meant. My confusions from the previous nights were now very distant. I easily made rapid progress in my tutorials.

Upon completing my study session, I did a breath-check. My results were pretty good: calm, deep, and slow. I smiled, acknowledging a feeling of health and relaxation, and lay down to sleep. Turning off the light, I sank into my soft bed. I slept deeply.

RELEASE

Sam and I spent over a week diving at the same dive site, working on these mystical practices. Each day we would begin with a period of sitting meditation. We did several dives each day and I became more adept at the exercises.

Before each dive and at the end of the day Sam had me perform a breath-check. The results were consistently excellent after the last dive of the day. Soon I started to notice many positive changes in my breathing patterns at the beginning of the day as well. After a few days of diving and practicing the Mystic SCUBA exercises, I found that my normal breathing rate naturally became slower. I felt much more relaxed and was able to breathe comfortably from my abdomen.

One day, upon setting my SCUBA gear down after a lengthy surface swim back to the shore, I cut open a papaya with my dive knife. After cleaning out the shiny, peppercorn seeds, I handed half to Sam. As he accepted the papaya, I noticed that he was looking at me with a pleased grin.

"What is it?" I asked.

"What are you thinking about?" Sam asked back.

"Nothing," I answered.

"And how do you feel?"

"Great," I answered. Then it immediately dawned on me—I felt fine! I felt well, as though I had been cured of a headache or relieved of carrying a heavy load. I felt healthy. I found it easy to smile. I couldn't remember a time when I felt so wholesomely good.

"You are making progress," Sam said.

I smiled, noting the change. I appreciated Sam's encouragement. I really enjoyed the Mystic SCUBA exercises. I felt healthy, both physically and mentally, but more than that, I was starting to feel healthy in a deeper and more spiritual way.

A couple of times Sam and I took a day-long break from diving. Sam called them "desaturation days". He said that after we had been diving repeatedly for a few days, it's healthy to take a day off to reduce the likelihood of getting decompression sickness. On these days, we practiced some of the Mystic SCUBA exercises in a modified form while sitting on the beach.

Sam shared greater insight into relaxation, meditation, and deep breathing. I began to feel more energy in my body from practicing the exercises.

One morning, as Sam and I started walking into the calm waters of the cove, Sam abruptly stopped. He was just in front of me, touching the water with his left hand. I stepped up along his right side as he looked with some concern to the south of the cove.

"What's wrong, Sam?"

"We should exit," he answered. "We'll walk down to the boat ramp and enter the southern shallows."

"That's over a hundred yards down the beach," I protested. "We're already in the water here. Can't we just dive the shallow part of the reef here? We don't have to go deep."

Sam turned to head to the boat ramp, and said, "We should dive at the first reef beyond the boat ramp."

"But why?" I asked.

"That is what the ocean told me."

This struck me as odd, yet I remembered Sam saying once before that the ocean had spoken to him. Sam had said that the ocean told him where I was when I nearly drowned, trapped on the reef.

I followed Sam and asked, "Are you saying that the ocean told you that we should dive out by the boat ramp?"

"Yes."

"Just like the ocean told you before where I was stuck during my diving accident?"

"Yes."

We started walking across the beach, close to the small crashing waves, heading towards the boat ramp.

A moment later I said, "Wait a minute, you're telling me that you can talk to the ocean? Like it's a person? That's so strange! I don't understand what you mean or how that could be."

"The ocean is not a person, like you or me," Sam said. "Yet, the ocean is a spirit. I talk to the ocean every time I dive. You see, the ocean is a body, a body of water. And just as your body holds your spirit, the ocean holds a divine spirit. Many large bodies of water have magical spirits."

"Really?" I was fascinated.

"Sure," Sam answered. "Haven't you ever heard of the Lady of the Lake?"

I nodded, remembering the Arthurian legend about the spirit of the lake that gave King Arthur his magical sword, Excalibur.

We started carefully crossing over some rugged lava rocks. Sam continued, "Water has energy. Water has consciousness. Water has light. The deepest dimensions of large bodies of water are home to very generous and wise spirits.

"One of my favorite lake spirits is Lake Michigan. Viewed from the shores of Chicago, billows of light come ceaselessly forth from the center of the lake and wash over the downtown Loop and Gold Coast neighborhoods especially. The lake constantly gives its energy of life, success, and balance to the city. Lake Michigan has a beautifully bright spirit."

Sam continued, "There are old Native American tales about how Lake Michigan gave the tribes living at its shores many boons. In one story a tribe's chief stood alone at a barren beach during a bitter winter. The chief was worrying about not having enough food for his people to last the winter. Just then, he looked down and saw that there were dozens of large berry bushes in the lake. When he reached into the cold waters to take the berries, his hands grasped nothing. Puzzled, the chief examined the berry bushes he saw. He discovered that what he saw was a reflection. Turning around, he found that the bountiful berry bushes had magically sprung up behind him though they were nowhere to be seen when he had come to the beach. There were enough berries to feed all of his people for the rest of the winter."

As we neared the boat ramp, Sam went on, "Ancient Hawaiians called the giving, life-bringing spirit of the ocean *Ali'ikai*. I ask this spirit if I may dive into her prior to every dive. Diving into the water is embracing the ocean. It is a union with her spirit."

Reaching the boat ramp, Sam said, "Sometimes the sea says 'Not now.' And I don't dive. I respect the information that the ocean tells me. Sometimes the ocean tells me other things like where a drowning diver is or where there is a better energy for a diver to release her tensions."

"How do you talk to the ocean?" I asked.

"You can speak out loud or speak the words in your mind," Sam answered. "Simply intend your communication. Be clear and honest. Address her respectfully, the same way you would address anyone of great power."

Sam and I started to enter the water by the boat ramp. "I also like to touch the water in my communication with the ocean. I feel her messages more deeply that way." Sam reached down and touched the water with his left hand. I had seen him do this prior to many of our dives.

"You should get into the habit of asking the ocean if it is OK for you to dive into her prior to your dives," Sam said. "Why don't you ask her now?

Ask the ocean if you can enter her. Be still and listen for an answer before taking any other action."

I looked out to the blue sea and asked aloud, "May I dive into you?" I listened quietly for a moment, touching the water with my hands. The water felt warm and gentle, but I heard nothing. I marveled at the glistening blue seas before me for another minute or so, but still couldn't detect the ocean's answer.

I looked to Sam. He nodded and said, "Good."

"But I didn't hear an answer."

"It takes time to hear the ocean's spirit," Sam said. "Yet her answers are readily visible in feelings. So for now trust your feelings. If you have a positive feeling after requesting a dive from the ocean, then the ocean has accepted you. However, if you have distinct bad thoughts or feelings, then you should not dive.

"So how did you feel?" Sam asked. "Did you feel positive or negative after you petitioned the sea?"

"Positive," I answered. "The ocean seemed warm and beautiful as I awaited an answer."

"Good," Sam said. "That is a positive feeling. Now, let's kick out to the reef and dive."

We did a short surface swim to the shallow reef. Sam gave me the thumbs-down dive hand signal and we began our descent.

During the dive, I practiced both relaxation exercises and experienced a powerful release of tension. It was as if every fiber of my being was released from invisible binds and floated free. I felt an exquisite peace in my physical being as I lay flat on the sandy ocean floor.

Sam tapped his tank with his dive wand to signal that the exercise was done. He showed me his dive computer. We had been at 24 feet for 90 minutes. Sam then pointed to my air gauge. I'd usually be out of air before reaching 90 minutes on a dive, but on this dive I had used just a little more than half of the air in my tank. Sam signaled me to ascend.

After our beautiful dive, I felt relaxed and energized. I smiled easily. Upon reaching the shore, Sam said, "You know something? I think you're healed. You have untied the knot of tension within you that had greatly threatened your life." I thought about it for a moment and then smiled in recognition.

"You have learned to let go of the tensions in your body," Sam said. "I'm certain you are no longer in danger of breaking the first rule of SCUBA!"

I laughed freely.

We disassembled and packed our SCUBA gear and drank from our water bottles. Sam said, "Tomorrow we will meet here at the usual time, but from here I will take you to a less known dive site. Rest well tonight and give yourself enough time to meditate in the morning. This will be a special place."

I stopped off at the dive shop on the way home to refill my air tanks for the next day. As I handed Michael my empty tanks, he mentioned that I looked changed. Instead of giving me his usual sermon of trivial facts, Michael looked at me intently and said, "There's something different about you, Vanessa. The first week or so that you came in here, you looked like a bump on a log." Then after a pause, he said, "But in the past day or so, you've been smiling. You look relaxed and healthy. You're not as tense as you used to be." Michael paused again, and then said, "Yep, just breathing underwater sure can transform your spirit."

His observations seemed to be completely in line with my spiritual experiences with Sam and Mystic SCUBA. *Michael must know Sam, or practice this too*, I thought. Michael smiled at me the way Sam did when I was making progress with my practice.

"Are you?" I paused.

"What?" Michael asked.

"Do you do Mystic SCUBA?" I asked. Michael, looking a little embarrassed, laughed as if I was poking fun at his comments. His deep look quickly vanished and he handed me some new tanks, saying, "Remember, it's always good to plan on coming up with 500 PSI in your tank. If your tank pressure gets too low, moisture may get in the tank and cause corrosion."

I could tell that Michael was still a little embarrassed about what he had said. I felt awkward. It was out of character for him and baffling to me. Too uncomfortable to pry further, I thanked Michael for the tanks and then headed home.

PLACES OF POWER

The next morning I met Sam at what had become our usual place. When I reached the completely packed parking lot, Sam was double-parked. He signaled me to follow him, started his Jeep, and pulled onto the road. We drove just a few miles down the road and then turned in to a pebbly ocean side pullout. We were a fair distance from the ocean.

Sam got out of his Jeep, fetched his dive gear bag from the back, and put it into the trunk of my car. Hopping into my passenger seat, he said, "OK, let's drive on. Our dive site is a half a mile from here." We drove down the road a little further and then turned in to another pullout. Sam explained, "We will enter the water here. There is a strong current that will sweep us back to a sandy beach exit by where I parked my Jeep." Opening the door and grabbing his dive bag, he said, "Let's kit-up. We'll have to walk almost a quarter mile to get to our entry."

We geared up, drank as much water as we could, and then started for the ocean. Halfway to the water's edge, the heat had become extremely uncomfortable. The hike, the sun, my heavy equipment and my wetsuit were an intolerable combination. I started taking more frequent breaks, bending forward and putting my hands on my knees to rest my back. As we neared the water's edge, I could tell that we were on high cliffs above the ocean. Getting as close as I would dare, I said, "How exactly are we going to enter the water?"

Sam smiled and said, "We're going to leap into the deep. Follow me, I'll show you. It's actually very safe."

Sam walked back away from the water's edge and to the south. "Ah ha," he said, "there it is." He pointed at what first seemed to be a large hole in the ground. We walked over to it. Sam signaled me to follow him as he started stepping down steep steps into the hole. It was large enough for both of us to enter and had a sturdy lava rock floor. The hole was an opening to an underground cave. I took a few steps in behind Sam. Sam turned on his dive light as the darkness of the cave engulfed him. I turned my dive light on as well. The cave floor descended rapidly as the cavern opened up to be large enough to drive a truck through.

"This is an old lava tube," Sam said. "It is a place where Hawaiian spiritual leaders of antiquity would come to practice rituals. It is a very sacred place. It is a spiritual place of power."

I felt cool and comfortable in the cave. I was out of the sun, and there was a cool breeze. I remembered Sam talking about places of power when he had surprised me by meeting me at my favorite morning swimming cove the day after he saved my life. I remembered seeing movements of subtle energy there when Sam had instructed me to still my mind and gaze in that place.

"Is it possible to see energy here?" I asked.

Sam stopped walking, paused, and said, "In a spiritual place of power everything is energy. In a spiritual place of power the unseen-world is more visible than the seen-world."

Sam stepped over to the right and sat down on a large flat earthen shelf protruding from the lava tube wall. He signaled me to sit next to him and then switched off his flashlight. After sitting down, I fiddled with my flashlight switch and turned it off too. It was pitch black in the lava tube. We had descended far from the entrance.

My tank was propped up on my lava rock seat and I sat comfortably. A moment later Sam said, "The best way to see the energy of this place is with your eyes closed. So close your eyes, still your mind, and see the energy here."

I closed my eyes and easily became still and quiet. The cave felt comfortable and inviting. I found that I naturally brought my focus to my navel chakra. After a minute or two I started to feel a subtle warmth from within my abdomen. Another minute later I began to feel a strong sensation of pulsing energy. The bright energy originated in my navel and moved throughout my body. This pulsing vibration felt beautifully warm and full. My body felt light and relaxed. The fatigue from my exertion trekking to the cave was gone. I felt a bright peaceful balance and physical well-being.

The pulsing energy from my navel seemed to extend beyond my physical body. I felt the bright vibration of energy in my aura several inches beyond my fingertips. I became aware of the multidimensional structure of my aura as it buzzed with energy around my whole body. The energy seemed to fill me and charge me.

"Now," Sam said several minutes later, "what did you see? What did you experience?" All was pitch black again when I opened my eyes. I seemed to have shifted into a bright internal awareness when my eyes were closed.

I explained my experience to Sam. I added, "I had a strong awareness of light and energy, but it wasn't really visual like the time you had me gaze at the lava rocks at the cove. This energy was very tangible, almost physical."

"There are different ways to see different energies," Sam said. "When you're able to still your mind, you are able to unlock many subtle senses for awareness. Subtle senses are similar to physical senses. If a manta ray were swimming by, the principal way for you to apprehend the information of the time would be to see the manta with your eyes. However, if you were ascending from a dive and a speedboat was rapidly coming to a point of collision with you, the principal way for you to apprehend that information would be by hearing the speedboat with your ears. In mysticism you develop many subtle senses of seeing, feeling, and knowing so that you are able to apprehend subtle, energetic and unseen-world dimensionality that can expand your awareness of life, keep you from danger, and aid you in reaching your goals."

Sam continued, "The cove where you practiced gazing the other day is a beautiful place of natural power. The innate natural energy of that particular cove is best perceived through gazing exercises and spiritual seeing. The cove has a luminous energy you can see. The energy there moves in a beneficial pattern of vibration that has a positive effect on you. Spending time there, and especially seeing the energy of the cove can relax you, expand your awareness of life, and bring you into a natural balance that is as beautiful and serene as the cove.

"Many beautiful places in nature are places of power like the cove. I call them 'natural places of power'. The Hawaiian Islands are filled with many wonderful natural places of power. And although the cove is uplifting and empowering in many ways, it is unsuitable for helping you learn the spiritual lesson that I am teaching you today."

"Why is that?" I asked.

"Because this is a 'spiritual place of power'. This lava tube is not like any natural place of power. There is a distinct spiritual power innate to this place. And the primary means of observation in this particular spiritual place of power is feeling and inner awareness. This place has a tremendous vibration and a specific energetic pattern that you can feel. Spending time being attuned to your feelings here has a precise spiritual effect on you."

In light of my feelings of an intense buzzing sensation in my aura moments earlier, what Sam was telling me made sense.

"The effect of the intense energetic vibration of this place on your aura and field of attention is quite profound. The spirit of this place is so powerful, so bright, that its energy envelops and fills your being with light, like a sponge dunked in water. Filled with the spiritual power of this land, your attention is elevated and you become aware of a greater truth. This place's strong spiritual power is quite suitable to help you learn today's spiritual lesson."

"Is it really that big of a deal?" I asked. "I saw energy at the cove and felt energy here, but the difference doesn't seem that significant to me—just two cool experiences."

"Oh, but the difference is the crux of mysticism!" Sam said. "Attending the proper places of power is like the difference between one of your favorite dance songs and a classical masterpiece. And like the difference between a conversation about how to replace a bad o-ring on a tank valve and a spiritual communication."

"Are you saying that my cove is just common and this place is special?"

"Not exactly," Sam responded, "both are places of power. Both are very beneficial when attended for the appropriate reason."

Sam continued, "Listening to a classical Mozart masterpiece, just like spending time in a spiritual place of power, is elevating. A Mozart masterpiece is a timeless artistic expression that can transport you to a refined awareness of life. Yet if you wanted to let loose and dance on a Saturday night at a club, you might find a Mozart masterpiece to be rather limiting."

I laughed.

Sam went on, "As well, profound spiritual communications about the dharma, awareness, and Samadhi are extremely enlightening, just like spending time in a spiritual place of power. Yet if the o-ring in your tank is nicked, a talk about cosmic consciousness would be impractical for getting you going on your dive. Rather, practical instructions on o-ring installation would be a more helpful communication for what you need to do."

Sam paused, and then asked, "Which pair of fins did you bring with you for this dive?"

"My longer, stiff fins," I answered. "You said that there will be a strong current on this dive, and although it causes more tension in my feet and ankles, I thought that it would be safer to have the extra power in my kicks."

"Exactly," Sam said, "you chose the fins that give you the power you need for the currents you are facing. Likewise, we choose places of power, as we would choose which fins to use. This way, we choose to go to powerful places that elevate our consciousness to learn the lessons we need to learn. And there are many types of places of power that are particularly conducive for specific spiritual endeavors."

"So how do you know what places to go to that are useful for your purpose?"

"In mysticism we learn to see the spirit of all things," Sam answered. "You cannot know a thing merely from its physical appearance or surface expression. Yet when you see its spirit, you know its essential nature. The subtle awarenesses that you gain from practicing Mystic SCUBA give you the ability to see the spirit of all matters. Once you know the spirit of places of power, you gain an important awareness that you can use to elevate and transform your consciousness.

"You have likely never been to a place of spiritual power before, so the profound transformative spiritual energy here is new to you. Yet it is not that hard to see the spirit of this place when your mind is clear."

Sam paused and then asked, "So tell me, what is the spirit of this place? I have told you that this is a place of spiritual power, but I have not told you the distinct spirit of this location. Take a moment to still your mind and reflect on the spirit of this place."

I quieted my mind. Sam's insights became very clear to me. My mind was unbound and the truth was simple. I could see the shining spirit of the lava tube. "This is a place of healing," I answered.

"It is easy to see and comprehend the truth in a place of power," Sam said. "In a place of power you're able to make rapid transformations of attention and grow in wisdom. You are right; this is a place of healing, spiritual healing. This cave is powerful, and the waters outside of the cave have an even greater healing power."

"What other types of power can be found in these places?" I asked.

"Though this is a place of healing power," Sam answered, "there are many other spiritual powers that places can have. Later today I will take you to a place of power that helps you gain a spiritual realization of light and consciousness."

Fantastic, I thought. The idea that there are sacred places where you can gain spiritual realizations filled me with a sense of wonder.

Sam said, "In the Southwest of the United States, there are spiritual places of power that afford you views into many magical dimensions of life. There you can gain abilities of spiritual vision and dreaming, or even gain the knowledge of how to control the winds and the rains."

As a kid, I had visited a Native American reservation in Arizona and learned about some of the tribe's spiritual beliefs. "So the Navajo rain dances really work?" I asked.

"Certainly," Sam said, "Native American shamans have a deep connection with sacred lands. Through that connection they learn the ways of the weather."

Sam continued, "In the Himalayas, there are spiritual places of power that lead into beautiful mystical realms. *Shambhala* for example, is a fabled hidden kingdom located somewhere in the Himalayan range. Shambhala is known to possess powerful secret spiritual teachings. The secret *Kalachakra Tantra* teachings of Tibet are known to have originated in Shambhala.

"Legend has it that Shambhala is protected by a psychic barrier so that only the spiritually pure can find the kingdom. Tibetan lamas of old would spend a great deal of their lives in spiritual development before attempting the journey to Shambhala. There are even guidebooks to Shambhala. However, the guidebooks describe the route in such vague symbols that only the most adept seekers of enlightenment can understand them."

"So Shambhala is a hidden place of spiritual power?"

"Not really," Sam answered, "Shambhala is a kingdom that exists in another dimension that happens to be located metaphysically close to ours. There is a place of spiritual power in the Himalayan range that can elevate your awareness high enough so that you can enter that realm."

"Fascinating," I said, "so you just go to spiritual places of power and 'Pow!' you can control the rains or leap into Shambhala!"

"It's not just automatic," Sam responded. "You have to work hard at it. The shaman and the lama are able to access the power of these places because of their spiritual discipline. In Mystic SCUBA you unlock the powers of places through meditative practices and spiritual considerations. You can only avail yourself of the power of a place by working with its power properly. Working with any form of energy or power, from electricity to money, from fire to martial arts, requires attention and discipline. Places of power are aids to your success because the currents of energy in places of power aid your discipline.

"Those seeking Enlightenment have long utilized places of power such as the Southwest of the United States, the Himalayan peaks, the Nile, the Ganges, and the Hawaiian Islands. The energies of these places are extremely helpful in aiding realization.

"For Mystic SCUBA there are particularly helpful spiritual places of power, such as this dive site. Awareness, transformation, and enlightenment can be gained rapidly by diving in spiritual places of power.

"Many of the dive sites throughout the world are natural places of power. Many dive sites have very good energies that are congruent with peace, calm, clarity, and relaxation. Dive sites are chosen for their natural beauty and accessibility. We can't dive too deep and can't dive in difficult conditions. Humans can only dive in pristine ocean locations. The marine life and natural beauty at these beautiful dive sites are the physical manifestations of the energy of the locations.

"Though many dive sites are natural places of power, there are a few that are spiritual places of power, like the dive site we are about to enter. All of the Hawaiian Islands have natural places of power for diving and a couple of the outer islands have dive sites that are spiritual places of power.

"Practicing Mystic SCUBA exercises at spiritual places of power like some of the Caribbean walls, Channel Island pinnacles, Hawaiian craters, Thai seamounts, or the Great Barrier Reef, affords divers tremendously enlightening power dives."

"Where is the most powerful place to dive in the world?" I asked.

"I will take you there," Sam said, "in the days to come."

I grinned.

Sam switched on his flashlight again, and said, "OK, you have absorbed the part of this lesson that takes place above water. Now we should move on so that you can learn the greatest truth of this lesson where the power of this location is strongest: under the sea."

I switched on my flashlight and we continued walking down the steep cavern pass.

POWER DIVES

After a few minutes, the lava tube became slightly brighter with the light of a distant exit. I could hear the gentle splashing of calm ocean waves not far ahead. Still descending, we came to a left-leaning bend in the lava tube that glowed softly, illumined by a delicate light. Coming around the bend, I could see that the lava tube plunged almost straight down into a glimmering pool of blue ocean water. Sam and I switched off our flashlights. A sparkling blue radiance illuminated the whole cavern. Sam and I moved to a ledge just before the lava tube dipped straight down. The ocean water seemed quite deep below us. Small, swelling waves gently pressed up against the ledge about five feet below where we stood. I could see that the lava tube continued straight down for about 30 feet beneath the sparkling surface and then opened out toward the bright sea. A pair of ornate butterfly fish glided in, along the bottom of the lava tube wall, their delicate orange stripes glowing along their narrow midsections.

"Welcome to your first power dive," Sam said as we stood at the ledge gazing into the shining water.

"What is a power dive exactly?"

"To power dive is to seek enlightenment while diving into a place of spiritual power," Sam answered.

"Well, isn't that what we've always been doing together?"

"No," Sam shook his head, "till now we've been working on the preliminary practices. It's true that the dive site where we met and trained is a place of spiritual power, but we have not yet attempted to access its most wondrous powers. We have stayed mostly in the shallows, working on basic relaxation and breathing exercises. In Mystic SCUBA it is essential to have deep breathing, relaxation, and a focused attention in order to experience a profound spiritual transformation on power dives. On power dives, we depart from the Mystic SCUBA practices that are focused on the physical body and aura. Power dives have specific spiritual focuses."

"What's the spiritual focus of this power dive?"

"Healing," Sam answered. "We will take advantage of the powerful currents of healing in these waters just below us."

"But I thought I was healed already," I responded. "Yesterday you said

I was healed of the physical and mental tensions that almost got me killed. And isn't healing a physical focus?"

"Not when it's spiritual healing," Sam said. "You have healed your physical and mental tensions by practicing the preliminary Mystic SCUBA practices. Yet there is another dimension of healing that you shall experience now: spiritual healing. This is a place of power that heals your spirit."

I was uplifted by the notion of spiritual healing. I felt this was exactly what I needed, to be healed of my confusion with what to do with my life.

"To begin," Sam said, "take a moment to be conscious of your pain. Hold the awareness of your pain in your mind for a moment. Before stepping into the ocean, inwardly ask the sea to heal you of your pain. The ocean heals all pains—be they physical, mental, or emotional—by healing your spirit. It's not that your conditions of physical pain or disturbing emotions will go away during this dive (though they certainly may), but rather that the power of these healing waters extends to you a new perspective and understanding of your pain. When you understand your physical and emotional pain with a greater perspective, you are better able to cope with your life and with your pain.

"After a giant-stride entry," Sam continued, "we'll descend to the bottom, then exit the lava tube at about 40 feet. You should continue to ask the ocean for healing while you descend. As you reach the lava tube exit, ask the ocean to show you the source of your pain. Ask from your heart, and then listen for an answer with your heart. The ocean will almost immediately give you a message about your pain. Be open to the subtle information the water may provide about the cause of your pain, the conditions of your suffering, and how to enhance your healing. It's not necessary that you cognitively become aware of the ocean's answer. Just trust that your authentic intention for healing is reflected back to you as healing energy from the water.

"After requesting healing from the ocean, and being open to information about your pain, the final step is to give your pain to the ocean. This place of healing power simply absorbs your pain. All pain—physical, mental, or emotional—has a spiritual origin. The water heals your pain by healing your spirit.

"To give your pain to the ocean, focus on the essence of your pain. Bring your attention to the spiritual origin of your pain. Intend to address that spiritual cause. Then simply open your arms in an outward gesture and let your pain go. Imagine your pain leaving your body and being absorbed into the depths of the sea. Exhale during this gesture, relaxing your body."

"Doesn't dumping my pain on this place of power hurt or dishonor it?"

"Not at all," Sam said. "This place is the very energy of spiritual healing. If you were sitting in a very warm room, the fact that you were very cold because a moment earlier you had stood outside for an hour during a snowstorm would not affect the warmth of the room. Though you are cold, the room is warm. The warmth of the room brings you into its condition. When you come to this place, your pain is transformed into freedom and knowledge by the power of this location."

"Amazing," I said, relishing the notion.

Sam continued, "After you let go of your pain and are cleansed by the power of the ocean, you'll practice another exercise that is excellent to work on in this place of power. The second exercise is a *sutra* practice. Sutra literally means 'a thread that holds things together'. In Buddhism, sutras are often canonical scriptures, yet in this practice we adhere to sutras in their root form, as aphoristic statements or expansive slogans. You will begin this exercise after you exit the lava tube. During this exercise you simply repeat again and again either or both of these sutras: 'I am love.' 'I am peace.'"

"'I am love' is a sutra?" I asked. "That's all there is to it?"

"Sure," Sam said. "'I am love' is a powerful spiritual aphorism. As you practice, you see that these sutras are most profound. You will find that 'I am love' is the thread that holds all things together. You may also condense these sutras by just saying 'love' and 'peace'."

"I just say the words? What's that going to do?"

"Don't just say the words, **mean** the words," Sam said. "An old friend once asked me the same question. She was a busy woman, very involved with her work. I pried her away from her job for a couple of weeks to learn about Mystic SCUBA. She was uncertain that the sutras would have any significant results. Yet I told her the same thing I'm telling you: Mean the words. She gave it an earnest try. During this exercise she entered into such a profound state of peace that she experienced Samadhi. After the dive she sat quietly in a beautiful silence. One of my students asked her about her experience during the dive. She said, 'I just felt love.'"

I was inspired by the story. "Will I experience Samadhi on this dive too?"

"It's possible," Sam said, "but only if you can relinquish all thoughts, and even expectations—and become love and peace through the heartfelt intent of your *sutras*.

"Now, because of this dive site's strong current, we'll be moving over the reef quite quickly as soon as we exit the lava tube. We will just go with the current the whole time, without stopping on the bottom. I will direct you to the exit after about 60 minutes of practicing the sutra exercises. So now, let's prepare for a power dive."

Sam and I put on our fins. We turned our air on and checked all of our equipment. I prepared for my giant-stride entry. Sam stepped into the water first. I brought my pain to mind. I paused to ask the water for healing. When I asked for healing from the ocean for my confusion about what to do with my life, I immediately sensed a welcoming and kind feeling enveloping me. After Sam gave me the OK signal, I held my equipment in place and leaped forward into the ocean.

Expelling the air from my buoyancy vest, I fell beneath the gentle waves. The rocky lava tube walls widened as I fell toward the exit. During my descent, I continued to ask the ocean to heal me of my confusion and pain. I began by speaking my request silently in my head, but then wondered whether English was really a good way to communicate with the spirit of the ocean, so I tried to convey my request without any words, just silent intent.

As Sam and I exited the lava tube into the current, I opened my arms toward the deep and asked again, exhaling as Sam had instructed. I felt as though something were being gently removed from my body—coming to the surface, dissolving into the sea, and then being washed away. I heard a very distinct sentence, or rather felt it—it wasn't really words, but somehow I heard it: "Beyond fear there is only love." I knew undeniably that this was the ocean's message to me about my suffering. With those words, I suddenly understood my situation from a clear perspective. I could see the tangled mess of fear, confusion, doubt and self-limitation that was holding me back from moving forward, becoming powerful, and aiding the people I wanted to help. The simple truth of the ocean's message uprooted my pain, pulled it out from where it had settled in my body, and tossed it away.

My confusion was gone. Instead of feeling worry, I just knew that everything would work out perfectly. I felt very peaceful and quiet, but also expansive. Without my fear, confusion, and doubt, my mind was filled with infinite possibilities.

My heart felt as if it opened and the ocean's love flowed in, filling the most hidden recesses of my spirit with luminosity. The feelings of love within me were unattached to any thoughts of any thing. The love within me was infinite and without origin. It was vast and yet peaceful and simple.

With unrestricted love, I opened my arms as wide as I could, offering my love back to the ocean and feeling sublime harmony.

I looked over to Sam, who was floating very quietly over the reef, looking like part of the ocean itself. Inspired by the ocean's liberating message of healing, I began to repeat the *sutras* in my mind. "I am love… I am peace…"

I affirmed, "Without fear there is only love and peace."

"I am love… I am peace." I continued, letting go, letting the truth of the words sink in.

"I am love… I am peace.

"I am love…"

My mind became still as I drifted motionless over the coral outcroppings in the gentle current. Gazing into the glowing blue ocean, I experienced all-encompassing peace and joy. I smiled broadly beneath my regulator. I felt complete. I felt whole and connected to my heart, my spirit.

As the current flowed to an end, Sam signaled me with his dive wand and gave me the ascent sign. We slowly ascended and kicked a short distance back to shore. Exiting the ocean, Sam and I walked on to a sandy beach. I felt elevated and serene. Sam just smiled at me and nodded. We walked in silence for a couple hundred yards along a seldom-used footpath up to Sam's Jeep. We loaded our SCUBA gear still assembled, and drove up the road to my car.

MYSTIC LOGBOOK

At my car, I disassembled my SCUBA equipment and loaded it properly into my gear bag. It was around noon now, at the height of the day's tropical heat. Sitting down in the shade of my car as Sam attended to securing the SCUBA tanks, I pulled my dive logbook from my gear bag. I quickly logged my dive and then put my logbook down.

"You log your dive profiles after each open water dive," Sam remarked, closing the trunk of my car.

"Yes," I answered, "I am careful to log all of my dives."

"Why do you log your dives?"

"To keep a record of how many dives I've done, what dive sites I've been to, my dive profiles at each site, and any other interesting facts or things that I had experienced on the dive."

"That is indeed important information," Sam said. "It helps you remember where you've been and what seen-world experiences you've had during your dives. Yet I wonder, do you log your unseen-world experiences as well?"

"Um," I thought about it. "I don't think so. I'm not sure."

"In Mystic SCUBA," Sam said, "it is very important to log the spiritual, mystical, and enlightening experiences you have while diving. Recording your undersea awareness is important. It helps you remember where you've been inwardly and what unseen-world experiences you've had."

"How do I log my mystical experiences?" I asked.

"If during your dive you feel positive feelings, you should describe them in your logbook. If during your dive you have subtle awarenesses, seeings, or intuitions, write them in your logbook. Of course, log any magical experiences. Log all experiences of expanded awareness encountered from looking into the deep blue, flying over coral reefs, or seeing marine life."

"OK," I said, "I think I understand what I should log, but how do I log it? How do I log the amazing spiritual experience I just had on my dive when I can't even think of any words for it?"

"Just describe the experience in your logbook in a simple, straightforward and complete way. Logging a spiritual experience is a written testament of what you saw in the seen-world and what you experienced in the unseen-world. Describe what you experienced and felt in detail."

"Oh, but writing out all the details of a dive is so boring," I said. "My

Open Water Diver instructor made me write down every detail of our dives, looking up fish species and coral names. It was drudgery!"

"Can I see your logbook?" Sam asked. I handed it to Sam. He opened it to my first few dives that were logged during my Open Water Diver course.

He read aloud my log entry for dive number three. My dive log included my dive profile, the skills I performed on that dive, and details of the different marine life I came across. After reading it, Sam asked, "How does that make you feel?"

"Pretty bored actually," I said. I didn't really care to know that I saw hard corals and yellow tangs at a depth of 35 feet.

"Yes," Sam said as he flipped through my logbook, "these facts do little in expanding your awareness. In Mystic SCUBA it isn't necessary to log every detail about your dive. Besides helpful and healthful information about your dive site and dive profile, in Mystic SCUBA just log anything that touches the unseen-world. During Mystic SCUBA we enter a consideration of the spiritual. During your dive, when you experience insight and awareness of the mystical unseen-world, you should note that in you logbook. The other incidentals about what fish you saw, what coral you saw, and what your buddy did are not necessary unless related to a mystical experience."

Sam paused for a moment and then asked, "Isn't there a mention of dolphins in your logbook?"

"Yes," I answered.

"What was it like seeing dolphins while diving?"

"It was great," I said.

"How did you feel on that dive?"

"Good. I remember it being really fun."

After a minute of perusing the pages of my logbook, Sam said, "Ah, here it is. Dive number 22. I noticed this one when I was reviewing your logbook for your Advanced Open Water Diver course."

After mentioning the dive location and profile, Sam read aloud from the notes section of my dive log: "'As I floated, observing the reef fish, I heard a clicking sound behind me. At first I ignored it, but then it got louder. I turned to see what the sound was and to my amazement, there were two spinner dolphins less than 20 feet from me!!! They were just slowly swimming by. I could see them so clearly! One seemed to be grinning at me! Their graceful movements were so captivating. They were the most wondrous creatures! I floated entranced and delighted for a short but precious time. Then the dolphins turned and quickly moved out into the deep. A few seconds later, they were gone. It was amazing!!'"

Beaming, I remembered how fantastic that experience was.

"How does this log make you feel?" Sam asked.

"Amazing!" I answered. "That was such a fantastic dive! I loved it!"

"This is what I mean," Sam said. "Your words bring you back to the feeling, the undersea awareness that you had experienced on this dive. A moment ago when I asked you about the same experience, your feelings were vague. Your awareness of this magical moment was distant and amorphous. Without these written words in your logbook, you wouldn't be able to remember the magic of this experience so clearly."

"I see what you mean," I said.

"And was it such drudgery to write that in your journal?" Sam asked.

"No," I answered, "it was fun writing about such a wonderful moment."

"All magical experiences are fun to log. When you put spiritual experiences down in the structure of written language, you create a connection between the seen-world and the magic of the unseen-world. Like poetry, the words reach into a deeper awareness. The act of writing down your mystical awarenesses encodes your words with light and power, making them the doorway to the experience. At any point in the future you can reopen your logbook to read about your mystical diving experiences and again touch those precious dimensions that you found while diving. Reconnecting to the magic of your spiritual diving experiences is very helpful in reinvigorating your spiritual practice in between diving trips."

Sam continued, "It's also very important that you fill out your dive log right after you complete your dive. The awareness of your mystical experience is still accessible and fresh in your mind directly after your dive. Minutes later, you start to forget how you felt underwater. Your undersea awareness and mystical experiences become distant."

Sam handed my logbook back. I reflected deeply on my power dive. Noticing how my magical experiences on the dive were quickly fading, I jotted down some succinct log notes to capture the awareness, and extraordinary feelings of peace I experienced during the dive.

"Follow me in your car to the next dive site," Sam said when I had finished with my dive logbook. "It's north of here, not far from where I stay."

"OK," I said. As I stood up to get in my car, I noticed how my feelings of peace gave way to a strange physical feeling. I felt like my body was not solid. I felt as if I were in a dream.

"I feel a bit woozy," I said.

"Eat some of these," Sam said, tossing me a bag of peanut M&M's. "They will help you acclimate to the rougher energy fields of the road. Your attention is so accustomed to a higher awareness now from practicing the Mystic SCUBA exercises in that place of spiritual power that you will need to bring your attention more solidly back to the physical world."

I opened the bag of M&M's and ate a few.

"After mystical experiences, you have to make sure you get into your car before you drive," Sam joked.

I felt more grounded immediately.

Sam continued, "When you shift through powerful energy fields, there can be a disassociating effect on your aura and attention. It's important that you watch your self after entering and leaving places of power. Being spacey is a real danger for mystics. You must use your will power to shift your attention back into the physical, seen-world so that you don't have an accident or hurt yourself."

"I understand," I said, pressing my attention to the weight of my feet and feeling more grounded.

"Sometimes, it's a good idea to focus your attention on your navel chakra when feeling a bit spacey. That centers your energy into your will power."

I began to focus on my navel. I felt a bright warmth there that seemed to wake me from my dreamy attention.

"And a little sugar works wonders! The physical body can experience a drop in blood sugar as a reaction to moving through different energy fields. If we eat some sugar, the body quickly rebalances."

Sam gave me the OK sign and reminded me to drive carefully. I ate a few more M&M's and then started my car. Sam nodded agreeably and then jogged over and hopped into his Jeep. We slowly pulled onto the road and headed north. I felt much more grounded as I began to drive.

THE BEACH GUARDIAN

It took us about an hour to drive to the next dive site. Not far from the water, Sam pulled over to the side of the road and parked. I pulled in and parked behind him. I retrieved two fresh air tanks from my trunk. Sam and I assembled our dive equipment and donned our SCUBA gear. Sam made sure that we were well hydrated and that I carried my bag of papayas with me.

"We're going to the twin craters over there," Sam said, pointing toward a 40-foot high hill just in front of the water.

I noticed that the hill had an indentation on the top. It was a cinder cone, where at one time lava poured out from the earth. I could only see one crater on top of the cone. "I only see one crater on that hill. Where's the twin?" I asked.

Sam looked back at me with a smile and said, "We're going to dive into it."

We walked down just in front of the tall crater, less than a hundred yards from the road. There I could see a 20 year old, rusted, beat-up Toyota Land Cruiser parked on a platform of lava rocks next to the white sandy beach. I could see a small, blue tent on the beach next to the Land Cruiser with a couple of beach chairs, drink coolers, and articles of clothing around it. There was a large collection of seashells and dried corals in orderly piles and lines in front of the beach chairs. A man emerged from behind the tent. He was holding a puppy in one arm and carrying another on his shoulder. At the same time he was whittling what looked like a small red seashell with an odd carving tool.

He looked over at us with some concern, as four more puppies pranced about his ankles. He set down what he was carving, heading toward us. As he approached, his look of concern vanished into happy recognition. "Aloha bruddah Sam! Howzit?" he said with a broad smile while raising a puppy-adorned arm. Sam smiled and bowed to the man.

"This is Pono," Sam said to me as the man reached us, "and Pono, this is Vanessa. I'm showing her the ways of the ocean."

I smiled. Pono nodded favorably. Pono was a scruffy middle-aged Hawaiian with dark suntanned skin and tousled, sun bleached hair. He was broad-shouldered and pudgy, with a warm smile and kind way about him. He wore a tattered, unbuttoned Hawaiian floral shirt and a pair of navy blue knee-length shorts. Surprisingly, Pono was adorned with beautifully carved shell jewelry. He wore an intricately carved pink puka shell necklace, with each of the small shells tooled into the shape of plumeria blossoms. Around his neck he also wore a dazzling black shell necklace, weighted with a sea turtle pendant carved out of a spiraling multi-colored seashell, exquisitely sculpted and polished.

"These are for you," Sam said, pointing to the bag of papayas I was holding. "Vanessa brought them from home."

Taking Sam's signal, I handed the bag to Pono.

Pono looked in the bag and smiled. He addressed me in fast, heavily accented pidgin, "Ho'omaika'i 'iā 'oe! You gotta geev planny mahalo dat one malihini like you get da mana for meet cousin Sam ovah heeya! Dis guy can teach you any kine for da kai."

I thanked Pono by smiling, though I didn't really understand what he said.

We chatted with Pono for a while. He told us stories of vast schools of fish that he saw swimming in the Hawaiian waters 25 years ago. He told us of how even 10 years ago everyone on the island had a beautiful Aloha-spirit toward each other, but that in recent years tourism and greed had changed and hardened people. He told us how when he was a child he talked to the Hawaiian gods everyday and that as things started changing, he promised them he would take on the job of protecting the spirit of the land.

Pono tilted his head and looked down the beach, behind Sam and me. Then he squinted his eyes as if he saw something wrong. I turned around and saw a few divers coming down from their cars at the end of the beach. They were four large men. Two of them had double SCUBA tank setups and they all had various pony bottles, reels, and slates adorning their buoyancy vests. The fattest one in the back carried a large camera casing with four large strobe flashes in one hand and a harpoon gun in the other.

"Eh, I bettah get down to da oddah sidah da beach. Dose lōlō divers need me for kokua dem so dey no break da kapu!" Pono said "A hui hou!" to us as he turned with his puppies and went down the beach.

Sam bowed to Pono as he left.

"Bye," I waved.

"What a funny character," I said when Pono was halfway to the group of divers. "It sure sounds like things have changed for the worse in Hawaii. It must be very upsetting to someone who grew up here." I paused for a moment looking at the tent and cooler next to the Land Cruiser and then said, "It looks like he lives here. I feel bad for him, being so down on his luck."

"Pono is aligned with a powerful force of dharma, a force of truth," Sam said. "Places of power sometimes open their hearts to enrich the lives of a special custodian or guardian. Pono is a special and fortunate being, in touch with the gods and serving the land as a guardian. He lives a richer and happier life than most people in Beverly Hills."

I hadn't thought of it in such a way. I watched Pono far down the beach as he ambled along with his puppies about him. The turquoise waves gently broke on the white sands of Pono's paradise beach. In reflecting on Sam's words, I now saw Pono as happier, richer and freer than anyone I knew.

The four divers were loud and boisterous. I could hear their laughter as they plodded along toward the ocean waves. When Pono reached them they stopped and folded their arms, standing around him defiantly. Pono calmly scratched one of his puppy's heads as he spoke to the group. They were all very large compared to Pono. After a few moments, Pono started to point out areas in the ocean to the divers. They seemed to look with great concentration. They dropped their folded arms and seemed to be captivated by Pono's words.

Turning to the large man with the camera and the harpoon gun, Pono pointed at the harpoon gun and then back up toward where Sam and I were standing next to the blue Land Cruiser. The man seemed to consider Pono's words for a moment scratching his head, but then handed Pono the harpoon gun and shook his hand. With that the group of divers quietly walked into the ocean to dive. Pono set down the harpoon gun and sat, playing with his puppies.

"Wow," I said, "Pono sure has a way of dealing with people. I didn't think those big, over-geared-up divers would ever listen to him."

"Yes," Sam said, "Pono is a master at deflating egos. And as you know, SCUBA divers' egos can become more inflated than a fully filled buoyancy vest."

I laughed and then asked earnestly, "Why is that?"

"It's mostly because of gear," Sam replied. "Gear is important in SCUBA diving, so some divers attach their egos to their gear, thereby increasing their self-importance. Then they just have to keep adding gear to be fulfilled. First it's a mini pony air tank, which can fit in your buoyancy vest pocket for those eight additional breaths of air that just might save your life on a dive where you forgot to watch your air gauge. Then it's the red dye that you spill out at the surface so that the search helicopters can find you if a typhoon hits and you're swept far out to sea."

I laughed, considering the absurdity of some gear.

"I mean, you need the gear you need," Sam went on, "but you don't need to let your pride own your gear. Like with Mystic SCUBA, we use the meditative exercises of the art as tools to gain greater awareness, but not as a means of self-definition. Plus," Sam said, dramatically raising his pointer finger, "there is one principal reason that no one should be egotistical about SCUBA diving."

"What's that?" I asked.

"The reason is that when you're underwater," Sam explained, "every SCUBA diver looks completely ridiculous!" Sam put his hands around his eyes like they were oversized binoculars. Then he rounded his lips to the left, making a hyperventilating Darth Vader-like sound. His impression of SCUBA divers was so funny that I burst into laughter.

When my laughter began to subside, Sam went on, "People are often too self-oriented, too self-conscious, and far too self-important. What all divers should remember is that SCUBA diving is a fun exploration of life. When you dive, don't take yourself so seriously. Loosen up and relax. The point of SCUBA diving is not to focus on yourself; it's to focus on the beauty of the underwater world. There's nothing to accomplish on dives. There's just the wonder of ocean life to experience. So forget about yourself when you dive. As we go on this dive today, I want you to remember one thing: Every fish is precious."

"Every fish is precious?"

"All beings are equal. All are loved by eternity," Sam said. "Every fish is precious. Every fish, every person, every being is a mystery, a universe. Every fish is a humble form of the eternal. Every fish is as infinite in spirit as you or me."

I nodded, pondering the deeper, spiritual side of fish. Every fish is precious, I thought. Does that mean a fish is as important as a human being? Who's to say that any one life is more valuable than any other? I had recently glimpsed a disturbing TV news scene. A large boat was hauling in thousands of fish in a massive net. Shaking my head, I seriously considered, *Should I stop eating fish?*

Sam signaled me and said, "Let's get ready." We walked to the ocean's edge. As we performed a buddy-check to make sure our equipment was in order, the waves crashed and stretched across the sand to our feet.

"On this dive, we are going to go down to only about 20 feet. There you will see a deep crater that is large enough for both of us to sit in. We will enter the crater, let all of the air out of our buoyancy vests, and descend another 20 feet to the bottom. We will sit in there for about half an hour.

"During this time I'd like you to focus on your breathing. You should be able to breathe deeply and naturally in a comfortable sitting position. As we rest at the bottom of this crater, I'd like you to visualize that your inhalations are not of air, but of light. Inhale light. After your inhalation of light, visualize that your exhalation is light as well. Exhale light. Watch your bubbles as they arise to the surface. See that they are shining with the light of your breath. We will sit there meditatively breathing, inhaling light and exhaling light.

"This is another very strong spiritual place of power. With this meditation exercise it is easy to see that the air you breathe is actually the light of awareness, consciousness itself. Your attention to this essential light of life affords you spiritual insight and realization." Sam nodded to me and asked, "Ready to dive?"

I nodded back. We stepped into the ocean over the white sand. We quickly descended down to a high mound underwater at about 30 feet. The mound had a large, deep crater opening just as Sam had described. A single raccoon fish drifted over the sparse assortment of hard corals. *Every fish is precious,* I thought, as I considered the lone fish moving about the vast seascape. Sam and I finned over to the top of the crater. There we descended feet-first through the narrow crevice, to the sandy bottom. Upon reaching the bottom I carefully let all of the air out of my buoyancy control vest. Sam and I positioned ourselves to sit comfortably on the bottom.

I focused on my breath and tried to follow Sam's instructions. I realized that I wasn't sure that I knew what he meant by "light." As I exhaled, I watched my bubbles floating up to the surface and tried to imagine them as spheres of sunlight. As I breathed in, I tried to imagine inhaling the rays of the sun rather than oxygen molecules. But that wasn't quite it, I could tell. Sam was always talking about light, but he never really seemed to mean light in its physical definition. Maybe I'm thinking about it too hard, I decided.

I kept focusing on my breath, feeling each inhalation and exhalation, and after a few minutes, I realized that the air felt different. It wasn't just air; it felt like pure energy. I was breathing air—energy—light—life. I enjoyed the sensation of my body being filled with this light, this energy, releasing bubbles of light, and filling up with light again.

After about a half an hour, Sam gave me the ascent signal. I pressed the button on my low pressure inflator hose to add air to my buoyancy control vest. Sam and I ascended out of the crater and kicked along the rocky reef. As we headed toward shore, we saw a huge school of very small fish. Sam and I swam just alongside the massive school. The silvery fish moved and glided before me.

I moved closer to the dazzling band. Soon I found myself engulfed by the massive assembly of inch-long fish. Shimmering flashes of silver and blue surrounded me and filled my vision. The spectacle mesmerized me. I focused my vision on one little fish in the whole school. I followed the school and the single fish.

Sam is right, I thought, *I am no more important than this fish.* Then this realization struck me deeply. I was really no better than this fish and this fish's life was as important and precious as mine. Looking at the fish, awed by my realization, I thought, *You are precious!* All of a sudden I felt a simple, lighthearted freedom.

The school started heading out toward deeper water. Sam and I watched the gleaming mass move away in sporadic sprints and jetting turns. When the school was far away, we ascended and made our way back to shore.

UNDERSEA AWARENESS

Sam and I sat quietly for a few minutes. I looked to the north end of the beach where an outcropping of palm trees stood at the water's edge with their leaves rattling in the ocean wind. I felt a gentle swaying inside as if I were floating in the ocean waves. I gazed out to sea where a sailboat had just appeared on the horizon in the south. Sam turned and looked at me. I just sat peacefully, feeling the inner sway.

Sam leaned in closer to me and said, "Looks like you are still experiencing undersea awareness. That's very good."

I looked at him curiously, "What do you mean—undersea awareness?" I did notice that I was experiencing a calm, peaceful feeling that I sometimes felt after SCUBA diving.

"When you go underwater," Sam answered, "your awareness changes from the awareness of this world to the awareness of the water world. When you go SCUBA diving, you enter a completely different universe. In that non-terrestrial dimension, physics are different, our senses are altered, our awareness is shifted, and we perceive a completely different world. We perceive life through undersea awareness."

"I'm not sure I understand what you mean," I said. "I know things are different underwater. But is there more to undersea awareness than the aquatic atmosphere and marine life?"

"Yes," Sam said, "it's easy to see that things are physically different underwater, but what's not so apparent are the profound transformative effects on consciousness that one may experience through undersea awareness.

"Take this, for example." Sam reached into his SCUBA bag and pulled out a half empty bottle of water and a pencil. "This is you," he said holding the pencil in front of me. Then he put the pencil in the water bottle. Two thirds of the pencil was submerged in the water. The pencil rested diagonally against the side of the water bottle.

"See?" Sam said.

I looked at the pencil in the water bottle. I had seen this experiment done before by my Open Water Diver instructor. It was to show refraction, the bending of light as it changes in the greater density of water. The submerged part of the pencil looked larger and closer than the portion outside the water.

"That's refraction," I said.

"Yes," Sam agreed, "the greater molecular density of water heightens your vision of all things in the water world. Yet look at the submerged part of the pencil a bit more closely."

I gazed at it. The submerged portion of the pencil was a brighter color than the dry portion. It was shimmering and luminous. It looked somehow magical and alive compared to the top dry part.

"That's odd," I said, "I never noticed the beauty of refraction."

"Yes, it's magic," Sam said, "and colors are completely different underwater, too. Though some colors, like red, diminish in visibility to the eye the deeper you go, the colors that you do see underwater are magnificent and more alive than on land."

Sam pulled a SCUBA diving magazine from his bag. He paged through to a picture of an Achilles tang and said, "This is a common fish in Hawaii. What color would you say this fish's tail is?"

I looked at the picture. I was familiar with the Achilles tang. In the picture, the color of the circular formation by its tail looked like an unremarkable brownish orange. I answered, "Orange."

Sam put the magazine down. "Now close your eyes," he said. "Remember earlier today, in our morning dive we saw several of these Achilles tangs. In your mind's eye, see the color of their tails."

I closed my eyes and remembered the Achilles tangs that we had seen earlier. I envisioned their form and color in my memory. In my mind's eye, their tails were not orange, but rather a bright glowing tan color. I explained my vision to Sam.

"Exactly," Sam said, "even the most mundane colors are incredible underwater. Underwater colors are magnified and alive. And as you know from your Open Water Diver course, sound waves travel 400% faster underwater as well. The underwater world is often silent, but you can hear a boat engine or whale song over a mile away.

"As well, our sense of touch underwater is more intensely afferent. You simply move your hand and you feel the whole ocean! Cold and heat are transmitted through contact 20 times faster than in air. The senses of the body are tremendously heightened in water."

Sam held the bottle holding the submerged pencil before my eyes and said, "This is your mind underwater. Illuminated, bigger, brighter, magical."

As I gazed at the pencil, he continued, "Under water there is different logic. The sea, like any dimension, has its own logic. Learning to swim, surf, sail, or dive is learning an aspect of this logic, so that you can enjoy and use its power.

"Everything on land is order, but underwater everything is chaos. Yet all things that seem like chaos to us are really just a different kind of order. When we dive into what appears to be chaos, our ordered state of mind vanishes and we learn new dimensions of order."

Sam paused. "Underwater, things take on a totally different consciousness. If I show you a picture of a fish on land, it's in our ordinary attention. It is no longer of the sea." Sam held the picture of the Achilles tang in front of me, "The experience of seeing this fish in reality is very different from seeing this picture because the real fish exists in a dimension of undersea awareness.

"It is just as if you see a picture of a woman experiencing Samadhi. Your picture shows only what is ordinary to our surface awareness. If you were to actually sit with her, you'd enter her field of enlightened awareness and experience an ecstatic truth beyond our ordinary world.

"This, on the other hand," Sam said, turning the page of the magazine to a picture of a sleek speedboat, "this is in our ordinary attention. The experience of seeing this boat would be very similar to the picture. However, if this speedboat wrecks, it becomes a living reef under the sea."

Sam continued, "The depth limit for recreational diving is 130 feet. If you do a 130 foot dive, that is a very deep dive and must be done with planning and great care. However, 130 feet isn't so far up here on land. It's just over to that palm tree there, but underwater it's dimensionally very different."

Sam pointed to a palm tree that didn't look too far away. *That's so true!* I thought. From my experience doing a deep dive with Sam, 100 foot dives did seem like a very big deal.

"When you're underwater, sea logic sets in your mind the same way. Underwater you experience a big difference in your awareness of life. Awareness changes underwater. Your attention becomes attuned to the ways of water. Your state of mind shifts as you acclimate to the element of water. You see life in deeper dimensionality. Underwater awareness is heightened awareness."

I nodded with a deepening sense of what Sam was explaining.

"This is very important to the mystic," Sam said, "because if life can be such seeming chaos, so different from the orderly conditioned reality of our every day lives, then perhaps life isn't limited to anything. Seeing this shift in awareness gives you the ability to examine awareness itself. And as you examine awareness you will find that awareness is just love."

Awareness is just love, I thought, fascinated by the statement, but not really grasping its meaning. I was absorbed in what Sam was saying. I had felt some of what he described, but had no words to understand it till now.

Sam asked, "How did you feel about the dive?"

"Great," I said. "That was a fantastic dive."

"What did you like about it?"

"I'm not sure. The coral here is very sparse, but beautiful in its own way. The school of fish was beautiful. I really did come to see that every fish is precious. And going into the crater was quite an amazing experience. Sitting down there and breathing light seemed to create a magical atmosphere. It's hard to explain, but this dive was just very magical for me."

"Yes," Sam said smiling, "because you can see the magic. Not everyone experiences undersea awareness. You know, most people would have considered this to be quite a boring dive. There are few fish here, though there are some colorful ones. There are a lot more rocks than coral. The school, while large, was filled with small unremarkable fish. The crater is kind of interesting, but there's nothing to see in it. And we just sat around at the bottom in the sand the whole time."

I did agree with Sam's points. The details of the dive were kind of dull, but for some reason I still felt that the dive was wonderful.

Sam continued, "The reason that this dive was so great for you was that you are able to connect to the magic, the energy of the ocean's essence. Through that connection, you gain undersea awareness. If you cannot see the magic of the undersea world, you would be bored with many dives."

I had seen this contrast in my experience sometimes when I would go out on a dive boat operated by the local dive shop. On some of the dives I would come up exhilarated because of the beauty of the undersea world. Yet back on the dive boat, I would hear other divers say, "This isn't as good as the Bahamas," or "The dive was OK, but I didn't see any big fish." I wondered why, when I would experience so much beauty and excitement while diving, others would be bored by it.

Sam continued, "In places of power, it is easier to connect with the energy of water, which enhances your undersea awareness and makes your dive magical.

"Many people enjoy diving with dolphins, turtles, rays, and whales. When we see these animals in their ocean home, we psychically connect with them. This connection allows us to experience the awareness of water similarly to the way these amazing animals do. This also makes it very easy to connect with the power of the ocean.

"Fish see the water in deeper dimensions than humans do. Fish see the water as their home. We only see water. Water holds deeper dimensions of life. We gain some awareness of that connection by spending time with fish. Many marine animals, especially marine mammals have a great psychic facility. We experience this feeling, connection, and awareness more greatly with dolphins, manta rays, and whales."

"I love diving with dolphins," I said. "Once, I dived so close to a dolphin that I was able to touch it."

Sam looked at me with stern eyes, "There are only two conditions whereby you should touch any animal underwater as part of your recreation as a Mystic SCUBA diver. The first condition is that you learn from an expert what the ramifications are of your touch to an animal. Did you know that many fish have a protective coating on their skin, and that the oils on the human hand destroy that coating? A fish could then get sores or painful parasites in the area you touch. So before you think about touching a fish, you should ask a marine biologist if your touch would be harmful to the fish.

"The second condition is that you ask permission. Just because it is fun for you to touch a marine animal, it certainly may not be fun for them. Underwater animals do not touch nearly as much as humans do. Fish generally only touch to reproduce and are touched when being eaten by a bigger fish. They don't do a whole lot more touching than that. Humans tend to explore things with their hands, but we must refrain from this intrusive, potentially dangerous curiosity when we dive underwater.

"Mystic SCUBA divers have great respect for marine life. We honor the world of water that we experience by not trashing it. Where some divers may litter, crash into coral, or grab hold of turtles, we do not. It is our respect for the ocean and all of its life forms that grants us a greater awareness of life. If you ask an animal that you know your touch will not harm, the animal may give its consent for you to touch it. If you cannot positively understand the animal's communication to you, then do not touch."

"But how can you tell if a dolphin gives its consent?" I asked.

"The same way you know when it's OK to pet a dog that you come across on the street," Sam answered, "with care and awareness. If you come across a cute dog, with care you can tell if it is comfortable being petted by you. You should also extend this care in approaching marine life. If you see a sea turtle or eagle ray, swim in a parallel fashion to it. Do not swim as fast as you can right toward it. When it is aware that you are there, you can slowly narrow the distance between you.

"Marine animals feel the intensity of our stare. Though you are excited to see a dolphin or whale underwater, relax and know that the greatest factor for getting close or touching the marine animal depends on if it does not feel threatened by you and is comfortable. So if you are relaxed and communicate your desire to be closer, just as you would when coming across a dog or cat on the street, you have a greater chance of being closer to the marine animal."

I took Sam's words to heart.

"Tomorrow, let's meet here again," Sam said. "We will take a day off to desaturate because we've been diving for several days in a row. Let's meet here at our usual time and do our morning meditation together. After that I will bring you to one of my favorite terrestrial places of power. Make sure that you bring warm clothing and sturdy shoes for that. After that, we will return to my hotel for a nice dinner. The restaurant there is excellent, and the attire is island-chic, so bring a dress, too."

"Sounds great," I said, intrigued by Sam's plans and curious about terrestrial places of power.

Sam and I walked back up to the cars and disassembled our SCUBA gear. It was early in the afternoon, but we were done for the day. Sam bowed and reminded me to bring more papayas for Pono the next day. "I'll bring plenty for him," I said cheerfully. Sam pulled away in his Jeep, heading north. Starting my car, I turned around to head south for my long drive home.

That evening, after a few hours of struggling through my programming studies, I began to pack for my meeting with Sam the next day. I packed a wide variety of clothes, including a jacket for the visit to Sam's above-sea place of power. I didn't understand why I needed a warm jacket in Hawaii, but I did as Sam suggested.

CRATERS OF LIGHT

The next morning I was up early, ready for the adventures ahead. On my way across the island to meet Sam, I realized that I had forgotten to bring papayas. I stopped off at a grocery store on the way and picked up a few papayas. Reaching the previous day's dive site a few minutes late, I parked behind Sam's Jeep and ambled out of my car down to the ocean side of the crater. Sam was sitting there.

"Good morning," he said and gestured for me to sit next to him.

"Good morning," I said, sitting down.

"During our meditation today," Sam said, "we will focus on the chakras as we do every day, but we will sit with our eyes opened, gazing out over the ocean in the direction of the underwater crater. Just gaze out toward the horizon. Let's begin."

I sat up straight and focused on my navel center. After a few minutes of concentration, I noticed that there was a subtle energy moving just over where the underwater crater must have been. Luminous fibers of light appeared like the energy I had seen with Sam at my favorite cove, yet this energy moved in a different way. Long white lines that sparkled like disco balls moved slowly from the water's surface to high in the sky. Soon the energetic light became foremost in my vision.

As Sam and I meditated on the heart chakra and the third eye, I could see a tremendous amount of light moving up from the ocean in great billows. As I continued to still my thoughts, I could see that the exceptionally bright energy originated from about 20 feet underwater. It was as if the underwater crater was erupting with light. I sat still, amazed in this spectacle of light for the entire meditation.

"OK," Sam said, and we bowed.

"Did you see that?" I asked. "There were giant columns of light shooting up from the crater underwater."

"Yes," Sam said, "When you meditate with opened eyes, gazing in a place of power, you can see the profound spiritual energy that is present."

"It's amazing!" I exclaimed. "The light looked similar to the light I saw at my favorite cove, but it was a thousand times more intense here."

"The energy in the crater is a thousand times more powerful than the cove," Sam answered. "And remember, yesterday you were sitting in that light."

Recalling my awareness of breathing light yesterday during my dive in the crater, I said, "I think I'm starting to understand the effects of places of power now."

"Yes," Sam said. "Seeing the energy from here that you were diving in yesterday gives you some perspective. It gives you greater awareness of the light of this sacred place. In this powerful light, it is possible to realize the limitlessness of consciousness through attention to your breath."

After sitting for a moment in silence, Sam and I walked back up the beach toward the footpath leading to the road. When Pono, who was sitting out in front of his Land Cruiser, came into sight, Sam said to me, "Let's go fetch your papayas. I spoke with Pono earlier today before you arrived. He said that he loved the papayas we gave him yesterday."

"Great," I responded.

Sam and I reached the foot trail leading up to the road. Sam continued, "Pono said that he could taste the power of the land in eating your papayas. I told him that they were from your yard and he said that your yard has the Aloha Spirit, unlike a lot of the papayas that are in the stores."

"What's wrong with the papayas that you get in stores?" I asked, now concerned.

"It's like what Pono was saying yesterday," Sam answered, "they have no Aloha Spirit. Pono has a subtle sensitivity to feeling the intentions of the farmers and whether the crops are harvested in balance with the land. Many farmers now have more greed than they did 20 years ago and some of them use farming techniques that are harmful to the land."

"Really? And Pono can tell just by tasting a papaya?" I asked.

"Yep," Sam said.

"Well, then I should tell you something," I said, a pained expression on my face.

"What is it?"

"My papayas are from the store," I explained. "I was running late today and forgot to bring papayas from my yard. I stopped by the supermarket on my way here."

Sam stopped and chuckled, "In that case, follow me." Sam turned and walked back down the footpath toward Pono. I followed Sam down and around Pono's rusty Land Cruiser.

Pono was sitting on a beach chair, carefully carving a small red shell. Several of his puppies tumbled about him. Seeing us walk over, he said, "Eh, braddah Sam! Howzit?" Sam smiled as we approached him. Looking to me, Pono grinned and said, "Sistah Vanessa, mahalo for da papayas yestah day. Dose papayas was some good!"

"You're welcome, Pono," I said, kicking myself for forgetting them today.

Sam reached into his pocket and pulled out a one hundred dollar bill. Handing it to Pono he said, "No papayas today, but please take this."

I was surprised that Sam was giving him so much money. Pono casually accepted the money in his left hand and looked at it. He seemed less excited about being given $100 than a papaya, but graciously accepted Sam's gift with a smile. Pono shook his head slightly, laughing. Then he smiled warmly and spoke some cheerful Hawaiian words to Sam that were incomprehensible to me.

Sam bowed his head to Pono, "Aloha Pono, I'll see you next time."

"Mahalo, Sam! Aloha, Vanessa!" Pono said waving as Sam and I turned back up toward the footpath.

Just out of earshot of Pono, I exclaimed to Sam in a loud whisper, "A hundred dollars! You just gave him a lot of money."

"Sure," Sam said, "he'd have really preferred some papayas from your yard, but money is useful to him as well. He has to go into town from time to time."

Sam paused and then continued, "I always support guardians of places of power. Their work has tremendous value to me. If Pono weren't here, this bright, yet delicate, location would be trashed by tourists and no longer a place of power."

I paused and looked at the pristine sands and glistening blue waves of the beach. I thought about my dive yesterday and turned to see a luminous glow where the underwater crater stood.

Without Pono, maybe I wouldn't have been able to experience and learn the amazing things I have here, I thought.

"Pono's work is valuable indeed," I said, after my reflection.

"Now follow me," Sam said walking back up toward the cars. "It's a short drive to the hotel from here."

BUDDHIST AESTHETICS

I followed Sam north for a few miles, passing a large popular hotel. A minute or two later we were pulling in to the Four Seasons resort. As we turned off the highway, we passed the resort's unassuming gate. *Wow, is Sam staying here?* I wondered. We rolled down a long delicate driveway lined with large flamboyant trees and flowering hibiscus bushes. I had never been to one of the five-star Hawaiian resorts before. I felt that we had entered into a new world, a Hawaiian paradise more perfect than I could have possibly imagined.

We pulled up to the front entrance, just before the lobby. My eyes widened as I took in a grand vision of an artistic white fountain. Glistening sprinkles of sapphire water sprayed forth from its carved marble conch shells. I was stunned, gazing at the impeccably cared-for grounds. As I stopped, pulling in behind Sam, he jumped out of his very dusty Jeep.

"Hello, Sam," the valet said, "back so soon today?" The valet wore an immaculate white uniform and an unusually shaped hat that resembled a British policeman's cap.

"Yes, James," Sam said, "but I'll be going out again later."

The valet nodded.

Another valet approached my car, opening the driver's side door for me. As I pulled my day pack out of the car the valet smiled at me, saying, "Welcome to the Four Seasons."

"Thank you," I said awkwardly, not quite sure how to respond.

Sam signaled me to join him. I walked with him through the expansive lobby. A stunning floral centerpiece of pink Hawaiian lilies filled the air with a charmed scent. We exited the lobby area, down a grand staircase. I felt like we were walking through a palace.

"This is your hotel?" I asked Sam, a bit shocked.

"Yes," Sam said.

We meandered down toward the oceanfront rooms. While we walked, I looked around at the beautiful grounds. Flowering birds of paradise sprung flawlessly over the hedges of the manicured landscape. The luxurious simplicity of the building's architecture was stunning, yet I was starting to feel uncomfortable about the whole situation.

As we neared Sam's room, he pulled out his key.

"I can't believe you're staying here!" I found myself blurting out.

"Why is that?" Sam asked as he opened his door to reveal a beautiful oceanfront suite.

Walking in and looking around, I said, "This must cost a fortune! Why would a Buddhist monk want to stay in such an expensive place?"

"Buddhist monks love beautiful accommodations," Sam replied matter-of-factly. "In the Far East many of the Buddhist monasteries are as lavish, grand, and beautiful as the king's palaces! Buddhists like places that shine. Buddhism itself is a beautiful aesthetic.

"Many tropical five-star resorts are built on natural places of power," Sam said. "The people who come to these places use the rejuvenative energy of the location to revitalize themselves so that they can become more successful. The people who come to resorts like the Four Seasons have a lot of money and usually very little free time. They thrive on these places of power to maintain and increase their wealth and well-being."

Sam continued, "These days, I believe the monasteries of the Far East are poor places for spiritual practice. The enlightened founders of the monasteries lived long ago. Monasteries have become social traditions, conditioned by patterns of habit and bureaucracy. Though monasteries are good institutions for ethics and conceptual understandings, they often lack the freedom and luminosity that is so plentiful here. I no longer spend time on retreat in the Buddhist monasteries. Rather, I come to five-star resorts for my spiritual retreats.

"Five-star resorts have beauty and decorum, but no conditions and concepts of spirituality. The intent of the architecture and the place of power is for peace, serenity, recuperation, and fun. This place is more Buddhist than any monastery I've ever been to."

"But, how does a Buddhist monk pay for a suite at the Four Seasons?" I asked curiously.

"I work in a business consulting firm with some of my students," Sam answered.

"You work? At a job? Like everyone else?" I asked incredulously. "I thought that if you were a monk, you'd have to sit around all the time meditating or something."

"No, not at all," Sam said. "Monks in my lineage all work in the world. In some lineages the monks are poor and ask the community to feed and support them. In my lineage the monks are wealthy and support and feed our community."

This was very different from my concept of Buddhist monks, and it was intriguing to me.

Sam continued, "There was a time when I was traveling in Thailand that I saw two monks ask a family for food as holy alms. The family didn't even have enough food to fill their own stomachs, but religiously gave a portion of their daily meal to the monks anyway. Watching the mother and father worrying and deciding between feeding the monks and nourishing their children made me feel great pity. Why should monks cause so much duress and be a further strain in a poor and struggling community?"

I saw Sam's point.

Sam explained, "In my tradition, the most wise, powerful, and intuitive beings in the community use their strong minds and spiritual insights to better the lives of all the people. I use software automation and effective project management methodologies to improve the efficiency of supply chain execution for food distributors. Through my work, I help businesses organize, manage, and access information for vital business processes. With my aid, food distribution companies can be more organized and efficient so that there is a greater abundance of food for all families—and I can afford to visit places of power like this to increase my power and capabilities."

"That makes a lot of sense to me," I said. "I once thought that spiritual practice was selfish. I thought that it was just dwelling on your own happiness and forgetting about others who are suffering. What you're telling me is very interesting. It has a lot of bearing on what I'm considering to do next with my life."

I explained my interest in helping people in Ethiopia to Sam. I told him about my idea of working as a computer programmer to be able to microfinance small businesses in the developing world. I told him about the boys I was helping and their summer businesses. I told him about the mothers I had met and their visions for the small businesses they wanted to start. Sam was very interested in my plans. We talked about the possibilities that microfinance could offer.

Sam said, "If you make enough money, you can have the things you need to expand and increase your power, so that you are better able to aid the lives of many."

I agreed, deciding at that moment to get a high-paying job in technology to fund many ventures in Ethiopia and all over the developing world. The decision was clear and simple, without any of the confusions I'd felt earlier.

Telling Sam my resolution, he remarked, "Such powerful resolve to serve the dharma is the result of your expanded awareness in this place of power."

I smiled.

Sam brought me out to his patio. The white sand beach lay just before us. We sat quietly facing the blue sea as Sam explained what we were going to do with the rest of our day.

"We're going to the top of the volcano," Sam said.

"You can just drive there?" I asked.

"You can, in a Jeep!"

I laughed.

Sam continued, "The volcano is a very strong place of spiritual power. It has a very fast-moving energy field that vibrates so strongly that it pushes away much of the human aura of this planet. On the volcano it is easy to meditate and to have subtle visions. Within the aura of the volcano you can let go of your ordinary view of the world. We will go to the mountain to see a spiritual vision. If we stop at the store for water and provisions, by the time we reach the 10,000 foot elevation of the volcano, it will have been 24 hours since our last dive and we will not be in any danger of decompression sickness."

Sam and I changed into warmer clothes and left the Four Seasons.

BREATH HEALTH

Sam and I drove far beyond the coastal resorts, and then the Hawaiian towns and ranches, to the long empty roads of the island's center. On our long drive, we talked about how to successfully set up a microfinance program and about the computer programming job market. I found Sam to be very practical about both matters.

As we ascended up the mountain road, we found ourselves entering a thick mist. "Weather conditions can change rapidly up here," Sam said, as he turned on his headlights. As we continued along past craggy red lava rock formations, a gentle rain pattered on the soft top of the Jeep. Sam, looking to the left side of the road, began to slow down. A moment later, we came to a complete stop. Switching the Jeep into the low four-wheel drive gear, Sam turned to the left and we drove off the paved road and up a rough lava rock side road.

We bounced along on our steep ascent. I couldn't believe even a Jeep would make it up the rugged ground. As we ascended high up the mountain, we emerged from out of the wet clouds. Looking up into the stunning blue sky, I saw the magnificent contrasting red crater peaks.

After another exhilaratingly bumpy hour, we reached the top of the volcano. Zipping up our jackets, we stepped out of the car. The air was cool and crisp on the mountaintop. Sam and I hiked up a footpath to a ledge facing the west. The sun was high in the sky. There were clouds completely covering our view of the ocean. To me the top of the volcano looked like a cross between an alien planet and Heaven.

Sam and I sat down on a red dusty mound. I felt a little bit dizzy while acclimating to the altitude. "Breathe deeply," Sam advised. "Deep breathing will help you adjust to the higher altitude. Deep breathing always helps your body to gain balance and health."

I began to focus on deepening my breaths.

"Deep breathing is very healthy," Sam said. "The deep breathing that we practice in Mystic SCUBA has many substantial health benefits. For example, it prevents illness."

"How's that?" I asked.

"Increased abdominal movement during deep breathing helps oxygenate and circulate your blood. With a greater circulation of oxygen-rich blood, your resistance to illness is strengthened.

"Deep breathing also aids digestion."

"Because of the oxidation process you mentioned before?" I asked.

Sam answered, "Yes. Also, the extended movement of your abdomen during deep breathing massages your digestive organs. This helps expel toxins and improves digestion. The physical relaxation and meditative states of mind you experience while practicing deep breathing in Mystic SCUBA decreases ulcers and other psychosomatic digestive disorders."

"And," Sam said, "deep breathing reduces high blood pressure. Deep breathing causes your blood vessels to dilate, which enables them to carry more blood. This increases the volume of blood flowing through the arteries to your brain."

Sam pointed to his temple saying, "And that's why deep breathing is so beneficial for your mind." Sam explained, "Good circulation of oxygen-rich blood is necessary for healthy brain performance. Your brain not only governs physical health, but also emotional and psychological health.

"If you start to get upset, depressed, stressed, or in any other way mentally unbalanced, taking a few deep breaths has a powerful effect on your health and well being. Deep breathing improves physical health, which directly improves mental health. With a greater circulation of oxygen-rich blood, your physical health immediately begins to improve and your mind becomes clearer and better able to cope with disturbing thoughts and emotions."

"That makes sense," I said.

"And, deep breathing helps you stay young. Deep breathing increases your vitality. It conserves energy, lowering your metabolic rate. In deep breathing, your body relaxes while your heart rate normalizes, decreasing by almost 25%. While deep breathing, your breathing rate decreases from about 16 breaths per minute to a healthy five breaths per minute.

"The deep breathing you practice in Mystic SCUBA doesn't only aid your immune system, blood-pressure, digestion, and mental acuity, but it also improves many other aging factors, including vision, hearing, skin elasticity, reaction time, and physical strength.

"Deep breathing slows aging and aids rejuvenation. At the age of 60, you can have the health and vitality of a 30-year-old."

This was interesting to me. I remembered having lunch once with two co-workers in San Francisco. Of these two gentlemen one looked to be in his 60's. He had grey hair, wrinkles, and was about 50 pounds overweight. The other looked to be in his 30's with a full head of dark hair, smooth skin, and an athletic physique. During lunch, the grey-haired man asked the dark-haired man, "How old are you?" The dark-haired man answered, "46." Shocked, the grey-haired man said, "I'm 46, too!" I wondered what it was about their lifestyles that had created such a drastic difference.

BREATHING DEEP

Sam said, "Now that you are comfortable practicing deep breathing and you have an understanding of the health benefits, let's talk about something that you can only do in SCUBA diving: breathing deep."

A bit perplexed, I said, "But Sam, what more is there to tell me about deep breathing? You already taught me all about deep breathing and I've been practicing it everyday on our dives for over a week."

"I mean breathing while deep underwater," Sam said showing me the thumbs-down descend dive hand signal.

"Oh," I said, raising an eyebrow.

"Breathing underwater using SCUBA gear offers unique health benefits," Sam said. "We will begin by discussing how the partial pressure of oxygen affects the body as we breathe during SCUBA diving." Sam explained, "In SCUBA diving you are always breathing a higher partial pressure of oxygen than above water because of the physics of pressure on air. The partial pressure of oxygen in SCUBA diving increases the benefits of oxygen throughout the body."

I scratched my head, perplexed again. Though I had heard about the partial pressure of oxygen in my SCUBA diving classes, I wasn't following what Sam meant.

Noticing my puzzlement, Sam explained, "As you may remember from the supplemental reading in your Open Water Diver class, Dalton's Law states: 'In a mixture of gases, such as air, each gas exerts its individual pressure independent of other gases in the mixture. The independent pressure of a gas is its partial pressure – that is, the part of the pressure exerted by the gas.'"

I didn't remember Dalton's Law. As I considered the subject further, I did remember my first instructor saying something about the partial pressure of oxygen causing oxygen toxicity, a kind of diving malady that could cause a diver to go into convulsions at great depths. My instructor told our class that we wouldn't have to worry about it as long as we stayed within the depth limits of recreational SCUBA diving. Yet because I didn't have a lot of knowledge about under what conditions oxygen toxicity could occur, it caused me concern.

Sam continued, "If you take a gas mixture like regular air underwater, the atmospheric pressure increases upon the gas the deeper you go. The partial pressure of each gas in the mix also increases proportionately to its fraction in the mix."

I listened closely, though the subject was unclear to me.

Sam paused for a moment and then reached into his backpack, retrieving a PADI Instructor's Manual. Flipping through the early pages of the binder, he opened it to a page with a familiar illustration on it.

I remembered this illustration from my initial certification course. The simple picture helped me understand what Sam meant. It was a before and after picture. It showed a balloon at the surface just above the ocean. There were a dozen or so dots drawn at random within the balloon, the dots representing the oxygen molecules that are present in air. The second part of the picture showed the same balloon under the surface of the ocean. The balloon was now much smaller because the pressure of the water compressed the air in the balloon. The dots that represented the oxygen molecules were now very close together.

"Oh, yeah! I remember now," I exclaimed. "The air volume gets reduced under a greater pressure the deeper you go."

"That's right," Sam said, "and the oxygen in the air becomes more compressed."

"Yes," I said, understanding clearly.

"The greater the compression of oxygen molecules," Sam said, "the higher the partial pressure of oxygen."

"I understand perfectly."

"Good," Sam said with a smile. "Now, let's take a look at the numbers that support this." Sam pulled out a blank underwater writing slate with an attached pencil, so that I could follow along.

"The partial pressure of each gas in the mixture is a multiple of the gas's percentage in the mixture by the total absolute atmospheric pressure. So for example, the partial pressure of oxygen in air, or 'PO2', at a depth of 132 feet is expressed as 1.05 ATA, meaning total absolute pressure."

Sam recited the equation while writing it on the blank slate for me to see,

The absolute pressure is 5 ATA

132 feet ÷ 33 feet/ ATM = 4 ATM, meaning atmospheres of pressure

4 ATM + 1 ATM, for the Earth's atmosphere = 5 ATA

Air consists of 21% oxygen

5 ATA x .21 = 1.05 ATA

I nodded, trying to keep up with Sam's calculations.

"This means that when breathing air at 132 feet, you're breathing five times more oxygen in one breath than on the surface. Oxygen, the most vital nutrient for the body, becomes enhanced at depth."

Referring back to the balloon illustration in the instructor's manual, Sam pointed to the larger balloon at the surface, "You may only be filling your lungs with three or four of all these oxygen dots right?"

"Right," I said.

"But if you take the same complete inhalation from this balloon," Sam pointed to the smaller balloon underwater, "you will inhale almost all of these oxygen dots in one normal breath."

"OK, I get it," I said. "You get more oxygen."

Sam went on, "In light of your understanding of the importance of breath, and the many beneficial aspects of oxygen for your body, you can see that breathing a greater partial pressure of oxygen at 132 feet is five times healthier for you."

I interrupted with my nagging fear, "But I thought that if you breathe too great a partial pressure of oxygen that you can get oxygen toxicity?"

"Yes," Sam said, "exposure to oxygen with a partial pressure greater than approximately 1.4 ATA to 1.6 ATA can cause central nervous system toxicity. However, the maximum partial pressure that you will reach when SCUBA diving within recreational limits is about 1.05 ATA. At a maximum depth around 130 feet, the partial pressure of oxygen that you breathe in air is highly beneficial to your health and far from toxic."

I felt reassured that I wouldn't be in danger of getting oxygen toxicity.

Sam went on, "Just breathing a higher partial pressure of oxygen greatly benefits your brain. It increases neural energy metabolism in the brain, stimulates inactive brain cells, and improves sustained cognitive performance."

Sam explained, "Science has proven many benefits of breathing oxygen-enriched air decades ago. Breathing a higher partial pressure of oxygen beneficially stimulates cells, increases basal metabolism, neutralizes toxins, and provides increased energy for athletic performance. It can help cure headaches, immune system suppression, circulation problems, digestion problems, depression, muscle aches and pains, poor concentration, obesity, and even cancer."

"Cancer?" I interrupted. "Is that true?"

"Sure," Sam said, "remember, cells that are oxygen deprived can turn cancerous. And cancerous cells improve with greater exposure to oxygen.

"I once knew a Divemaster in Monterey who was diagnosed with inoperable lung cancer. Being a practitioner of Chi Gung, he believed in the healing power of air. He decided to practice deep breathing exercises while using enriched air Nitrox in his daily diving. He dived five to six days per week at a depth of 100 feet. With 40% oxygen in his air mix, the partial pressure of oxygen that he was breathing was 1.6—which was allowable under the rules of his technical Nitrox certification. He calmed his mind and practiced abdominal breathing."

Sam continued, "About eight people out of ten with lung cancer die within two years, and less than 2% with tumors like his survive past five years. Despite these statistics, he was miraculously healed. His cancer went into remission. Now 10 years later, he is cancer free and feeling healthier than ever."

"Wow!" I said, figuring that the higher partial pressure of oxygen must have really been a significant factor in his cancer's remission.

"Most importantly," Sam said, "through deep breathing and Mystic SCUBA exercises, the higher partial pressure of oxygen creates an instant state of heightened attention.

"Although the brain only makes up 2% of the body's overall weight, it utilizes 20% of its available oxygen. Greater cerebral blood flow with a higher partial pressure of oxygen acts as a super nutrient to the brain, and is the physical foundation of the enhanced experiences of awareness during Mystic SCUBA."

Air: The Mystic's Explanation

"Now that you have an understanding of the physical aspects of air in SCUBA diving, it is important to understand the subtle, energetic, and mystical benefits. In considering the mystical and spiritual aspects of air, there are many profound benefits to the health of your aura and the peace of your mind."

I listened closely as Sam continued, "In mysticism, just as in Chinese medicine, energy precedes physicality. Anything and everything physical is an outcome of its energy. When we focus on energy before physicality, we find there are many options for transformation and awareness. If we are only aware of the physical world, we are much more inflexible and limited."

Seeing my blank expression, Sam explained, "For example, in medicine if you can heal cancer in its subtle energetic form prior to its physical formation, the pathology of that potentially life-threatening illness never affects the body."

"Is that possible?" I asked. "Are you saying that cancer can be healed before it appears in the physical body?"

"Yes," Sam said, "Chinese medicine and other energetic forms of healing pay attention to the aura. An acupuncturist can heal a congestion of energy in the aura that would eventually manifest as cancerous cells."

"As we had discussed before, in Chinese medicine acupuncturists stimulate energetic points in the aura to balance its energy. When the energy of the aura is healthy, the physical body will follow the flow of energy to good health. Similarly in Mystic SCUBA, focusing on the breath in the element of water balances the energies of the aura and heightens the awareness of the mind. In Mystic SCUBA, the aura and physical body become balanced and healthy, as the mind and consciousness expand."

"I understand that deep breathing is healthy for the body, but how do you know that it is especially good for the aura and the mind?" I asked.

"Ancient spiritual masters in India and China taught that the foundation for spiritual practice is in cultivating the vital energy of life found in air," Sam said. "Air has energy. The spiritual masters understood it pragmatically: Without air you die, so air has a powerful life force. Just as air nourishes your physical body, air nourishes your aura.

"Indian Yogis and Taoist Chi Gung masters founded spiritual traditions on exercises and meditations focused on breath. They observed that we transform air into life energy and that the awareness of that energy itself transforms consciousness."

"Interesting," I said, intrigued by the ancient spiritual understanding of air's energy, "but why is it especially helpful in SCUBA diving?"

"Breathing a greater partial pressure of oxygen at depth is equivalent to supplying the body with super-energy," Sam answered. "Breathing air during SCUBA at 33 feet infuses your aura with twice as much energy as breathing at the surface. At 66 feet your aura is three times as energized by the air you breathe, and at 133 feet your aura is five times as energized. With a much greater amount of life energy in each breath, it is easier to increase awareness of the spiritual essence of life itself!

"The energy of air is comprised of *yin* and *yang*. Yin and yang are the fundamental complementary, yet opposing forces that make up everything in the universe. Nitrogen is the yin part of air. Although considered by science to be an inert gas in air that the physical body doesn't use, nitrogen's auric energy actually sustains the subtle body. So, nitrogen is crucial to the health of your energy body, supplying the aura with the most vital life energy. Oxygen is the yang part of air, supplying the physical aspect of your being with the most vital life energy. Oxygen nourishes the physical body. Nitrogen nourishes the aura.

"Increasing the partial pressure of nitrogen in the air you breathe during

SCUBA greatly energizes your aura. It has the same compounding effects as oxygen at depth. Also, when you ascend slowly and safely from a dive, nitrogen bubbles slowly expand in your blood. This moderate super-saturation causes a cleansing effect in your aura. The safe 'silent bubbles' scrub toxicities out of your aura.

"Of course, if you ascend too quickly you can get decompression sickness. If the nitrogen bubbles grow too rapidly the scrubbing bubbles will tear holes in your aura. Then the physical body will be damaged."

"So, just the fact that you breathe at depth and dive safely cleans your aura," I said, nodding positively. "And I understand that oxygen is good for your brain, but how does breathing underwater have an expansive effect on your mind?"

Sam answered, "Yogis in India realized the relationship of air, life, energy, and consciousness thousands of years ago. Patanjali, an enlightened yogi of ancient India, said, 'Breath practice is the heart of the human body. By mastery of the energy of breath, the perfect disciple can walk over water and thorns without touching them, and attain cosmic powers to control water and levitate the body at will.'

"Yogis developed and perfected breathing techniques and exercises called *pranayama*. The techniques not only increase the practitioner's health, vitality, and life span, but also help them attain super-conscious states of mind and mystical powers."

"Is Mystic SCUBA like pranayama?"

"Yes, SCUBA by nature is very similar to many of the ancient Indian breathing meditations," Sam nodded. "*Vipassana* or 'insight' meditation is an ancient discipline that is still widely practiced. Mystic SCUBA is perfect vipassana. In vipassana meditation, you practice awareness. You focus on seeing things as they are, without concepts, reactions, judgments, or conditions. In vipassana you observe everything you do as you are doing it. As you sit, you observe your breathing and posture. As you walk, you observe the feelings of your steps and the sensations of your balance.

"It is, however, somewhat difficult to cultivate awareness of things as they are. Your mind is so conditioned by habit that you can hardly see what's really going on outside of your habitual awareness. If you were bound to a wheel chair your whole life and then were suddenly able to walk, your first steps would be a new experience. Vipassana would be easy in this case. But since walking is something very routine for you, it is very difficult to break through your conditioned awareness of walking to become conscious enough to experience the actuality of walking.

"On the other hand, in SCUBA diving, the experience is so fresh and so different that the mind is directly aware of the many subtle feelings and sensations, actions and reactions, and the actuality of the experience. SCUBA diving is so different for you because your awareness is completely unconditioned to the alien atmosphere. Therefore, your experience underwater while SCUBA diving is a more complete and direct experience. In SCUBA diving, vipassana meditation is practically effortless."

"Wow," I said, "there are many similarities between vipassana and SCUBA diving."

"That's right," Sam said, "the focus of vipassana breathing meditation is on developing awareness of the breath. Similarly, in SCUBA diving, the first rule is to always be aware of the breath. Even in the course of recreational SCUBA diving many divers note that in their early dives, their air consumption rate is very high, and that they just seem to suck up air. Though many start out breathing fast and shallow in SCUBA, after some time their breath naturally slows and deepens. In Mystic SCUBA, attention is paid to natural, deep, slow breathing. Slow breathing is healthy breathing. Attention to breath is the first rule of recreational SCUBA diving and the increased attention in Mystic SCUBA meets the principles of perfect vipassana and *samatha*."

"What is samatha?"

"Samatha is another form of Indian meditation often practiced by monks and easily experienced in Mystic SCUBA. Samatha is a Sanskrit word meaning 'tranquility'. One of the predominant concentration techniques in samatha meditation is a focus on breathing. Through samatha meditation on the breath, your mind becomes so still that you can experience profound spiritual mind states known as *jhanas*. Jhanas afford you great happiness, insight into the nature of life, peace, and balance. Many SCUBA divers report having such experiences sporadically, and in Mystic SCUBA, jhanas are commonly experienced. Jhanas are beautiful states of spiritual awareness, but are not direct experiences of enlightenment. The union with Nirvana is only experienced in Samadhi."

I thought back to several occasions when I felt extremely happy while SCUBA diving. My feelings of happiness seemed magical and very different from anything I had experienced on land. *Could these be jhanas?* I wondered.

Sam went on, "In Taoism, practitioners learn about the integral relationships between breath, the physical body, the aura, and enlightened states of consciousness. The ancient Taoist masters created breathing exercises and meditations called Chi Gung. Chi Gung is an effective way to cultivate and circulate energy to all areas of the body. In Mystic SCUBA, deep breathing observations similar to Chi Gung help cultivate and circulate energy the same way."

"It's like the Orbit exercise I practice," I said.

"That's right," Sam said. "And underwater, the increased partial pressure of oxygen acts as super energy. When circulation of this super energy is increased, the aura is energized, stimulating a higher spiritual awareness."

Sam paused and then went on, "Ancient Taoist Chi Gung masters said that most people only use a small percentage of their brain. They said that with a greater energy of air circulating in the brain, practitioners could unlock the unlimited capabilities of the mind. These masters taught methods allowing practitioners to open new brain functions and to become more conscious of their infinite possibilities.

"These masters taught breathing exercises, physical practices, and meditations that afforded many of the powers that are associated with martial arts and Chinese medicine such as Light energy—walking on water or the tips of the blades of grass; Yang energy—a protective formation of the aura that turns arrows, swords, and spears away inches before touching the physical body; *Tomo* energy—the ability to make the body warm even when practicing without shelter in the coldest winters; and *Dur Chi*—the ability to heal any disease by the touch of the hand. There are hundreds of such powers documented by the ancient Taoist masters."

Sam looked from left to right and all around, smiling. I was still thinking about everything he had said about breathing and air. Sam seemed to be acknowledging something particular. I followed Sam's eyes to see what he was observing. I saw nothing unusual, though I was impressed by the encompassing beauty of the land.

"There are powerful guardian spirits here," Sam said. "They are the guardians of the Hawaiian Islands, ancient spirits that have been here long before man. They are saddened and unhappy about what man is doing to the islands. But they constantly offer the light of their divinity to the islands and all of their inhabitants. I am a friend to these spirits."

"How can one become friends with these spirits?"

"It's easy. All you have to do is offer your friendship to them from your heart. It's also a nice gesture to offer your service in helping them with their work of guarding and protecting the light of Hawaii."

"Like Pono?" I asked.

"Yes," Sam said, "just like Pono." We sat in silence for a few minutes. My breath formed misty billows in the cold high altitude air. I peered all around from the white clouds to the cinder cone peaks, eager to glimpse the presence of the guardian spirits Sam spoke of.

Then Sam broke the silence, softly saying, "Let's meditate now."

I closed my eyes and began to concentrate. My mind was filled with visions of fish, coral, and undersea life. I felt as if I were floating underwater. A moment later I opened my eyes and thought about what Sam had said about being friends with the guardian spirits of Hawaii. I immediately felt a deep reverence for them. In a genuine way from my heart, I offered my friendship to the spirits and promised to guard the beauty, power, light, and energy of the Hawaiian Islands.

I didn't notice an answer from the spirits and decided to keep practicing meditation. I closed my eyes again to concentrate. Again my mind was filled with underwater scenes. I continued my focus and then suddenly all became very still. What seemed like moments later, I opened my eyes. The sun was setting into the clouds. I felt bright and peaceful. Just as the last of the sun sunk out of view, Sam bowed. I followed, bowing as well.

Looking at me Sam said, "You have seen the vision."

"Vision of what?" I didn't remember seeing anything but fish before I could still my thoughts.

"You have seen a vision of the unseen-world," Sam answered.

"I don't know what you mean," I responded. "I didn't really see anything."

"Well, did you have a nice meditation?" Sam asked.

"Oh," I wondered, "I don't know. I think that I may have fallen asleep. It seems as though we just sat down to meditate a few minutes ago, but so much time has passed."

"Do you feel groggy, as if you've just wakened from a nap?" Sam asked.

"No," I answered, "I feel clear and awake."

Sam paused for a moment and then said, "In your meditation, you went beyond time. You were not sleeping, you were beyond thought. In places of power it's easy to look beyond all structures of this world, to see the unseen-world, and experience perfect stillness."

"Was that Samadhi?"

"Samadhi is an indescribable ecstasy," Sam answered shaking his head. "When you experience Samadhi, you'll know for yourself and won't need to ask me. Yet this was *jhana*, a very good meditation. You're on your way."

I smiled.

"We should head back now," Sam said. "It will be dark soon."

We stood and returned back down the path to Sam's glowing Jeep, alight in the reddening light of the sunset. Before departing the volcano, Sam looked from left to right, smiled, and then bowed. I closed my eyes and thanked the guardian spirits.

ENLIGHTENED DINING

Sam and I drove back to the Four Seasons in quiet serenity. By the time we reached the resort, I was very hungry and worn-out from the long drive. I quickly showered and changed into my dinner clothes. The shower revived me from my tiredness. Sam said that we had reservations at the Four Seasons' fine dining restaurant. He was wearing beige slacks and a Hawaiian hibiscus floral print shirt. After I finished putting on my makeup, we walked briskly across the resort to the restaurant.

Arriving just a little late to the picturesque restaurant, Sam and I approached the smiling maitre d' at the reservations podium. "We have a reservation for 9:00," Sam said. "Room 124."

The maitre d' glanced at her reservations book and then showed us to our table. We were seated steps away from the beach, next to an oil-burning torch.

As Sam perused the menu, I looked around, taking in the beauty of the restaurant architecture. From the open dining room facing the sea to the blue glass shell chandeliers, the restaurant was a vision of decadence.

"I really like Buddhism," I said, "but it sure is different from what I had expected."

"How so?" Sam asked, closing his menu.

"Well, this place is so chic and ritzy," I said, "before, I wouldn't think a place like this would have anything to do with Buddhism, but now it makes perfect sense."

Sam smiled.

"And you are not quite how I'd picture a monk," I said. "You SCUBA dive, you don't wear robes, and your name is Sam. Sam is such an ordinary name. I figured if you were a Buddhist monk you'd go by something exotic sounding, like Peaceful Mountain or something."

"Actually, Sam is my spiritual name," Sam responded.

"Sam is your spiritual name?" I asked. "What's that mean?"

"A spiritual name is a name that reflects your spiritual nature. You receive a spiritual name when, as a student on the pathway of enlightenment, you reach such a level of transformation that the karma represented by your birth name can no longer identify you. Transformed by spirit, you are named by spirit."

"That sounds wonderful," I said, "but how does such a common name like Sam reflect your spiritual nature?"

"My full name, as given to me by my teacher, is Samvara," Sam answered. "It is a Sanskrit word. Samvara is the name of an advanced spiritual doctrine. My friends and students often call me Sam for short, which I am very comfortable with. In Sanskrit the Sam part of Samvara means 'the ecstatic play of life.'"

"So magnificent!" I exclaimed. "Can I have a spiritual name too?"

"You do have one," Sam said. "In time you will discover your spiritual nature and your name."

"But what if I pick the wrong name?" I asked.

"When it is time, you can't be wrong," Sam answered. "And in our tradition spiritual names are given to students by their teachers."

"Oh," I said, "then when can I get a spiritual name?"

"When the time is right, you'll know your name," Sam answered, "till then, don't worry about it; there's so much to explore on the pathway to enlightenment."

Just then, the waiter came to take our order. After quickly reading the menu, I selected a green salad and the truffle risotto. I was careful to choose something I thought would be agreeable to Sam. When the waiter came to Sam, Sam ordered a beet salad and the Ahi tuna entrée. I was shocked! After the waiter left, I asked Sam, "You eat fish? I thought Buddhist monks had to be vegetarians."

Sam answered, "Oh yes, I enjoy fish. I prefer a vegetarian diet but often supplement it with fish. Not all Buddhist traditions require a vegetarian diet. I follow a diet strictly in accordance with Chinese medicine. This diet views food as medicine to balance the energies of your subtle physical body. My Chinese medicine diet prescribes that I even eat chicken and lamb at times to strengthen my aura and maintain physical and energetic health. Also, in my Buddhist tradition there are some spiritual tasks that require that the monks eat beef."

I was still a little taken aback by this. I said, "Isn't it bad karma to eat animals? After your speech about 'every fish is precious' and the importance of being respectful to all marine life, I would never expect that you'd eat a fish."

Sam answered, "If it were bad karma to eat animals, then it would also be bad karma to eat plants. Both animals and plants are equally alive. People tend to be particularly aware of animal deaths because people can understand the point of view of animals better than the point of view of plants.

"Nourishing your body and sustaining your life is good karma. I eat fish with the same care and awareness of death as when I eat cauliflower. I am aware that I take life to sustain my own life. Though it seems incongruent, unfair, and irresolvable to some, this is the truth of life, the dharma. I also know that one day I will die. I am equally at peace with this awareness. Life and death are truths that no being can escape.

"What's important is to respect the natural balance of life. Fish eat fish and maintain the natural balance of life. The awareness of balance is a far greater truth than the fear of death."

Sam paused for a moment, setting his napkin down and then continued, "I use this to guide my dining choices, while maintaining a natural balance of marine life." He reached into his pocket and pulled out a small folded card. "This is my Audubon Society seafood wallet card. It categorizes and color-codes seafood, reflecting their abundance, humane farming, and environmentally-friendly fishing methods." Sam held out the card for me to see, pointing to the Ahi tuna and saying, "See, I selected the Ahi tuna here in the green section and avoided ordering the red snapper here in the red section. This way I can eat the seafood I love while maintaining the natural balance of marine life.

"It's best to make shopping and dining choices that do not support over-fishing, over-hunting of animals, or abusive, inhumane, and unbalanced farming practices. Organic foods are happier foods. They are raised naturally with more care."

I started to understand how thoughtful Sam was in his considerations for food.

"Having said this," Sam said, "I would also agree that a 100% vegan diet is best for many forms of spirituality. Meat tends to lower the vibratory rate of your aura which can introduce a level of mental activity if you are unmindful."

"Well, if vegan is better for spirituality, why don't you just eat vegan?"

"I said that it is best for many forms of spirituality," Sam said, "but not for Buddhist mysticism. If your spiritual path were to sit in a cave in a Himalayan mountain and meditate all day, then it would be best to be vegan. For Buddhist mystics however, it is necessary for us to be very active in our physical and subtle physical lives. With greater activity, our physical and subtle bodies require more attention and nourishment.

"You could say Buddhist mystics are more like professional athletes. An Olympic swimmer requires different foods than, say, someone who swims for fun a few times per week. A pure vegetarian tends to be unable to acclimate to and assimilate the powers and dimensions that help Buddhist mystics toward enlightenment."

A moment later, the waiter appeared, serving us our salads. Sam and I began to eat, and boy was I hungry! Shortly after we finished our salads, the entrées were served. The food was impeccably presented on large white plates, garnished with finely chopped herbs and swirled sauces. I had been to some nice restaurants in the past, but with the view and perfect ambiance, the Four Seasons was beyond compare.

Sam spoke to me about résumé writing during dinner. He recommended that I target temporary programming contracts instead of fulltime programming jobs. He said that programming contracts had a higher hourly rate, that they would give me the mobility to work anywhere in the world, and would allow me to take time off whenever I wanted to.

He talked to me about marketing myself for the highest contracting rates in technology. As we talked about how to do it, the prospect of becoming successful in this line of work grew in my mind. At the end of our dinner I saw the fact that I could be making a top income in technology as a distinct possibility. Working in technology now seemed just as exciting as what I wanted to use the money for.

Later as I was sipping tea and nibbling on a small macadamia nut covered chocolate cake, I became curious about Samadhi again. "How can I experience Samadhi?" I asked Sam. "Do I just keep meditating and then 'Pow,' it happens?"

"Sure," Sam said.

Unsatisfied with Sam's vague answer I asked, "But what do I do to experience it? What's the most direct route to Samadhi?"

Sam answered, "You don't really do anything. Just keep practicing your Mystic SCUBA and then when the time comes I'll put you into Samadhi."

"You can just put me into Samadhi?" I asked excitedly.

"Sure," Sam answered. "When you have done the preliminary practices, I will open the doorway to Nirvana."

"How's that possible?" I asked. "I mean, it's not something I have to strive for and do myself?"

"Not at all," Sam said. "You don't have to strive for a truth that you already possess. You just have to learn to let go of striving enough so that I can point you to the truth of who you are."

Sam paused for a moment and then continued, "Samadhi is being all of awareness, the perfect truth of life. It is the greatest spiritual bliss, the highest ecstasy. Samadhi is the unity and essence of all consciousness. Yet Samadhi is not that big of a deal, though it is very rare in this world.

"I can put you into Samadhi because my teacher showed me how. There are endless doorways to Nirvana. My teacher has taught me one that I can open for others, just as he opened it for me. This way to Nirvana is underwater Samadhi. You must dive and meditate to experience it."

Sam explained, "Esoteric teachers teach by transmitting enlightened states of consciousness to their students. In Zen they call it 'the passing of the lamp'. In Tibetan Buddhism they call it the empowerment of *Dharmakaya*. I have received these transmissions from my teacher and now am able to share the way."

"So that's the big secret shortcut to Samadhi!" I exclaimed. "You can just put me into it?"

Sam shook his head saying, "It's not a secret. It's the truth. And it's not a shortcut. It's the way. Just as a doctor is the way to healing and a locksmith is the way into a treasure chest, an enlightened teacher is the way to Samadhi."

"Wonderful!" I said cheerfully. "Can you put me into Samadhi tomorrow? I think I'm ready now."

Sam shook his head and said, "One of the most important things about being ready is being patient," Sam signaled the waiter for the check and was silent.

Buddha's First Meditation Teacher

After dinner, Sam and I returned to the suite. I really wanted to ask him when he planned on putting me into Samadhi and what it would be like, but I didn't want to seem impatient. I decided I would just work hard on my Mystic SCUBA lessons so that Sam would realize that I was ready as soon as possible.

We sat down to meditate in the living room. As soon as we began, visions of the undersea world permeated my attention. In my mind's eye, I saw colorful reef fish, coral formations, and the blue colors of the deep. These visions were very similar to my meditation experience on the volcano earlier. I just kept concentrating, expecting that the visions would subside and that I would be able to reach the same timeless peace that I had atop the volcano. After a few more minutes, I realized that I was deeper and deeper in the underwater world of my visions. Sam interrupted the meditation, asking me, "Are you able to concentrate well?"

"Yes," I answered, "or, no. I'm not sure actually." I explained, "My mind is kind of still, but I keep seeing intense visions of fish and underwater scenes."

"This is progress," Sam said. "Before when you meditated, you were filled with the thoughts of yourself and your conditioned world. Recently in your meditations the power of your Mystic SCUBA experiences has caused you to yield your conventional thoughts of this world and yourself to a new awareness of underwater attention. This shift in your awareness primes your consciousness for transformation. Shifting from state of mind to state of mind enables your mind to become flexible and open instead of rigid and closed. It is necessary to still and stop all thoughts in meditation, even these very different thoughts. For a period of time in the beginning, it will be helpful for you to use Buddha's first meditation teacher."

Sam stood up, went into the bedroom, and returned with an iPod. He plugged it into the living room stereo system. A moment later soft, melodic music filled the room.

Sam sat down next to me again saying, "During his lifetime in India, the Buddha's first meditative experience was in listening to a song played by one of his courtesans. The song honored the spirit of a sacred place of power in the Himalayas. As the Buddha listened to this music, he was mystically transported to that place and beyond thought. It is very beneficial for beginners of meditation to learn what the Buddha learned from this mystical teacher."

Sam then closed his eyes and began meditating. I straightened my posture and closed my eyes, concentrating on my navel center. For the first few minutes I felt distracted by the music. The music was beautiful and smooth, yet I spent a lot of attention listening to it and even judging it. After a few more minutes, I realized that my mind was becoming more still and that I had no more visions of the undersea world. My meditation was pleasant, but a bit of a struggle, especially in the beginning. I felt I did a much worse job than earlier in the day on top of the volcano.

After our meditation, Sam bowed and said, "You did well. Meditation is good. I have an extra copy of this CD for you so that you can practice your meditation with this aid whenever you want to." Sam retrieved the CD from his room, and handed it to me. "Like the song that aided the Buddha in his first mystical experience, this pure music describes the spirit of spiritual places of power that can help you the same way. Practicing properly in this way will bring you to a stronger mind and greater awareness."

I nodded, open to Sam's encouragement.

"It's getting late now, and you have a long drive home," Sam said.

"Please come pick me up here tomorrow morning, and we will go up to dive the North Shore."

"Sounds great," I said as I stood up and collected my things.

"Good night." Sam bowed to me as I left the suite.

I retrieved my car from the valet and drove home, recounting the many adventures and lessons of the day. At home I played the CD Sam gave me on the portable stereo in my room. I turned the volume low and set the CD to repeat. As I became comfortable in bed, I felt as if I were swaying in the waves of the ocean. The beautiful instrumental music was like a soft lullaby, soothing me into a restful slumber.

WATER

In the morning Sam took me back up to the top of the volcano. "Why are we going back up the mountain? I thought we were going to dive the North Shore," I asked.

"Oh, we will," Sam said, "we'll dive the North Shore later, but right now there's something I have to show you."

When we reached the top of the volcano, we got out of the Jeep and walked to the western ledge. The clouds were thick and high in the sky, yet just below the peak of the volcano. It looked as if we were sitting just above a sea of clouds. As the wind blew towards us, the clouds seemed to crash on the mountainside like waves meeting the shore. The farther I gazed out over the heavy cloud layer, the more the clouds seemed to move like flowing waves. Aside from the color of the clouds, the sky began to look identical to the sea.

Just then something fantastic happened. A dolphin leaped up from the clouds less than 100 feet in front of us! It was a Hawaiian spinner dolphin. It breached the surface of the clouds the same way I've seen them breach the surface of the water so many times.

How could this be? I wondered, bewildered and amazed. After the dolphin splashed down into the clouds, I turned to Sam. *Had he seen the dolphin too?* Sam smiled affirmingly.

I began to ponder how this could happen. *Were my eyes playing tricks on me? Did I just see what I thought I saw? A dolphin jumping out of the clouds?* And then all of a sudden, the dolphin breached the clouds again right in front of me! Instead of splashing back down into the clouds, this time the dolphin floated up over to me. The dolphin levitated before me, sounding off a cheerful call. I was amazed. To my further astonishment, I noticed that I was floating in the air with the dolphin! We were being drawn out into the clouds, away from the volcano. I could no longer see Sam. I splashed in the clouds, playing with the dolphin. The dolphin and I flew towards the sunset.

Just then, I started to hear a ringing sound. The dolphin seemed more distant from me. The ringing sound persisted and the dolphin faded away.

A moment later, I became cognizant of opening my eyes. It was morning.

I was in bed at home with the covers over my head, and my alarm clock was sounding. *It was a dream,* I thought. *What a wonderful dream!*

As soon as I met Sam at the Four Seasons, I excitedly told him about my dream. "Wonderful," Sam said. He smiled with an uncanny similarity to his expression in my dream. "That was a very good dream indeed." The flash in Sam's eyes seemed to suggest a deeper significance than I was aware of.

Sam invited me to meditate with him on his patio. My meditation was filled with beauty and wonder, borne from the feelings of my dream. After our meditation, we loaded our dive gear into the Jeep and headed to the North Shore.

When we arrived at the dive site, we assembled our dive gear. "Today we are going to do a Mystic SCUBA exercise that takes advantage of water's natural healing power," Sam said. We sat in the shade of a palm tree not far from the edge of the water. Sam fetched a couple water bottles from his dive bag and handed one to me.

"Now that you understand the importance of air and breath, let's talk about water. Water is the second uniquely important factor for health and awareness in Mystic SCUBA. We've spent so much time and attention on learning about air and breathing because respiration takes practice, relaxation, and attention. To gain the health and spiritual benefits of water, all you have to do is dive into it."

I smiled.

"So let's talk about water inside-out. When considering the health benefits of water, you must first understand that the greatest benefit for your body comes from drinking it. Water is part of every cell and fiber of your body. It is a commonly known fact that your body is 75% water. Therefore drinking the proper amount of water is helpful for maintaining good health for all aspects of your body.

"Water generates cellular energy. All chemical reactions for physical operation and good health require water. Water also enhances the performance of your body's enzymes and proteins.

"Good hydration prevents and even cures many diseases including migraine headaches, early adult-onset diabetes, and, most importantly for SCUBA divers, decompression illness."

In my Open Water Diver classes, I had learned that dehydration could dispose divers to a higher risk of getting decompression illness. I had made it a habit of drinking plenty of water before and after all dives.

Sam went on, "Water has also been a means of exercise for thousands of years. Aquatic exercise increases your heart efficiency and lung capacity, while improving endurance, increasing flexibility and range of motion."

I nodded. I was very knowledgeable about the healthful benefits of exercising in water from my years on the swim team.

"Aquatic exercise has been practiced well before recorded history," Sam continued. "The earliest artifact relating aquatic exercise dates back to 2500 BC in the form of an Egyptian hieroglyph for swimming."

I added, "My swimming coach used to tell us that the first swim meets were held in Japan in the 1st century BC. And the ancient Greeks included water exercises and swimming as part of their military training. That was the origin of the swimming events of the Olympic games."

"Very interesting," Sam said.

I continued, "I love the sport of swimming! Swimming always relaxes and refreshes me. And I feel like it allows more freedom of movement than any sport on land. It really helped me build my strength and coordination. Plus, swimming causes far fewer injuries than aerobic exercises on land. There's just a lot less stress on your joints."

Nodding, Sam said, "For building strength, viscosity is the physical property of water which resists movement. The density of water creates a greater friction than air as you move in it. It increases the resistance against your muscles by a factor of 12, making them work harder. This makes it possible to build greater strength in the water than on land.

"Buoyancy is the physical property of water that makes objects float in it and seemingly counteracts gravity. It lessens the burden of weight during exercise, reducing joint compression and injury.

"Water is also therapeutic. The buoyancy and viscosity of water make it a beneficial medium for treating pain and injuries. Warm water touching the body causes vasodilation, which draws the blood into the surface soft tissues. This increases blood flow and brings more oxygen to cells. When the water is at or above 86 degrees, the muscles loosen and become less tense. Pain lessens and spasms decrease.

"Cold water touching the body causes vasoconstriction, which slows the circulation of the blood. This reduces pain and inflammation. When the body gets cold, the body attempts to conserve heat by directing blood away from extremities towards the body core, increasing the amount of blood in the torso.

"Hot tubs, saunas, whirlpools, and ice are all mediums of hydrotherapy. Water can be used to soothe tensions and relax your body. Water therapy can heal muscle aches, spinal cord injuries, and joint pains. Water therapy can also aid in the treatment of other conditions such as arthritis, fibromyalgia, and stroke recovery. It is also very soothing, balancing, and relaxing for mental tensions."

WATER: THE MYSTIC'S EXPLANATION

"In the past couple of weeks water has healed me in so many ways," I observed. "In the same way that air aids spiritual practice, water must, too."

"That's right," Sam said. "Water is the most spiritual of elements. Enlightenment is likened to water. Enlightenment flows and changes. It is the origin of life, the sustainer of life, and the destroyer of life. Enlightenment is mysterious from the surface, and can only be known by diving to its depths.

"Lau Tzu, the founder of Taoism, said that the way to enlightenment was to live in the consideration of water. He said, 'A person's higher nature is like that of water; it benefits all things without striving. It takes to the low places shunned by others. Water is akin to the *Tao*; in all the earth there is nothing weaker than water, yet in overcoming the strong, hard, and immoveable, there is nothing more superior; there is nothing so certain.'

"Taoist Chi Gung practitioners often practice near water, because flowing water helps the flow of energy in the body. Buddhist monks often meditate near water, because moving waters still the mind."

"Wow," I said. "Water is a very deep element."

"It is," Sam chuckled at my unintended pun. "Water is the archetypal symbol of life's fluidity. It is the element of intuition, revealing the primordial, unconscious mind.

"Water is the womb of life. It embraces us with unconditional love. In water's depths reside emotional release. Water is the vessel that carries us to the mystical shores of the unseen-world."

"I always feel wonderful in water," I said. "I feel more at home in the warm oceans here than in my hometown on the mainland."

"Yes," Sam said, "the element of water is our origin. We humans understand water to be our beginning. Many indigenous cultural cosmologies regard water as the origin of life.

"We also scientifically understand this, knowing that our evolutionary ancestors crawled out of the primordial ooze."

"Interesting," I remarked.

Sam went on, "Water is healing to our spirit. We spend the first nine months of our lives in the water element. We experience a primal comfort by being in water. When we're in water, we naturally feel still. Our minds and body become quiet automatically.

"Water is also where your aura heals. We pick up toxicity throughout the day. When we travel through different fields of energy and experience, our aura often becomes weakened and fatigued. Talking to and interacting with people, especially if they're upset and imbalanced, often exhausts our aura. For many people, driving home in traffic from work tremendously burdens the aura. Shopping in malls wears on the aura. Even celebratory events and places such as parties, clubs, and crowded restaurants drain the aura.

"Yet water is like magic. You'll notice that you will instantly feel better if you take a shower after traveling, shopping, or being in a place where there are many people. You will feel recuperated, balanced, and awake. This is because water neutralizes toxic or otherwise imbalanced energies in the aura. Water instantly washes the aura clean. When your aura is clean, your energy body is healthy. When your energy is unhindered and healthy, it is easy and natural to feel happy. This is why people sing in the shower. This is also why it's a good idea to take a shower before meditation."

"Why would we feel tired from just being around other people?" I asked.

"The world is filled with tremendously heavy human aura. There are so many people inhabiting our planet that our auras bump into each other. This causes us discomfort and aggravation, and makes us unbalanced and confused. People become very irritable and uncomfortable when they don't have enough space and are too close to even one other person's aura."

I remembered a couple of population studies from a biology class I took at Stanford. They seemed to agree with Sam's conclusions. I told Sam, "In a behavioral experiment I read about in school, researchers put people of the same and opposite sexes in very small (10 foot by 10 foot) living quarters for a period of one month. The results of the study were that at the end of the month the sets of couples reported an average of over 200% more thoughts about sex and violence in daily journals."

"Yes," Sam said, "this is because their auras were too close for too long. This is a similar situation to our condition throughout the whole planet."

Sam continued, "In India they say that the universe has four ages. The first age is the Golden Age where people are close to the gods. The next ages become more and more physical. The gods seem more distant and spirit yields to matter. The fourth age is called the *Kali Yuga*, the Dark Age. According to the Buddha and Indian lore, the age we live in is the Dark Age. The reason that it is dark is because there are so many people on the planet that our agitated auras bumping into each other block out the light of spirit.

"So as I had mentioned earlier, water neutralizes the toxicity of aura. Water cuts aura. When you bathe, swim, or shower, you get some temporary relief from the toxic human aura of the planet. Surface contact with water definitely helps a lot, but when you dive you can experience something truly amazing. When you dive, the human aura tremendously lessens and eventually stops. The aura-neutralizing nature of water decreases human aura dramatically, the deeper you go. Diving to a depth of even 20 feet cuts you off from a significant amount of human aura, so that you can feel greater spirit. The tremendous weight of the human aura cannot reach 130 feet below the surface due to water's neutralizing nature. So when you dive, you can cut yourself off entirely from the agitated minds of this crowded world."

"What's it like to be below the human aura of our world?" I asked, intrigued.

"It's magic," Sam said with a smile. "It's perfect." His eyes twinkled as if he were beholding an utterly beautiful vision.

A moment later Sam continued, "Masaru Emoto, a doctor of alternative medicine from Japan, knew that water is a very receptive element and wondered how it would respond to human attention. He experimented by focusing different intentions on water. He subtly noticed that when water was imbued with positive intentions, the water felt different. The aura of the water would change.

"Though the aura would change, the water physically appeared the same. He looked for physical aspects and differences in the intention infused waters so that he could prove that attention affects matter. In freezing the water he found his proof. As he cooled the water, crystals began to form. The crystals in imbued water looked different from the crystals in water that was not imbued. The crystals in water that was imbued with bright intentions such as love, gratitude, and friendship formed fantastic shapes of beauty and balance. The crystals in water that was instilled with dark intentions such as hate and envy were deformed shapes that are terrible to behold."

"That's incredible," I commented. "Why does water get so affected by intentions?"

"Water absorbs attention," Sam responded. "Water is energetically shaped by it. Similarly, water's energy is absorbed into our auras. This is where the tradition of holy water came from. A person of great purity and light can imbue water with her attention. Then others can touch the water and connect with the purity and power of the spiritually adept person.

"Also consider that every cell of your body is mostly made up of water. This adds insight to the Buddha's teachings, 'You are what you think. All that you are arises with your thoughts.' If attention on a bottle of water could fill it with a beautiful aura and spectacular crystals, imagine what effects positive attention on yourself could produce within you?"

I was amazed.

Sam then stood up and signaled me to follow him with his hand. "I'd like to show you something over here."

I stood and followed him. We walked over to one of the tidal pools formed by lava rock at the ocean's edge. Sam reached down and dipped his cupped hands into the pool, saying, "I'd like to tell you about some of the teachings of Zen and water as expounded by the revered Zen master of ancient Japan, Master Dogen." Lifting his water-filled hands from the rocky pool, Sam reached over to me saying, "Hold this." I cupped my hands and Sam poured some of the water from his hands into mine.

Sam continued, "Master Dogen once said that water is the actualization of the ancient Buddha way. He said, 'Abiding in its phenomenal expression, water realizes completeness. Because water has been the self before any form arose, water is emancipated realization.'"

"Water is alive," Sam said. "It's magic. Look at the water. Feel it in your hands. Master Dogen said, 'Consider not how you see water, but how water sees water. Since water has realization of water, water speaks of water.' "

I looked at the water in my hands. I saw it in a new light. It somehow seemed more magical. I felt as if it were aware and ancient.

"Not all beings see water in the same way," Sam continued speaking of Master Dogen's teachings, "'Some beings see water as a jeweled ornament. We only see their jeweled ornaments as water. Some beings see water as blossoms. Ghosts see water as raging fire. Dragons see water as a palace or a pavilion. Some beings see water as a wish-granting jewel. Some see it as a forest or a wall. Some see it as the dharma nature of liberation, the true human body, or as the form of the body and essence of mind.'"

Sam continued, "With the awareness of water in its original aspect, we can heal our auras, advance our spiritual practice, and shift our attention."

After a few moments, Sam opened his hands slightly and let the water slowly fall back to the tidal pool. He nodded, signaling for me to do the same. The falling water droplets were like jewels and blossoms in the light as they fell. The sound of the water landing in the pool made a trickling melody.

DEEP MEDITATION

Sam and I returned to sit by our gear. Sam picked up his water bottle, made a toasting gesture with it, and then took a sip.

"Do you understand what I mean when I talk about the Kali Yuga, the Dark Age, and how water cuts aura?"

"Yes, I think so," I responded, "I understand logically, at least."

"Good," Sam said, "because now we will do a dive that will let you feel what I mean. Today we are going to do a Mystic SCUBA exercise that takes advantage of water's natural ability to neutralize the toxic aura of the world.

"In ancient times, up to even 100 years ago, seekers of enlightenment used to go high into the mountains to meditate. Going above 10,000 feet in elevation allowed seekers to get above the heavy aura of the planet. As the world's population increased, seekers had to climb even higher. Today we can't go high enough. Even the Himalayan peaks do not breach the darkness of our planet's aura. So we can't go up. But we can go down!"

Sam began explaining our dive plan and the mystical exercises. "This is a good location for a deep dive," Sam said. "Today we're going to do a multilevel dive. We will dive to 99 feet for 10 minutes, to 66 feet for 10 minutes, and up to 33 feet for 20 minutes before we do our safety stop and ascend.

"Because water cuts aura, the deeper you go, the higher your spiritual energy can ascend. When you descend to about 33 feet, significantly less aura presses on your energy body. At this depth, it is much easier to open your navel center. When you descend to about 66 feet, there is even less aura pressing on your subtle physical body. At this depth it is much easier to open your heart center. When you descend to about 99 feet, again there is tremendously less aura pressing on you. At this depth, it is much easier to open your third eye."

"So as I go down," I said, "it's easier for me to bring my energy up?"

"That's right," Sam said.

"During your descent on this multilevel dive," Sam went on, "you will shift your focus to the correlating chakras. You will concentrate on your navel center as you reach 33 feet. Continue the focus on your navel center as you keep descending. Then you will concentrate on your heart center when you reach 66 feet. Continue the focus on your heart center as you keep descending. Finally you will concentrate on your third eye as you reach 99 feet. That's where we'll stop our descent.

"We will remain at 99 feet with a soft focus on the third eye for 10 minutes or for the maximum bottom time according to your dive computer. Then we will ascend to 66 feet and focus on the heart center for about 10 minutes. Then we will ascend to 33 feet and focus on the navel center for about 20 minutes. Finally we will do a safety stop and ascend to the surface."

Now ready, we entered the ocean amidst the large North Shore swells.

As we started our surface swim, I could see the sea floor steeply sloping beneath us. When the bottom looked to be about 90 feet of depth, Sam gave me the down signal. We let the air out of our buoyancy control vests. I watched my depth gauge and focused on my navel, heart and third eye as we descended.

I was surprised by the results. When Sam and I meditated on land, it was sometimes hard for me to identify and focus on the chakras; they were kind of indistinct and I had to really work to imagine connecting with them. However, underwater, the chakras were easy to find. As we free-fell deeper into the sea, it felt like energy moved to each of the chakras naturally, without my even trying.

At 99 feet, I felt amazing again, as I had on my first deep dive with Sam. As I meditated on my third eye, I felt a distinct, tremendous brightness and clarity for the entire 10 minutes we were deep. Next we ascended to 66 feet, and during the ascent I moved my focus from my third eye to my heart. I was peaceful and my mind was very calm. I felt a deep gratitude in my heart for the ocean and for Sam for showing me so much beauty.

At 33 feet I focused on my navel. I began to realize what Sam meant about water cutting the heavy aura of the world and aiding meditation. At 99 feet, meditation really was quite easy, but as we moved closer to the surface, it became more challenging. Meditating at 33 feet was definitely not as difficult as meditating on land, but it required noticeably more effort than meditating at greater depths.

AUMAKUA

After the dive, when we were back on shore, I felt wonderful. I was very happy about my meditative experiences while diving. I said to Sam, "I want to feel this way all the time. Should I dive all the time? If I become a Divemaster or an instructor like you, I can get a diving job and then just dive all the time."

Sam shook his head and said, "No, that's not necessary. While it is beneficial to take pilgrimages into the sea several times per year, diving all the time could become habitual, boring, and deaden your awareness. Some Divemasters become altogether bored with diving. Rather, keep Mystic SCUBA fresh and new. Seek to be open-minded in SCUBA diving instead of mired in habit. Consider Mystic SCUBA to be a powerful point of shifting your habitual consciousness instead of the routine of your life.

"SCUBA diving is like a powerful spa treatment. If you get a massage once in a while, it feels so good. With a good massage the knots in your muscles loosen, your shoulders relax, and the tensions in your back vanish. However, if you continue to get massages there is very little additional benefit. Your muscles are already loose and tension-free; what does it help to massage a relaxed healthy body?"

Sam continued, "You don't need to SCUBA dive every day to gain tremendous benefits from it. It is a powerful force of balance. Once you are balanced, there is no more to do. Like the volcano, a dazzling place of power, you don't need to be there all the time. Going there occasionally is more helpful to your aura and spirit."

Just then, as Sam was talking to me, a dolphin jumped high out of the water. It rose in the air so close to us that I could make out a bright twinkle in its dark eyes. As it sailed through the air at its greatest height, the dolphin flipped its tail up. The dolphin's majestic leap immediately reminded me of the cloud-leaping dolphin of my dream. I excitedly pointed to the dolphin. The dolphin splashed back down into the water.

"Did you see that?"

"Yes," Sam answered, "the dolphin is your *aumakua*."

"My what?"

Sam explained, "There are animals that one may enter into mystical relationships with. The native Hawaiians call them 'aumakua'. Aumakua are considered by Hawaiians to be benevolent guardian spirits that manifest in animal forms.

"After you do some dives with a mystical awareness, you find your aumakua. Your aumakua is your ocean totem. Each person has a special relationship to a specific variety of marine animal. When you make the connection with the animal, it opens certain dimensions of awareness to you."

"What do you gain from that?" I asked, intrigued.

"A connection with your aumakua gives you an awareness of your totem's view of life. You come to see deeper dimensions of the ocean world. This awareness has a positive effect on many aspects of your life and practice. The aumakua relationship gives you insight into your own magical nature. Your connection to your aumakua aids you in gaining the powers that are native to your aumakua's awareness."

I had never heard the word aumakua before, but Sam seemed to use the word 'totem' interchangeably. *Is the aumakua like the Native American totem?* I wondered. I had seen a small wood carving of a bear totem once. A friend of mine who was part Native American received it as a gift from his grandfather. It was said to have magical properties of strength and protection.

"Are aumakua found only in Hawaii?" I asked Sam.

"No," Sam answered, "many traditions of spirituality and magic incorporate the aumakua relationship. Native American shamans incorporate their rich knowledge of the totems into their tribal rituals and rites of passage. The Maya recognize and learn from the *nahual*, or spirit animal guides. Witches used similar relationships with cats. They called them 'familiars.' They used their familiars for insight into other worlds and spells. Wizards of old used the power of this relationship with hawks and other birds of prey to see into the future. As well, Buddhist monks of the Vajrayana lineage gain love and power from their relationships with terriers."

"I thought that a totem was a small carved figurine of an animal and that the figurine was somehow magical," I said.

Sam shook his head grinning, and said, "The figurine acts as a unifying reminder of the power and awareness of the animal spirit itself. The figurine is magical, but only because it is an intended symbol of the animal. The spirit of the animal is what is magical. Your relationship with that spirit allows the magic to enter your life."

"OK, I get it," I said, "the carving comes second to what it represents."

Sam nodded and went on, "In the Hawaiian spiritual tradition, when

160

you see your aumakua for the first time, you call to them with an ancient benediction. Sam looked out over the water and called in a smooth, melodious voice:

> I na ʻaumakua wahine a pau loa
> Owau nei o Vanessa
> ka pua keia i ke ao
> Homai i mana
> ʻEliʻeli kapu, ʻeliʻeli noa, ia la honua
> Amama, ua noa, lele wale

"This means:

> Aumakua
> Here I am, Vanessa, your sister
> Give me life energy
> Profound freedom
> Free to fly

"This is said to be a magical phrase that brings the blessings of your aumakua into your life," Sam explained. Repeating the words of the benediction in English once again, Sam looked to me and said, "Give it a try. Call out to your aumakua."

"It's OK to say the words in English?" I asked.

"Absolutely," Sam answered, "the words have more meaning for you in English, so English is best." He went on, "Words are really just syntax. With every prayer or spiritual benediction, what is of greatest importance is not the language, cleverness, or correct grammar of your words, but the intent of your words—what you mean when you say them. So it's fine to say the words in English as long as you mean what you say."

I asked Sam to say the words again. Then I repeated the benediction, calling out over the ocean to the dolphin that was somewhere out there.

Sam smiled serenely and we sat quietly for a moment. "These words are just a starting point to direct your attention," Sam said softly. "In Buddhist mysticism, when we find our aumakua, we acknowledge this relationship most importantly in our hearts." We both fell silent. I became aware of the sounds of the pounding surf.

"Dolphin is a good totem!" Sam said a moment later. "With the dolphin as an aumakua, you gain special insight into dimensions of a very wise happiness. The dolphin's way is playfulness, dreaming, and psychic communication. The dolphin brings you into a deeper dimension of harmony. The dolphin also aids you in developing higher intelligence."

"Really?" I said. "Just by having the dolphin as my aumakua, I get harmony, insights, and higher intelligence? All this just comes to me?"

With a judicious squinting of his eyes, Sam answered, "You begin to learn the mind, attention, and innate qualities of the dolphin's spirit as you explore and experience your mystical relationship with your aumakua. You don't just get anything, but you are shown the path that will lead you to awareness."

Sam paused for a moment, having managed my expectations, and then went on, "As the great teacher of ease and effortlessness, the dolphin helps you in learning to put forth effort without strain: right effort, natural effort. The dolphin aids you in allowing things to unfold naturally. The dolphin is the totem that teaches you to flow through life with ease and agility."

"That sounds so wonderful," I said. "I can really use help in learning to let my life flow with ease. I often find myself over-thinking what I should do and getting stuck."

"Yes," Sam said, "the dolphin is often the aumakua for those who tend to try too hard."

Well, that's definitely me, I thought.

Sam continued, "Your aumakua appears to you when you are ready for a powerful transformation."

I listened intently.

"The dolphin helps you develop comfort with change and transformation. It helps you to understand and see that change is the only constant in life. The dolphin helps you in dealing with activities during busy periods of your life. The dolphin provides strength and certainty for you during deep emotional and spiritual changes."

Could the dolphin be here now to help me with my career and life changes? I wondered.

Sam continued, "The dolphin facilitates experiencing the everyday world as miraculous. The dolphin helps you to become aware of and to trust in life as a phenomenal, transformative process. The dolphin nurtures qualities of innocence, simplicity, and purity. It helps you to release worries and enjoy life."

I was delighted that the dolphin was my aumakua. I kept watch in the area where I had seen the dolphin jump. I felt a special excitement in knowing that I had a magical connection to this amazing creature. In my heart I again repeated the benediction.

Just as I completed my heartfelt call, the dolphin jumped again, spinning high in the air. I was exhilarated! The dolphin's great descending splash caused a rainbow mist to shine in the sun. I looked to Sam, with a huge grin. Sam smiled back, sharing my excitement.

Still watching for the dolphin, I asked Sam, "Is the dolphin your aumakua too?"

"No," Sam said, "my aumakua is the manta ray."

I looked to Sam's carved manta ray pendant. "Is your necklace pendant similar to the carved wooden figurines of the Native Americans?"

"Yes," Sam replied. "My manta ray pendant reminds me of, and connects me with my aumakua."

"What is the mystical meaning of having the manta as your aumakua?"

"The manta," Sam said, "has taught me beautiful dimensions of graceful silence." Sam became quiet and seemed very distant for a moment.

I was very interested in the totems of the sea. "What are some other common aumakua for Mystic SCUBA divers?"

"For other great mystical divers I know," Sam said returning his attention to me, "there is the whale."

"Wow! Can you tell me about the whale?" I asked excitedly.

Sam answered, "The whale is a doorway to higher realms of knowledge. Like the dolphin, the whale allows you to connect with higher intelligence. The whale totem gives you a profound connection to higher planes of consciousness. The whale teaches spiritual expansion and supports honoring your intuitive nature and experiencing the vastness of life. The whale helps you in exploring the 'big picture' of reality. This totem helps you in remembering what is important. It calms and clears the mind, helping you focus on listening to the rhythm of your own nature."

"Magnificent."

"The whale is also the bringer of abundance. It helps you in creating abundance at all levels of your life. The whale increases your innate creativity. It nurtures confidence in your ability to create the life you dream of. The whale nurtures creativity and manifestation in all aspects of your life.

"Then there is the sea otter. The sea otter is another wonderful aumakua. It's one of my favorite of the ocean totems. The sea otter helps you access your playful child-self, raising your awareness of your spirited inner child. The sea otter keeps you light and playful, even while facing very serious matters. This totem helps you in finding a dynamic integration of work and play.

"The sea otter turns any task into a delightful game. It encourages the expression of humor and laughter by nurturing a sense of not taking life too seriously. The sea otter encourages you to experience life as a joyful, fun game. The sea otter supports surrendering to the spiritual mystery of life. It helps you increase a sense of freedom, lightness, and delight at being alive."

Sam sat quietly after describing the sea otter.

"Sam, what is the best aumakua to have?" I asked. "Is it the dolphin, the manta ray, the whale, or the sea otter?"

Sam paused for a moment, grinned, and then answered, "There is no best or worst aumakua. Like a dive mask, what makes it good is how well it fits you. How well you fit together is what enables you to see the ocean world with greater clarity. Though different masks have different sizes, dimensions, and features, what makes a mask good is your relationship to the mask."

Sam added, "Yet, just as there are some very good dive mask brands that are well engineered, there are some very auspicious aumakua. The dolphin is a very auspicious aumakua."

"What about Pono?" I asked. "Does he have an aumakua too?"

"Yes," Sam answered, "Pono has a totem that is very useful to his work. Pono's aumakua is the sea turtle."

I remembered Pono's stunning pink plumeria puka shell necklace and his large beautifully carved turtle shaped shell pendant. "And Pono wears a pendant of his aumakua just like you do?" I asked.

"Yes," Sam said, "Pono honors his aumakua and fosters his connection with the sea turtle by wearing a carved shell totem pendant. The sea turtle helps Pono gain a very grounded wisdom. It gives Pono a stronger connection with the energy of the world, and provides emotional and psychic protection. This totem helps one feel safe when dealing with intense situations and environments. The sea turtle facilitates focusing on the present moment and taking care of matters at hand. It helps you to slow down and appreciate the present, and provides support for solitary pursuits.

"The sea turtle is a force for accessing and acting upon your higher wisdom. It supports seeing through your own darkness and directly facing things that need attention. The sea turtle also encourages clarity of mind and seeing the truth at the heart of all situations."

"Did Pono carve his aumakua pendant?" I asked, remembering Pono's orderly piles of shells and that he was carving something the day I met him.

"Yes," Sam answered.

"I didn't realize that he was such an amazing artisan!"

"He is," Sam said. Holding his manta ray pendant between his thumb and index finger, he added, "Pono carved my aumakua pendant as well."

"Really?" I said peering closely at Sam's shiny golden pendant. "Yours looks somehow different. It looked like Pono had mostly white and red seashells and corals, but your manta ray looks like a shimmery stone with kind of a shiny opal-like depth."

"This is actually a coral pendant," Sam explained. "It is a very rare coral called Hawaiian gold coral. It is only known to be found at one dive site deep in these waters, atop an ancient underwater volcano. Hawaiian gold coral has this unique characteristic of a gemstone-like depth."

"It's exquisite," I remarked.

"All Mystic SCUBA divers in my school have paid homage to the Hawaiian shores," Sam said, "and have received a gift of an aumakua pendant from Pono's shells and corals."

"Will I get one too?"

"Yes," Sam answered, "when you learn more about your aumakua and complete your initial studies."

"I can't wait!" I exclaimed. "Do you think Pono can carve a dolphin out of a pink clam shell for me?"

"Let's not get ahead of ourselves," Sam said. "You have a lot more to learn and experience before you're done."

"Does everyone have an aumakua?" I asked. "What about those two over there? Do they have an aumakua?" I pointed far down the beach to a couple of surfers paddling in the ocean swells.

"Yes," Sam said, "everyone has the disposition of being open to a magical animal of the sea."

A large wave formed and one of the surfers, a tall blond gal caught it. She masterfully rode the wave, cutting left just ahead of the crashing crest.

"Her totem is the elephant seal," Sam said. "The elephant seal supports claiming your personal authority and spiritual power. The elephant seal nurtures a sense of well-being and strength. It helps you in connecting with the inner archetypes of nobility. The elephant seal helps you to develop courage and to face fears. It nurtures and enhances your self-confidence, encouraging leadership, achievement, and success."

"The other fellow there has the octopus as his aumakua," Sam continued, looking at the other surfer as he bobbed in the waves. "The octopus offers protection, intelligence, and a multifaceted detail-oriented attention. It helps you get past negative barriers and learn new skills. It is the doorway to a silly yet happy view of the complexity and learning of the world."

Sam paused and then said, "There are so many wonderful aumakua, and each totem offers many profound lessons."

"So, you can just see anyone's aumakua?" I asked.

"Yes, and I can teach anyone who wants to learn how to access the magic of their totem relationship."

"Are there any bad aumakua? Like man-eating tiger sharks? Would they be a bad aumakua?"

Sam said, "Well, I wouldn't say they're bad, but there are totems that reach into dimensions and powers of the dark side. Several of the older monks in my lineage have such aumakua. The dark powers can also be used for enlightenment if you are very skilled."

Sam paused and then said, "The shark aumakua has a tremendous, primal power. The shark gives you the strength for survival, adaptability, and constant vigilance. It gives you the awareness to hunt, stock, and attain anything. The shark's power is explosive, ancient, and unstoppable."

Sam continued, "Eels are of the lower realms. Eels offer visions of narrow and fleeting opportunity. With the vision of the eel you can find things that no one else would find. You can get into situations that you did not merit. The eel sees its way into un-destined advantages. Those who have eels as their aumakua seem resourceful and lucky.

"There's also the sea snake," Sam said. "The sea snake facilitates initiation into the deep transpersonal realms of power. The sea snake has the venomous power of death, yet also has the power of healing. It provides support for transformation of powers and skills. The sea snake helps you deepen and integrate your experience of the archetypal energies of death for awakening. The sea snake enables views into the deepest mysteries of creation.

"There are others," Sam said, "but we don't need to talk about them now."

"Sam, I'm just curious about one thing," I said. "In describing the different aumakua, you said very little about the manta ray, your own totem. You said much more about all of the other aumakua. Why is this? It seems that you would have a lot more to say about the manta ray."

"It is because I know the manta ray the best that I described it the least," Sam answered softly. "Actually, it's difficult to accurately say any of this in words. I can give you some high-level generalizations about the different aumakua, but to truly know your aumakua, you must experience your relationship with your aumakua.

"The way you find your aumakua is by being aware of, and interested in, the marine life you come across. As you recognize the relationship between you and your aumakua, you will recognize the spirit that the relationship brings you. My descriptions just give you a conceptual idea of what the connections to different aumakua are like. The truth of the connection is in its feeling. In your dream you had indescribable feelings from your connection to the dolphin's world. Those feelings are more real than words."

Sam and I sat in the sand. From time to time we would see the dolphin jump and spin out of the water. After a while, it seemed as if the dolphin had moved on out of the bay.

"It's time we prepare for our next dive," Sam said, standing up.

"OK," I sighed, feeling warm and tired in the sun. I stood up, grabbing a small smooth rock from among the few lava rocks in front of me in the stand. I reached back and was about to throw the rock toward the waves.

Sam grabbed my wrist before my arm could swing into a forward motion. "Never throw a rock in a place of power!" Sam warned sternly. "It disturbs the energy of the place and bothers local spirits.

"Though it is hot and you are tired, you cannot be messy with your attention. When practicing mysticism you must take greater care not to be sloppy. Be more mindful when you're in nature."

"Oh, OK. Sorry," I said awkwardly. "I'll be more mindful."

Sam started chuckling as he prepared his gear saying, "I mean really, what were you trying to do? Hit your aumakua with a rock?"

I apologized sincerely again.

"It's OK," Sam said with an accepting smile. "You're making progress. Finding your aumakua is a good sign."

I smiled.

"Just lay off the rocks," Sam said jokingly. "Throwing rocks at marine animals is not part of our Buddhist practice."

BEING THE OCEAN

Sam and I strapped on fresh air tanks. Once we were geared up, Sam said, "The next exercise that we are going to practice is called 'Be the Ocean.' This is a beautiful meditative technique. It is a profound practice, though it may seem simple. On this dive, we will go to 60 feet for around 30 minutes. At 60 feet there is a rocky bottom. We'll attach our reef-lines to a large rock, add air to our buoyancy vests, and float there. You will focus on connecting with the ocean as you float. You will become the ocean. After a period of this meditation, we'll make our way back up to the shallow corals."

"Be the ocean?" I asked. "How do I do that? What does that mean?"

Sam explained, "When you're down there secured by your reef-line, just gaze out into the deep blue of the sea. Look with a soft focus with the intention to see beyond the physical world. The ocean innately has tremendous energy, an enlightened spirit. Become still and quiet so that you can feel the energy of the ocean and connect to her spirit. The ocean has deep dimensionality within her blue hues. Peer with your inner eye into this infinite blue Goddess. Just relax your body and still your mind. Gaze into the ocean's depths. Look into the void of blue and join your mind to it.

"Witness the ocean. Bring your attention into the moment and just observe quietly. Connect with the luminous essence of the ocean. Be a bridge to her spirit. When you still your mind and focus on the ocean, you will become the ocean, you will join with the ocean's spirit. You will merge with the ocean and become the ocean herself."

"OK," I said, engrossed by Sam's description, "it sounds amazing."

"This is a very mystical meditation practice," Sam said. "When you meditate within the deep dimensions of the sea, your aura merges with the powerful movement of the ocean's spirit. Be the Ocean is a meditation that is guided by the purity of the sea's aura. As you practice, the ocean leads you to perfection in every moment. Meditation and spiritual practices are often difficult to learn and master. For a long time they may seem impossible and ambiguous. Be the Ocean helps you to have more direct and immediate spiritual experiences."

I was eager to try this exercise.

Sam and I prepared for the dive. We turned on our air and performed a buddy-check to make sure our equipment was functioning. We entered the waves and did a short surface swim to an area a little west of where we had descended on our previous dive. Sam gave me the thumbs-down signal and we descended to the bottom at around 60 feet.

The bottom was grey and rough. There were small sandy patches between the lava rock-strewn outcroppings. A brightly colored Christmas wrasse weaved in and out of the small, rounded hard corals that grew sparsely on the worn rocks. The wrasse's bright green scales glinted over its cylindrical red body. Just as the wrasse darted out of sight, I found a bare, sturdy hold for my reef-line on one of the larger rocks. Having rigged my reef-line, I added air to my buoyancy vest and floated up. Sam had already rigged his reef-line and was floating steadily a few feet from me.

I relaxed my shoulders and jaw. My arms fell down and to my sides. I observed my deep, slow breath. I quickly came to feel completely comfortable. Looking down the steep sloping bottom, I cast my gaze out to the deep, to the blue. Then I tilted my head up slightly, removing the deep sandy slope from my view. Now all I could see was the glowing blue of the ocean's depths.

I felt as if my eyes were shifting their focus slightly from nearer to farther as I looked out into the blue infinity. I blinked comfortably, yet seldom. The sound of my slowly exhaling bubbles began to feel very distant. The ocean's gentle surge softly rocked me to and fro on my reef-line.

As I continued to peer into the ocean's void, I began to feel a peaceful calm. I perceived an immense, blue perfection. Everything became so profoundly simple— elemental and perfect. It was just Sam and I and the blue simple perfection. *It's simple...so perfect...* were my only thoughts.

After a few beautiful minutes, we rewound our reef-lines and headed to the abundant corals of the shallow reef. There we sat in the sand amid spectacularly beautiful coral heads. Sam tapped his wand to get my attention. I turned, from my sitting position to see him next to me. He was on his knees facing me.

Sam pointed to his eyes and then to himself, indicating that I should watch him. While I looked at his face, he suddenly and impossibly disappeared. He hadn't moved. He just vanished! I hadn't stopped looking at him, but now instead of his body, I saw the sea. I blinked hard and shook my head, and for a moment, I saw Sam, but then he faded away again and became the sea.

It seemed totally unbelievable from a logical perspective, and yet, innately I knew it wasn't odd at all. It felt completely natural, and was completely in line with all the mind-blowing magical experiences Sam had shared with me since that first day I met him.

Moments later, Sam came back into view kneeling just as he started out in front of me. He gave me the OK signal and then motioned for me to follow him. We kicked along the reef, among the many invisible wonders of the sea.

Upon ascending I exclaimed, "That was amazing! How did you do that? You vanished right before my eyes. How can it be?"

"It is as all things are," Sam said, "a miracle." He went on, "I wanted to show you how profound this exercise is. When you practice Be the Ocean perfectly, you can completely transcend yourself and become a wave of consciousness within the ocean of life."

I smiled, filled with the amazement, awed by this new secret knowledge of life.

A PRECIOUS WAVE

Returning to shore, we sat down and began disassembling our dive gear. I felt peaceful, still, and relaxed. After I had unzipped and pulled off the top half of my wetsuit, I slowed down and turned my attention towards the beautiful ocean. Sam quickly disassembled his equipment. He brought his dive gear bag to the Jeep, loading it in the back. I stayed behind, watching the dazzling reflections of light on the water in the noon sun.

My mind became very still as I sat. I experienced a peaceful expansiveness similar to many of my Mystic SCUBA meditations. The waves crashed making bright sprays and revealing colorful rainbows. The ocean glowed with a pulsating light. The calm of my mind opened within me sensations of brightness and feelings of eternity. I felt as if the ocean was God and that I was in the presence of the highest and most divine of all wonders. It seemed to me that the ocean was aware of me. The ocean seemed to reflect my feelings through its glistening waves and blue depths, as if I were in peaceful communion with an infinite spirit. I knew a direct connection with the sea. The awareness of my communion with the ocean stirred in me a question from the deepest part of my spirit, *Who am I?* I felt as if I were not 'me', but that I was the ocean. Yet if I were the ocean and not the self I always thought I was, then who was I really?

Who am I? I wondered almost aloud.

"A precious wave," came a distinct, yet inaudible answer. The answer seemed to come from the heart of the ocean. "A precious wave," came the answer again. The second response was extremely clear in my mind and definite in origin: the center of the ocean. The surprise of hearing an answer from the ocean so loudly jolted me. My mind returned to this world and the ocean felt immediately distant. I then noticed that Sam was sitting next to me cross-legged.

A beautiful and particularly tall wave came in. The wave was a rich blue color at its base with a lighter aquamarine crest. As the wave crashed, Sam said, "We're all like waves: forming, growing, moving, and eventually falling and crashing. The motion of a wave makes it seem separate. But after death, after the wave crashes, the essence of the wave, water, is drawn back in to the ocean, the source. Though the wave is an individual form, it is always inseparable from the ocean itself."

I looked at Sam and nodded. *He must have heard the ocean, too,* I thought.

After a few quiet minutes, Sam began helping me to pack the rest of my gear. "Let's have lunch now," Sam said. "After lunch we're going to drive far to the Southwest and then do a night dive on a friend's boat." I agreed, grabbing our food.

After lunch and before leaving the beach area, Sam bowed toward the ocean. I bowed too.

ANCIENT SEAS

Departing from the beach, which was just at the end of a lush flowering valley, we slowly headed south over the crumbly dirt road in the midday sun. On our way out over the sloping knolls, the aromatic scent of blossoming plumerias filled Sam's Jeep with the tangy-sweet perfume of the tropics. As we continued on our long ride south, Sam told me about the friend of his we were going diving with.

"His name is Nakoa Ka Mea E Ka Maluhia," Sam said. "In Hawaiian it means 'The Warrior Who Brings Peace and Protection,' but you can just call him Nakoa. In this lifetime, Nakoa follows the Ho'opono Pono Ke Ala Hawaiian tradition of spirituality, but he is wholly open to all spiritual traditions."

"And," Sam added, "Nakoa's aumakua is also the dolphin."

I smiled. "Nakoa and I already have a lot in common."

Sam nodded. "Nakoa is a very unique and ancient being. He is an incarnation of Hawaii's first civilization."

"Are you saying he's somehow one of the original Polynesian settlers?" I asked with a bit of incredulity.

Sam continued, "Long before the Polynesian navigators paddled to these shores, another ancient race lived here. This was the civilization of Mu. The people of Mu were agrarian and peaceful. They had an advanced tradition of spirituality. The people of Mu were good healers and artisans. They also had a strong connection with marine life and the sea. Nakoa was one of the spiritual leaders of Mu. Nakoa knows the spirit of these waters better than anyone."

I was a little puzzled and skeptical of Sam's historical commentary. "I've never heard of Mu. I read a book on Hawaiian history, and they never mentioned a culture existing here before the Polynesians who discovered Hawaii. And you're saying that he has been here since then? Or that he's reincarnated from that time?"

"Yes," Sam said, "historians know little about Mu. The people of Mu lived in accord with the land. Their impact on the land was minimal and left few structures, tools, or artifacts as remnants of their culture. When the Polynesians arrived, the ancient civilization of Mu was already in decline. The Polynesians called the small-statured people of Mu, who by that time lived only in a few small hidden villages throughout the islands,

'Menehune.' Hawaiians still have stories of the magical Menehune today, but they are mostly just fables and fabulous tales. So what was history has now become myth.

"And yes," Sam continued, "Nakoa lived and died in Mu many times, many years ago. When the Polynesians became predominant in the land, Nakoa took incarnation in China. Now that the conditions for spiritual growth are again beneficial in Hawaii, Nakoa has reincarnated in these islands to reconnect with the awareness and powers that he had developed here so long ago."

I was dissatisfied with Sam's explanation of Nakoa's reincarnation. I remarked, "I've read about reincarnation, but I'm not sure that I really buy into it. If we have past lives, why can't we naturally remember them?"

"First of all, you don't have to buy into reincarnation," Sam responded. "You can think metaphorically, that stories of past lives are a way to describe your current condition of life. The past is dust anyway. What's most important for your happiness is this moment, now."

Sam paused and then said, "But to explain this discrepancy I will tell you how reincarnation works and why most people don't remember their past lives, if you'd like."

Raising an eyebrow, I looked at Sam, "OK, let's hear it."

"Reincarnation works exactly the same as dreaming," he explained. "In Buddhism we say that this life is a dream. Life seems real and physical and actual, but it is really very transient, no different from a dream."

"What do you mean?" I asked. "Life doesn't seem all that transient. Life certainly isn't like a dream to me. Life is real!"

"Of course life is real," Sam said, "yet, when you investigate the principal way that you perceive life, you will find that your awareness of life is just as a dream."

"What do you mean?" I asked. "How is this a dream now?" I knocked on the dashboard in front of me and turned my palms up in a quizzical gesture.

"To understand how this moment is a dream," Sam said, "you must consider how yesterday was a dream."

"I still don't get it," I remarked, now quite perplexed.

"Was yesterday real, or a dream?"

"Real, of course," I answered.

"Think back to yesterday for a moment," Sam said.

I thought about yesterday's events. I remembered my surprise when I found out that Sam was staying at the Four Seasons. I remembered the amazing view from the top of the volcano. I had an exceptionally peaceful experience meditating there. There was a special feeling of quiet for me up there high above the clouds. Then I giggled, remembering how shocked I was when Sam had ordered fish for dinner.

Sam nodded and went on to ask, "And how about your dream last night? Was your dream about the dolphin in the clouds real?"

"No, it was only a dream," I answered.

"OK," Sam said, "now just take a moment and think back to your dream."

I remembered the remarkable dream that I had during the previous night. In the dream Sam had taken me back up to the volcano. At the top, to my utter amazement a dolphin had jumped from the clouds as if the clouds were the sea. Delighted even though I couldn't figure out how a dolphin could be swimming in the sky, the dream had been viscerally exciting. It had given me a wonderful feeling that I couldn't quite put my finger on. Upon finishing my reflection, I looked to Sam.

"Now, what's the difference between your experiences yesterday and the experiences in your dream?" he asked.

"One was real and one was a dream," I replied matter-of-factly. "The events of yesterday really happened and the events in my dream were just in my head."

"Yet when you think back," Sam asked, "to both yesterday's experiences and your dream's experiences, how are they different in terms of your awareness?"

I thought about it. As I recalled going to the volcano with Sam in the dream, it seemed very much the same as my memories of going to the volcano with Sam on the previous day. My memories of the events and experiences yesterday didn't seem perceptually different from my memories of the events and experiences of the dream. I scratched my head, considering the similarities.

"What is the difference between your awareness yesterday and your awareness in your dream?" Sam asked. "Were you any less aware of life in your dream than in your experiences yesterday? Considering your awareness of life, there's no difference, is there?"

I thought about it, but found it difficult to answer. Though my dream had included something as fantastically impossible as a flying dolphin, it still seemed as real to me as having had dinner last night. I had never really considered things this way. As I examined my awareness of life in the dream, I found it was actually no different from my awareness of life yesterday. In fact, there were moments in my dream where I felt more aware of life than in any of my experiences yesterday.

"So," Sam said, "in terms of your awareness, your conscious experience of life, how are your experiences yesterday not a dream? And how was your dream different than your experiences yesterday?"

Again I considered Sam's questions, but found them difficult to answer.

"Your awareness of yesterday is as unreal as a dream. Or you can say that your dream last night was as unreal as yesterday."

"I think I see what you mean," I said. "In considering my awareness, there is no difference between yesterday and my dream."

"That's right," Sam said, "just as your awareness in this, the present moment, is no different from your awareness in your dream."

"This moment is no different from a dream?" I wondered aloud.

"Life is transient. Life is like a dream. Dreams are as real as waking." Sam became quiet after speaking. He sat motionless with his hands on top of the steering wheel as we moved down the long highway. Sam suddenly appeared to become very distant. The Jeep's interior seemed to take on an illusory quality, as if I were seeing it in the reflection of a pool of water.

Feeling a peculiar sort of unease, I peered at Sam with uncertainty. As my gaze investigated him, I started to sense that he was no more real than an apparition. *Just like a dream!* I thought with some alarm. I was seeing Sam as a dream, as if I were dreaming even though I knew I was really awake. I turned and looked out at the red, dusty Hawaiian earth and the blue sparkling sea beyond the western shore. It all seemed to be a vision, unreal.

"This is a dream!" Sam exclaimed knocking on the dashboard right above the glove compartment in front of me as I had done moments ago. The loud knocking sound startled me.

"OK," I agreed, shaking off what felt like a daze. "Life is no different from a dream. I agree with the Buddhist aphorisms," I said in wonder, mostly surprised by my own words. "But you said that reincarnation works like dreams. Tell me about reincarnation. How is reincarnation like a dream?"

"Well, you must understand something very important first."

"What's that?"

"In truth, life is not a dream," Sam said.

"But you just explained to me how my awareness of waking life now is no different than my awareness of life in my dreams. It's true: Life is like a dream. I just saw it! You, the car, the land, and the ocean; it was all a dream."

Sam shook his head saying, "Life is like a dream only when you are bound to half-sight. Life is like a dream only when you lack whole-sight."

"Half-sight? Whole-sight?" I asked. "What do you mean? What's the difference?"

"I mean the awareness of life. It is the difference between finite awareness of life and the infinite awareness of life," Sam answered. "Half-sight is a transient awareness of life. Half-sight is seeing life in a partial way, a limited way, an obscured way. When life is viewed with half-sight, life is veiled, life is as unreal as a dream."

"Half-sight is like SCUBA diving in conditions of poor visibility. Half-sight is only seeing what is happening right before your eyes and having no knowledge of anything else. When you can only see 10 feet in any direction because of dense particulates such as algae and sand in the water, you have a very limited view of the underwater world.

"With half-sight, you are cut off from some of the most extraordinary life-enriching experiences. For example, during a dive in Monterey Bay, a dive boat captain I knew saw two Humpback Whales slowly pass directly over the bubbles of four divers who were at a depth of 25 feet. The whales probably passed just 15 feet over the diver's heads. The captain was certain that the divers had witnessed the majestic whales. When the divers returned to the boat, they reported with great disappointment that they hadn't seen the whales at all because there was only 10 feet of visibility.

"With half-sight, you also misinterpret and misunderstand what you see, causing yourself stress and unnecessary suffering. Not long ago, a local Divemaster and his buddy were coming back into a shallow bay after a deep dive. The winds had become strong while they were out on their dive. As they entered the bay, the crashing waves had stirred up the bottom sediment and they could see less than four feet in any direction. As they swam toward the shore in the shallow waters, large gills came into the Divemaster's view a couple of feet ahead. It was a large slowly moving fish. A moment after he could see the gills, the tell-tale stripes of a tiger shark came into sight. His buddy, unable to see the stripes in the murky water, thought the shark was a dolphin and reached out to touch it. Fortunately the Divemaster pulled his buddy's hand back before he touched the shark. They were unharmed, but quite shaken.

"Yet whole-sight," Sam continued, "is seeing life beyond all dreams. Whole-sight is a true, eternal, and complete awareness of life. Whole-sight is unlimited, unobscured awareness. Your recognition of the waking moment as a dream is a step into whole-sight.

"Whole-sight is like seeing the whole ocean. There is no barrier, no limit to your ability to see the life of the ocean near or far. With whole-sight you are enriched by the majestic experiences of encounters with whales. With whole-sight you are able to see sharks clearly and live in balance with the ocean. With whole-sight your awareness of the underwater world is complete.

"With whole-sight you see that you are an eternal spirit. Your spirit is your present infinite awareness—your awareness now. Your eternal consciousness exists right now, here, present in this moment. You are present eternal consciousness moving from day to day, dream to dream, lifetime to lifetime."

"OK, I see what you're saying," I said. "Viewed through half-sight, life is a dream. But the truth is that life is not a dream. And that can be seen with whole-sight."

"You got it," Sam responded.

"But what's that have to do with reincarnation?" I asked.

"We reflect on the transient nature of life so that we can identify our eternal nature. The knowledge of half-sight and whole-sight not only exposes the dreamlike quality of life, but the dreamlike quality of lifetimes."

"Every night's dream is just like a new incarnation. You have new dreams each night, yet the greater truth of who you are is found in the waking. It is the same with reincarnation. You go from lifetime to lifetime as if your lives were dreams, yet your spirit is eternal.

"Consider the nature of dreams," Sam said. "When you go to sleep, you have experiences you call dreams. Like a movie in which you are the main character, each dream tells a story: a drama, a horror, an adventure, or perhaps a romantic comedy. Then you wake up to your waking life, which is again like a movie in which you are the main character.

"Your waking life seems much more real than your dreams because it has a greater continuity. Your dreams seem less real than your waking life because they are much more transient. Eventually, after experiencing the waking life movie for a time, the day comes to an end and you go back to sleep and experience dream movies again.

"Every time you go to sleep and dream, you think your dream is the only reality, just as you think this incarnation is the only reality. This is half-sight, the transient awareness of life. Yet life projects infinite movies upon the silver screen of your awareness. The truth is that you are a human being having many dreams over many nights. And it is the same with reincarnation. Your spirit is eternal, and you have many lives.

Your lives are experiences as transient to your eternal spirit as dreams are to your waking life."

"Interesting," I said, "but this gets right back to my original doubt: Why don't I remember my previous incarnations? I remember my dream last night. I remember my experiences yesterday. Why wouldn't I remember any past lives if I had them?"

"For the same reason you can never remember a previous night's dream while you are dreaming. Half-sight limits you to only be aware of the dream you're in. You have no knowledge or memory of any previous dreams. Whole-sight opens you to see and remember all dreams, all lifetimes."

"This sounds very compelling," I said, "but is it really true?"

"When you slept last night, you had a dream consisting of circumstances, people, and events. In the dream you had thoughts, feelings, concerns, fears, and desires. Your dream was an authentic experience of life, albeit more transient. Tonight when you dream, you will have a new dream with different circumstances, people, and events. Your thoughts, feelings, concerns, fears, and desires will be similar because they are habitual forms of consciousness associated with your eternal spirit, but they will play out differently in the new circumstances and situations.

"During your dream tonight, you will remember nothing of the events, concerns, and circumstances of last night's dream. You won't remember the dolphin jumping from the clouds or the volcano and its spectacular view. You won't remember the amazing feelings of your dream or what the dream showed you about life. It will be gone from your memory and awareness just as your past lives are gone from your current awareness. With half-sight, you can't remember your previous night's dream while you're having tonight's dream. With half-sight, you can't remember your previous life during this life."

"I see what you mean," I said, "but what about dreams where I stress out about a biology midterm or worry about the bureaucracy of my work or see a friend I knew from college?"

"These dreams only mirror the circumstances of your waking life," Sam answered. "This shows you the surface patterns of your life just as your repeating desires, thoughts, concerns, and fears show you a deeper pattern of self. You can learn about your habitual awareness by observing these patterns, yet what I'm bringing to your attention is not these common patterns. What I'm showing you is much more profound.

"Knowing what you did last year is half-sight. Knowing what you did last incarnation is whole-sight. Remembering the circumstances and relations of your waking life while dreaming is half-sight. Remembering the circumstances and relations of your previous dreams while dreaming is whole-sight. I'm bringing your attention to the limits of your transient awareness, to the fact that you can't see a more powerful pattern—the pattern of dreams, the pattern of lifetimes.

"Your principal way of perceiving life is in its transient form, though your spirit is eternal. When you're in a dream, you don't recall previous dreams, and you are unconscious of the deeper truth of who you are. This is half-sight, the transient awareness of life.

"The way dreams work is the way reincarnation works. In each dream you don't think you're dreaming and you can't remember any previous dreams. Tonight when you dream, you won't even know that you are dreaming. You will forget all about waking life; that you are actually laying down in a bed. In each lifetime you think this is your only lifetime, and you can't remember any previous incarnations."

Just then, what Sam had been saying really sunk in. *It's true*, I thought, though I had never been aware of it before. *I could never remember a previous dream while dreaming.* This truth of dreams intrigued me. *Is remembering past lives really just the same? Could Sam be right about reincarnation?*

I started to feel a little uneasy. I had never really wanted to believe that reincarnation could be real, but my new understanding of awareness and dreaming left a hole in the reality that I had thought was so solid. *Do I have past lives that I just don't remember because of half-sight?* I wondered. I sat pondering this for a moment.

"Do you remember your past lives and previous dreams?" I asked.

"Yes."

"What's it like remembering?"

"It is being awake in my dreams," Sam answered. "In my dreams I know that I am dreaming. And it is being awake in life. In this lifetime I am aware of my eternality."

"How do you move beyond the transient awareness of half-sight to the eternal awareness of whole-sight?" I asked.

"Now you're finally asking me a real question!" Sam laughed. "On the spiritual path, through meditation and Mystic SCUBA, you can awaken from the dream. You can see beyond the transient forms of life. You can learn who you really are: a condition of limitless light. Gaining whole-sight, you can see beyond the illusion of this life."

I sat quietly reflecting on Sam's words. I felt that I was on my way to seeing and knowing the truth beyond the limits of my dreams.

BIOLUMINATION

Sam and I rolled over a great expanse of the sun-soaked highway till we reached a pungent grove of pua keni keni trees. Pulling to the right of the grove, I could see a weathered wooden sign pointing to the old marina. Sam drove slowly along the winding road to the head of the inlet.

Sam said, "Tonight Nakoa will take us to the just right spot and we will dive. Nakoa won't be diving with us. He is going out there to perform a sacred Hawaiian ritual. You and I will participate in the ceremony. After Nakoa has completed the ritual, you and I will gear up and do a dark water dive."

"A dark water dive? Is that different from a night dive?"

"Yes," Sam said, "we will be somewhere out in the second current stream. The depth out there will be about 24,000 feet and there will be a strong current. We will dive to about 50 feet, tethered on to a line from the boat. There, we will turn our lights off and practice the Be the Ocean exercise for about a half an hour. Then we will slowly make our way up the line."

Our dive plan sounded quite daunting. At the same time, I felt that it would be a unique and incredibly fun experience. Though I have often enjoyed swimming over shallow reefs with a flashlight searching for Hawaiian shrimp and squirrel fish on night dives, the dark water dive Sam described seemed very different and much more intense an experience.

Passing through a gated entry, we pulled in to the harbor area where dozens of docked boats came suddenly into view. Sam parked the Jeep and we unloaded our dive bags. We walked down to one of the piers. As we approached a 40-foot green and white boat, a man came into view on the ship's bow.

"Sam," the man exclaimed, "it's great to see you again, brah!"

"Always a pleasure to see you again, Nakoa," Sam said, pressing his hands together under his chin as we walked closer to the boat. Pointing to me, he said, "This is Vanessa."

Nakoa smiled broadly and nodded to me as he stepped up to the pier. He looked to be a middle aged Asian-Hawaiian with long, thick shoulder-length hair and a sturdy build. He wore an unassuming Hawaiian shirt, plain shorts, and bounded toward us with no shoes. He met us just as we reached the stern of the boat. Sam began his gesture of bowing, but Nakoa flung his arms around him in a warm embrace. After hugging Sam, Nakoa hugged me too, saying, "Welcome, Vanessa!" Nakoa's welcome was genuinely warm and kind.

Nakoa quickly attended to our gear bags, helping us ready our equipment on the boat. There was a pale-skinned young man sitting at the bow of the ship. Nakoa introduced him as David, his student. "Vanessa, why don't you sit here with David while Sam and I go over the navigation and dive plan on the captain's deck."

"OK," I said, and sat down next to David. He smiled and greeted me. Sam and Nakoa went inside a room a few feet away where I could see them looking at a map.

"So, you're learning about Hawaiian spirituality from Nakoa?" I asked David.

"Yes," David answered, "traditional Hawaiian spirituality and much more, though I've only recently started."

"How long have you been studying with him?"

"Only about a week and a half," he answered, "but what an amazing time it's been!"

"Really?" I asked. "What have you been learning?"

"Nakoa teaches me to become aware of the sacred connection I have to the sea and its marine life. I came here on vacation from Seattle almost two weeks ago. I wanted to swim with dolphins, so I was asking around the harbor if someone would take me out to find them. Then I met Nakoa. He told me that he could take me to a place where I could swim with 200 dolphins. I was hooked!"

"Is the dolphin your aumakua?" I asked.

David looked a little surprised and said, "Yes, the dolphin is my aumakua. Are you and Sam students of Nakoa's too?"

"Not really," I answered. "Sam is a Buddhist monk and has been teaching me Mystic SCUBA for the past couple weeks. Sam teaches about the aumakua, too. My aumakua is also the dolphin."

"Wow, this is so fascinating!" David remarked. A moment later he scratched his head and said, "So, Sam is a SCUBA-diving Buddhist monk?"

I shrugged my shoulders and smiled, "Oddly enough, yes."

Just then, the boat began to move. We were pulling away from the pier and out of the harbor. When we had cleared the harbor and had entered the open ocean, Nakoa and Sam stopped the boat and came out to the bow with David and me. Nakoa was carrying a long wooden horn. He faced the west and blew his horn. After sounding a long deep call, Nakoa said some words in Hawaiian. He continued blowing the horn and chanting a Hawaiian song for a few minutes. I found it to be peaceful and meditative. Sam, David, and I sat reverently until Nakoa had finished. Nakoa lowered the wooden horn and nodded his head looking out to sea. Sam bowed. Smiling, Nakoa returned to the captain's deck and we continued sailing out to the open water.

"Was that the ceremony?" I asked Sam.

"That was the consecration of our spiritual journey," Sam replied.

I nodded, although unsure as to what he meant.

"We do that before each journey," David added. "Nakoa calls to the spirits of nature to be present on our journey. He pays respect to the gods, asking them to keep us safe and to teach us. That's just the beginning. We are heading out to do another special ceremony."

We sailed straight out to the west, far from land, before we finally came to a stop. Sam stood up and brought me to the back of the ship to prepare our SCUBA gear. Nakoa exited the captain's deck and spoke with David at the front of the ship. A few minutes later, I heard Nakoa's horn sounding again. Sam brought me back to join Nakoa and David. We all sat quietly for a few minutes.

Nakoa began speaking, "In this ritual, we will connect with cousin pilot whale. Close your eyes and let the waves of the sea reopen your memory so that you can experience a spiritual communion with our amazing marine friend. During the ritual, I will blow the horn and call pilot whale. Pilot whale will come, but keep your eyes closed and focus on the feeling of your connection. We will be sitting for perhaps a little over an hour, till the sun sets."

I closed my eyes. Nakoa sounded the horn several times in long deep tones. He called and chanted in Hawaiian. Then he was silent. I sat meditatively, open to the feeling of the ocean. After some time, I heard some splashing that sounded different from the waves slapping against the side of the boat. I was curious and wanted to open my eyes, but I kept them closed and focused on feeling out to where the sounds were.

A few minutes later, I heard a deep gasping inhalation. It was the sound of pilot whale breathing very near us. A minute later, I heard a large distinct splash off the starboard bow. I felt the pilot whales were with us! I could see them in my imagination. They swam around our boat communicating with us, aware of us. I envisioned myself playing with the pilot whales in the sea.

After some time, the warmth of the sun diminished, and it grew darker. No longer could I hear the splashing of the pilot whales. Just when I felt that they had left, Nakoa blew his horn and invited us to open our eyes.

The sun had set. I looked around from left to right. There were no whales in sight. Sam bowed and then invited me to gear up for the dive. I walked back to the stern of the boat and began donning my SCUBA gear. Sam carefully tied tethers from a long rope attached to the stern of the ship to our buoyancy control vests. We turned on our air and did a buddy-check. As we turned our lights on, Nakoa wished us a beautiful experience and blew his horn as we began our dive.

We did a giant-stride entry from the back of the boat into the dark water. We immediately drifted away from the boat in the strong current. Sam gave me the thumbs-down signal and we descended to 50 feet where we automatically stopped, since we were tied on to the rope.

Sam turned off his light. A moment later, I turned off mine. It was pitch black at 50 feet in the open water at the beginning of the moonless night. I was being pushed around in the current and felt my fins bump into Sam from time to time. I remembered that I was supposed to be practicing the Be the Ocean exercise and began to still my thoughts, gazing into the void of darkness all around me.

I couldn't tell which way was up or which way was down. I knew that I was tied on to a rope, but I began to worry about the rope snapping in the strong current, or the knot loosening. If I broke free in this current, I would surely be swept far out to sea. Worse, with my light off, and being negatively buoyant, I would probably sink hundreds of feet down before realizing which way was up.

I started to wonder if Sam was still with me. "What if he floated away in the current?" I contemplated. After worrying for a few minutes, I reassured myself that the rope was in good condition and Sam's knots were secure. Then I wondered if Sam had vanished as he had before when he demonstrated the Be the Ocean exercise. I looked for him, but realized that whether he had vanished or not, I would not be able to see him in the pitch dark water. Feeling calmer now, I resumed my meditative focus again.

My eyes were open, but I couldn't see anything. The darkness that spread before me felt infinitely immense. I didn't know where it went, where it ended, or what was out there. The endless darkness engulfed me and brought me feelings of great peace. I was suddenly struck by a sense of eternity and felt somehow connected to that limitlessness. I felt that I was as empty as the void that appeared before me. I came to see that I was that void, boundless and free. Then the grasp of the darkness left me. My awareness shifted into a bright, still, endless space. I felt the ocean's spirit. I sensed her limitless heart.

What seemed like moments later, Sam turned his light on. He checked his gauges and then checked mine. He gave me the thumbs-up signal and we slowly climbed our way up the rope. When we reached the surface, we were pulled back up on to the ship by Nakoa and David.

As we started our long boat ride back, I pulled out my dive logbook and began writing a detailed description of my experiences, feelings, and awareness on the dive. Just as I finished, David approached me. He inquired as to what Sam and I had done on the dive. It seemed strange to him that we would dive in the dark. I explained my experiences to David by reading my logbook entry to him. As I read aloud, putting my experiences into words, the story of my spirit merging with the limitlessness black ocean void sounded completely amazing! Yet, at the same time my story seemed utterly preposterous, even to me. For a moment I felt as if I were telling a tremendous fiction—recounting someone else's adventure as in a fairy tale—but in actuality I was succinctly recounting what I had experienced on my dive. Though I felt odd telling David my seemingly far-fetched tale, he listened closely with interest and appeared to completely accept what I had told him.

Sam began to disassemble his gear. Nakoa had filled a large tub with fresh water for us to rinse our gear in. I disassembled, rinsed, and bagged my gear almost as quickly as Sam. Then I took a fresh water shower and put on a pair of shorts and a T-shirt over my swimsuit.

I climbed up the steep staircase at the back of the boat to join Sam and David, who had made themselves comfortable on the upper deck. We sat looking out into the dark sea under the star-filled sky.

As we drew within a few minutes of land, Nakoa directed us to the starboard bow of the boat. "Aumakua is here! Look to the front," he said.

David and I quickly shuffled down the stairs and ran to the front of the boat. We looked from left to right, but saw nothing. "Look to the very tip of the bow," Nakoa called from the captain's deck. Sam had now joined David and me. Together we moved to the very front of the boat. Putting my hands on the railing above the front anchor, I looked down into the water. To my utter amazement I saw a luminous dolphin swimming in the pitch black sea just to the left of the tip of the boat! I couldn't believe my eyes. I had a feeling of excitement and awe not unlike my dream of the dolphin in the clouds. *Is this a dream?* I wondered, as I watched the dazzling dolphin move over to the right side of the bow. I looked up to see if Sam and David were seeing what I was seeing. David was bent far over the rail intently watching the dolphin, and Sam was standing just behind me with an excited smile and a nod.

Just as I acknowledged Sam's nod, I realized what I had seen. I quickly looked back down to the glowing dolphin. As it moved just slightly ahead of the boat, I could see a trail of small glowing particles left behind it. The glowing particles were of a memorable color, but I had never seen such a brilliant concentration of them before. It was bioluminescence, a glow given off by tiny marine organisms. This firefly-light was being caused by natural chemical reactions in the organisms as the dolphin moved past them in the water. The dolphin's swift swimming through the dark water created a magnificent bioluminescent blaze that outlined every movement and detail of its form. I could see the dolphin's glowing silhouette clearly in the dark.

We watched the bioluminescent dolphin in wonder for another exhilarating minute or two. As the boat approached the harbor, the dolphin drifted into the deep, out of sight. While we entered the harbor, the moon rose from behind the island's sloping volcano. I watched the moonlight dancing on the rolling waves till we reached the pier.

Sam and I grabbed our gear bags and offloaded them onto the pier with the help of Nakoa.

"Thank you, Nakoa," Sam said.

"Anytime bruddah Sam," Nakoa said. "Did you have a good time, Vanessa?"

"I had a wonderful time! It was truly amazing," I answered, as visions of the luminous dolphin played in my mind.

"Good night!" David called out from the upper deck.

"Good night!" I called back.

Sam and I rolled our gear bags along the wooden pier to his parked Jeep. After loading our gear, we headed out of the harbor toward the main road. Turning north toward home, Sam said, "Nakoa has invited us to dive with him again tomorrow afternoon."

"I can't wait!" I exclaimed.

Sam went on, "Tomorrow we will dive with your aumakua."

I was overjoyed. I love swimming with dolphins. On the few occasions that I had seen dolphins underwater, they would swim away after only a few moments. I was wondering if Nakoa would take me to the place where there were 200 dolphins to swim and play with, as he had for David. As Sam drove, I filled out my dive journal, recounting every detail of magic that I had experienced on the dive and on the boat with Nakoa, but I couldn't shake my growing anticipation for the next day's prospects of diving with dolphins.

As we drove back north to the Four Seasons, I started thinking again about reincarnation and the ancient civilization of Mu. "Did you know Nakoa in Mu in past incarnations?"

"During the age of Mu, I incarnated in Atlantis," Sam said.

"Atlantis? It was a real place? Where was it?"

"Yes, it was real," Sam said. "Atlantis was a very advanced civilization that had a beautiful tradition of enlightenment. Atlantis was located in the Atlantic Ocean, but because of a powerful natural disaster, there's almost no trace of it today."

"Was I in Atlantis too?" I asked.

"Yes," Sam replied, "you had many incarnations there. You were part of the Ocean Tribe. The populations of Mu and Atlantis were very small. It is unusual to bump into an Atlantean incarnate and even more uncommon to come across an incarnate from Mu. Both Mu and Atlantis had Ocean Tribes, peoples whose lives were centered on the sea."

"You mentioned Ocean Tribe before," I said, "when you read PADI's philosophy about SCUBA diving to me in the advanced course. You said that PADI's philosophy was akin to Ocean Tribe."

"Yes," Sam responded, "PADI was founded by two men who were incarnates from the Ocean Tribe of Atlantis. The spirit and philosophy of PADI comes from an awareness, respect, and love for the ocean that they had honored and cultivated for many incarnations."

"How can you tell if someone is Ocean Tribe?" I asked.

"It's easy to tell," Sam said. "One who is Ocean Tribe has an aura that is connected to the sea. One who is Ocean Tribe loves the sea and gains a deep awareness and knowledge through that love. If you find someone who loves the ocean with a spiritual quality, they are most likely incarnates from the Ocean Tribes of Atlantis or Mu where they made deep spiritual connections with the sea."

"Do you know Michael, the Divemaster at the local dive shop?" I asked. "Recently he said something to me that reminded me of the things you say about the ocean. Is he Ocean Tribe?"

"Yes," Sam said, "Michael is Ocean Tribe. He is an Atlantean too. The best Divemasters are often Ocean Tribe."

"I knew it!" I said. "But what is the Ocean Tribe, anyway?"

"Atlantis had a caste system," Sam said. "The Ocean Tribe was one of the castes along with the scientists, architects, lawmakers, healers, and the priests. The Ocean Tribe would swim, dive, sail, and surf, supporting the greater Atlantean society and for spiritual practice.

"The divers performed many functions for society including hunting fish and repairing docks and other water-touching foundations. They also retrieved crystals from the depths for scientific and spiritual use. They built and sailed great ships that they used to net fish, trade, and transport. They harvested seaweed and other aquatic crops. They also practiced surfing as a form of meditation. All Atlanteans meditated, and the divers practiced many mystical exercises similar to the ones you have learned."

We sat in silence for the rest of the ride. My mind was filled with the wonder of forgotten ancient civilizations, the magic known by the Ocean Tribe, and the magnificence of the bioluminescent dolphin!

When we arrived back at Sam's hotel suite, it was getting late. Sam fetched a DVD from his room before I departed. I switched the tanks and my gear from his Jeep to my car while he was away.

"Watch this when you get a chance," Sam said when he returned, handing me the DVD. "I think you might like this film; it's about your aumakua."

"Thank you," I said, looking at a picture of a dolphin on the cover.

Bowing, Sam wished me a safe drive home and invited me to meet him for morning meditation the next day. Joyfully accepting his invitation, I departed.

By the time I got home, my curiosity and excitement for my aumakua got the better of me and I decided to stay up late to watch the DVD. After I showered and changed, I sat in bed and watched the film.

Though I was tired, the film was lively and entertaining. I was immediately awestruck by the beautiful cinematography of the ocean. The movie was about the life of a champion breath-hold diver. He was a very innocent being with great purity of character. He had a magical connection with the sea and was the perfect portrayal of Sam's descriptions of Ocean Tribe. Most amazing about the film were his magical interactions with his best friends, dolphins.

When the film ended, I quickly fell into a deep slumber. What seemed like moments after shutting my eyes, I heard the ringing of my alarm clock.

OCEAN MANTRA

After waking up early and meeting Sam for a particularly still morning meditation, we headed out to the east side of the island to dive. "We're going to a very beautiful dive site this morning," Sam said. "You're going to learn another meditative SCUBA exercise. We'll meet with Nakoa later this afternoon."

I was excited about our upcoming adventures and anticipated a beautiful dive. When we arrived at the dive site, we parked and pulled our equipment from the Jeep. Sam began explaining our dive profile after we assembled our gear.

"This is a current dive along a sheer wall. We will enter the water here, and kick out about 100 yards. At that point we will be over the wall and in a strong southerly current. There we will descend immediately to 100 feet. The current will sweep us down and around the south peninsula there." Sam pointed to a craggy landmass jetting out into the ocean far south of us.

"From there we'll have to do a moderate kick for a few minutes toward the shallow corals. The current will lessen as we descend and will end when we are sheltered by the peninsula in the coral shallows. There we will do a safety stop and make an easy exit. Once out of the water, I will hike back up here and drive the Jeep down to pick up you and the gear. The steep wall around the peninsula is the most beautiful part of the experience."

I had never done a sheer wall dive before. Hawaii doesn't have many wall dives, and I hadn't heard of any on this side of the island.

"We will dive to 100 feet for 10 minutes and then slowly make our way up, to end the dive in the shallow reef around the peninsula where there is no current. Once we reach 100 feet you will practice a *mantra* exercise."

"Mantra?" I asked risibly, "Isn't that like when Buddhist monks say 'Yummm'?" I held the 'mmm' sound for a comically prolonged time.

"Yes," Sam answered, smiling in amusement. "It's something like that."

"But what is a mantra?" I asked more sincerely. "Why would someone say one?"

"Mantras are sacred syllables," Sam answered. "One who chants, speaks, or thinks a mantra creates a connection to divine powers and awareness."

"I don't get it," I said, growing puzzled. "How could just saying a word connect you to powers?"

"Mantras are not really words," Sam replied. "They are actual experiences."

I raised an eyebrow, interested.

"Mantras connect you to the experience of divinity. Mantras open you to expanding experiences of awareness."

Before I could ask Sam what he meant, he continued, "The other day on your first power dive, when you were drifting outside of the lava tube, you told me that the ocean's message for you was 'Beyond fear there is only love.' You said that you could hear the words."

"Yes," I responded, "somehow, I could clearly hear the words."

"And that message which you experienced brought you to a direct awareness of love, infinite and filled with wonder," Sam said. "That knowing beyond fear—that there is only love—is eternal and limitless. It is truly divine awareness."

I remembered the experience and smiled.

Sam continued, "That's why mantras are so powerful—because words cannot contain the infinite wonder of actual experience."

"So the words 'Beyond fear there is only love' are a mantra?" I asked.

Sam laughed, shook his head and said, "I'm saying that the words 'Beyond fear there is only love' are insufficient in conveying your actual experience of that vast love. Only the act of moving beyond your fears and into love could ever give meaning to the words. Only the experience of that very wonder has meaning.

"When the message of the ocean freed you from your fear and engendered your love, only then did you have a context for the words 'Beyond fear there is only love.' Yet the words cannot contain the actual experience of the love and liberation that you felt on that dive. Essentially, there is no way to express the experience in words. The experience exposes an infinitely greater truth than the words can describe."

"So a mantra," I said, "brings you into an expanding experience in the same way that love does. Mantras are themselves spiritual experiences."

"You got it," Sam said.

"But why are these holy syllables meaningless sounds? The sutras that we practiced outside of the lava tube make a lot more sense to me. 'I am love' and 'I am peace' are more meaningful to me. Those sutras seemed to really help me enter into divine awareness. And when I was learning the call to my aumakua, you had me do it in English because my words were more meaningful to me and I could more easily focus my intent with familiar words."

"Yes," Sam said, "intention is extremely important. Sutra practice is a very accessible way for you to learn to focus your intent. Sutras, the aumakua benediction, and prayers are powerful primarily because of your focused intent, yet authentic mantras have an innate spiritual power that exists on its own, separate from and prior to your intention. Combining mantras with noble focused intentions is a most enlightening practice, but today your practice will be focused solely on the innate spiritual power of mantras."

"How can words have their own spiritual power?"

"Mantras," Sam answered, pointing upward, high over the horizon, "are words that flow forth from divine energy fields. In Buddhism we believe that there are many divine energy fields that are as real as Hawaii's sugar cane fields and as infinite as the sky. All beings recognize these universal energy fields such as love, compassion, and gratitude. With whole-sight we see that these divine energies exist on their own as dimensions of enlightenment, as fields of awareness in the unseen-world.

"All beings may ascend into these fields of awareness. One may experience these divine energy fields when someone, something, a situation, or in your case earlier, the ocean's message of healing, inspires you to enter unconditional love. Or you may experience other divine energy fields when moved to compassion from the awareness and understanding of another's suffering. All beings can experience these higher, more noble dimensions of life from time to time. Yet the power of unconditional love and selfless compassion are seldom experienced by most people.

"In Buddhism we make a disciplined practice of ascending into these divine energy fields on a regular basis. One of the ways that we can invoke these fields of awareness is through the use of mantras. Like all energies, these divine energies have a movement, a feeling, a vibration. Similarly, words produce a movement in the form of sound waves and physical vibrations. Words that have a physical vibration that harmonizes with the vibrations of divine energies are mantras. A mantra in this way is a vehicle to divinity. A mantra enables you to access divine energies that expand your awareness.

"I'll show you what I mean," Sam said. "Listen closely to the three words that I will say. Still your mind and feel how these words affect your awareness."

I sat up straight and relaxed my shoulders. I closed my eyes and began breathing deeply from my abdomen. Sam was silent for quite a long time and all I could hear was the ocean's gentle waves caressing the shore.

A moment later, Sam spoke in a slightly louder than normal voice. He calmly and slowly said, "Aumakua." The bioluminescent dolphin that I had seen the night before came to my mind and I smiled. Sam repeated "Aumakua" in the same way. I began to remember my previous dolphin dream and my conversations with Sam about it. I started feeling really excited about being able to go diving with Nakoa later to see dolphins. "Aumakua," Sam repeated for the third time. I was brimming with anticipation about my upcoming dolphin dive.

Sam again sat in silence. After a moment, amid my wondering if Nakoa would take me to the dive site with 200 dolphins, I noticed that my breathing had become shallow. I quieted my mind again and deepened my breaths. A moment later, Sam spoke, "Aye," articulating in the same way as when he had said "Aumakua" but there was something about this word 'Aye' that almost shocked me. Being one syllable, Sam's slow enunciation was soon over. "Aye," Sam repeated. Though the tone was the same, this time it felt as if Sam spoke from a deeper, more powerful place. Something about the word now seemed rougher. "Aye," Sam said again. Shocked by the intensity of the sound I abruptly opened my eyes. Sam was sitting peacefully before me in silence, with his eyes closed. I felt uncomfortable. I closed my eyes again, but I wasn't sure if I wanted to experience another mantra.

After sitting for a few quiet moments, Sam spoke, "Om." He spoke this word a touch more quietly and held the 'O' sound for an extended time. I felt relieved because this word felt less harsh. This word immediately soothed me. "Om," Sam repeated. The sound made me feel quiet and peaceful. My mind became very still. Sam repeated "Om" for a third time. I sat in a meditative silence for a long beautiful moment. Upon opening my eyes, I remarked, "The last mantra was very beautiful."

"What was your experience of awareness when you heard me say 'aumakua'?" Sam asked.

"That was nice," I said. "It got me very excited about dolphins. All I could think about was my experiences with dolphins, our conversations about them, and especially that I would have a chance to dive with them today."

"Very good," Sam said. "It is very positive for you to have those thoughts and feelings because the word aumakua is not a mantra."

"What do you mean?" I asked. "I thought you were demonstrating mantras for me so that I could see what they were like."

"I used the word aumakua," Sam responded, "to show you the difference between words and mantras."

"But the word aumakua seemed to spark a lot of magical thoughts in me. Isn't that what mantras do?"

"No," Sam answered, "mantras do not start thoughts. Mantras initiate expanded awareness. Aumakua is a word that you just learned yesterday, but you already have many thoughts and concepts associated with it. Without the conceptual associations, 'aumakua' is nothing."

"OK," I said, following Sam, "but aren't all words like that?"

Sam shook his head and asked, "What was your experience of awareness when you heard me say the next mantra?"

"That kind of shocked me in an uncomfortable way," I said. "It definitely got my attention, but it was somehow rough and almost prickly."

"That's right," Sam said, "that was a mantra. 'Aye' is a self-defense mantra. It is not uncommon to hear this mantra being practiced in martial arts schools. You had no associations to it, but it had an energy that had a significant effect on your awareness."

"That's true," I said as I imagined an old Asian karate master breaking a board while yelling "Aye!" *I did experience something much more visceral than the thoughts triggered by the word aumakua,* I thought to myself.

"But is self-defense a divine energy?" I asked Sam.

"You can use the divine energy of 'Aye' to keep yourself from harm," Sam said. "If something threatens to harm your life, 'Aye' connects you to the dharma of defense and continuation of life. 'Aye' may also be used in defending another's life. Defending and continuing life has a strong dharma."

"That makes sense," I said.

"And what was your experience when you heard me say the last mantra?" Sam asked.

"That was actually very peaceful and calming," I said. "'Om' seemed to soothe me instantly from the discomfort I felt from the previous mantra. Just as you ended speaking the first 'Om' I recall a strong feeling of liking the mantra. The second 'Om' gave me a strong feeling of peace and joy. Then my mind was still and I was meditating kind of automatically without struggling with thoughts at all."

"'Om' is considered to be the highest of all the mantras," Sam said. "In Buddhist cosmology, 'Om' is regarded to be the most ancient sound, the origin of all mantras. This mantra was first described in *The Upanishads,* one of India's most ancient spiritual texts, as an all-encompassing mystical field and the ultimate goal of meditation.

"Ancient spiritual teachings, not unlike recent breakthroughs in quantum physics, describe all things in existence as fundamentally made up of vibrating energy. Spiritual masters have described their experience of this energy as a psychically audible humming vibration that encompasses everything. The ancient masters said that the sound a person can make which most resembles this universal vibration is the syllable 'Om.'"

Fascinated, I asked, "So the sound of the universe boils down to a two letter syllable?" I sounded out the mantra, "Om... Om..."

"Actually," Sam said, drawing a somewhat familiar character resembling the shape of the number three into the sand with his dive wand, "Om is a Sanskrit word that does not consist only of a two-letter syllable, but is composed of four distinct elements."

Sam finished his drawing of the Sanskrit character, adding a small circle over a wavy line.

"The first three elements," Sam said, "are the sounds: 'Ah', 'O', and 'M'. The fourth element of this mantra is the silence which precedes and ends the sounds."

The 'Ah' is pronounced like the 'Ah' in the exclamation 'Ah Ha!' The vibration of the 'Ah' sound initiates awakening in your transient mind. Consider 'Ah' to be the sound of you. You are the infinite universe manifesting in a particular awareness. When practicing the 'Om' mantra 'Ah' is most subtly expressed. It is more intended and felt than pronounced.

"The sound 'O'," Sam went on, "pronounced like 'Oh' as in 'Oh, I forgot my dive mask!'" I giggled as Sam continued, "The vibration of the 'O' sound brings all things into balance and unity within your mind. Regard 'O' to be love. Love is the sound of universal unity.

"'M' is hummed with your mouth gently closed." Sam hummed harmoniously for a moment and then went on, "The vibration of the 'M' sound directs your mind to pure, unobscured consciousness. Feel that 'M' is perfection. Perfection is your absorption into love.

"The fourth element is perfect stillness," Sam concluded. "After you have spoken the three syllables, you experience the silence of 'Om.' The silent element brings the ascending vibrations of the three sound elements into the perfect unity of being. Regard the silence of the fourth element as enlightenment itself."

"There's quite a lot to this seemingly simple syllable," I said.

"Yet it's not so hard," Sam said. "Just be mindful of the four elements while intending awareness of their nature."

"OK, I think I can do that."

"Speaking or thinking the mantra 'Om' enables you to transcend dualistic awareness. 'Om' is the bridge which leads your mind beyond this transient physical world to the inexpressible unseen-world. It gives you whole-sight, revealing the all-embracing blissful truth of life."

Sam paused for a moment, and then said, "Now you are ready to do the exercise."

I was intrigued, eager to try it for myself.

"To start," Sam said, "stand comfortably with your feet about shoulder width apart. Let your arms hang at your sides with your palms facing your legs. Begin a full inhalation. Inhale gently, breathing to your abdomen. Always follow the essential principals of relaxation and deep, natural breathing. As you inhale, bring your focused attention to your heart chakra. Feel the breath filling your heart center with a bright warm light. Prepare to sound the 'Om' mantra with attention to all three syllables in one seamless breath.

"As you begin to make the 'Ah' sound," he continued, "raise your arms out and up along your sides with your palms facing down. Then as your voice shifts, naturally to the 'O' sound, extend your arms to the front at heart level. Bring your hands together in front of you with your palms facing up." Sam's hands glided smoothly as he spoke. I followed his movements carefully.

"Then, gliding from 'O' to the 'M' sound," Sam continued, "bring your hands to your heart center. Make sure you match the duration of your mantra with the exhalation of your breath. Finally, in the silence after the 'M' sound, let your hands slowly drop palms facing upward as you begin your inhalation and focus on your heart. Breathe gently and deeply. Repeat this exercise several times. I'll let you know when to end."

"OK," I said, "I'll give it a try."

I stood up and dusted off the sand from my shorts. I stood facing the ocean with my feet apart and hands at my sides. I relaxed my shoulders and focused on deep breathing for a while, as was my routine now in preparation to begin all Mystic SCUBA exercises.

After a very deep abdominal inhalation I began quietly calling the 'Ah' sound and raising my arms. My transition to the 'O' sound seemed disturbingly abrupt to me as I extended my arms out. The 'M' sound immediately felt comfortable and healing.

After a long, slow sounding of 'M,' I let my hands slowly drop to my sides as I began a gradual inhalation through my nose. My eyes naturally came to a close. I felt a great peace in the stillness after I had completed making the sound. When my lungs were full and my hands reached my sides, I began to repeat the exercise, sounding the 'Ah' and raising my hands.

After I had spoken the mantra a few more times, Sam quietly instructed, "Mantras are not words, but are rather more like music. Mantras are vibrations, intonations, which, just like music, transcend the barriers of the seen-world and lift you to the unseen-world. When you speak or think 'Om', the vibration of the mantra moves throughout your body and your aura, peacefully harmonizing the very center of your being, your spirit."

I continued practicing the mantra exercise for several minutes. I tried to see the mantra Om as a tonal vibration that harmonized my spirit with eternity, but found myself distracted and began losing focus. My mind was mostly calm, but I was often self-conscious of my physical stiffness in raising my arms and the awkward transitions I made in articulating the 'O' sound after the 'Ah' sound.

"Relax and open your mind," Sam said gently. "During this exercise, when you chant 'Om', you create a vibration within yourself that attunes your awareness to the essential vibration of being. In the silence of the fourth element, there is ever deeper stillness, emptiness, and no thought."

Sam's words seemed to invisibly direct me toward harmony. My arms flowed effortlessly with the sounds of the mantra. Though my verbalization of the 'Ah' may not have been perfect, I let go of dwelling on it and brought my mind more deeply into the awareness of the mantra. My experience of peaceful stillness of the silent points after the 'M' sound verged on bliss. After another couple of minutes of practice Sam signaled me to end.

Sitting back down next to Sam, whose broad smile didn't escape my attention, I said, "That was quite a beautiful experience, but still, I'm not sure I did it so well. I felt too stiff in my shoulders and I'm not sure if my breathing was deep and slow enough. Also, I was really struggling with the articulation and meaning of the 'Ah' and the 'O' vowels."

Still smiling, Sam responded, "You did just fine. This exercise is the simple combination of sound and movement. Intoning this ancient sound with relaxed breathing and movement has a natural balancing effect on your body, emotions, mind, and spirit."

"Plus," Sam said pointing to our SCUBA gear, "it's much easier to do this exercise underwater."

"Oh?" I asked, perking up.

Nodding, Sam said, "We will practice this mantra exercise on our dive."

"Fantastic!" I said.

Sam instructed, "As you practice this exercise underwater, it is not necessary to actually verbalize the mantra. You can simply say it internally as you exhale slowly and naturally. And remember to maintain your buoyancy. This is a drift dive; we will not be sitting on a sandy bottom or hooked to a reef-line. You must remain mindful of your depth and surroundings as we glide past a sheer wall in the current.

"We will be at a depth of 100 feet and will continue practicing the mantra exercise for about 10 minutes. I will signal you when it's time to ascend. We will do an extra long safety stop while playing in the coral shallows. Do you have any questions?"

"No," I said, "sounds great! Let's do it."

We geared up, buddy-checked our equipment for proper function, and then headed into the water. The long surface swim out was a bit tiring, though we kicked at a slow pace. Now far away from shore, I noticed that we were moving very fast. The current had suddenly become very strong. We were rapidly being carried further out towards the open sea. I looked down into the water and saw the bottom about 40 feet below.

Sam gave me the thumbs-down signal and we started our descent. As soon as my head was submerged, I could see the edge of the drop-off. The current carried us swiftly over the drop-off. The sea floor plummeted from 40 feet to an unfathomable oblivion! Being pulled out to sea with no bottom in sight ignited a primal dread in me. I quickly stopped my descent and kicked up to the surface.

My heart was beating fast and I couldn't breathe very well. Anxiety washed over me. I had to get out. I couldn't do this dive!

I started swimming back against the current toward our entry point. A moment later Sam appeared next to me breathing hard as he kicked against the current.

"What's wrong?" Sam asked.

"I can't see the bottom! We're getting pulled out to sea!" I panted.

"The current at the surface is much stronger than at 50 feet below," Sam said. "We must descend now or we will surely be pulled out to sea."

I looked down into the water. There was only blue everywhere. We had moved far away from the wall in the current. I shook my head, "I can't!"

Sam said calmly, "Look at that palm tree parallel to us on the peninsula and kick as hard as you can."

I looked. I saw the lone palm tree in line with us on the peninsula. I began kicking even harder. Though I was giving my strongest effort, I was losing ground quickly in the current.

"You cannot swim back against a current this strong," Sam said, "and there is no action I can take to save you now. This situation makes you tense. Tension limits your awareness; your thoughts and actions become impaired. It is essential to practice your mystical discipline now. Your life is at stake! You must descend, because in this current, you've got a one-way ticket on the slow boat to Tahiti. It's your choice."

At that, Sam began preparing himself to descend. It looked like he was planning on going with or without me. I knew that what Sam was saying was true. I didn't need to panic. I just needed to descend. Sam swiftly began his descent without another word.

He's leaving me! I shuddered.

Gathering my focus, I thought, *I need to calm myself.*

"Om," I chanted, "Om." I wanted the peace that I had felt on shore while doing the mantra exercise. I stopped my frantic attempt to kick back to shore. I spent a moment catching my breath. I watched the land to see how quickly I was being drawn out to sea.

"Om," I repeated, as I began relaxing my body. I let my body fall limp and breathed into the tension in my shoulders. "Om," I repeated. I then began practicing deep breathing. "Om," I chanted a few moments longer. My body relaxed and my mind became calm. With a clear head now, I was ready to dive.

I grabbed the low-pressure inflator hose on my buoyancy control vest and let all of the air out. To my surprise, Sam hadn't abandoned me. He had only descended a few feet below me and was watching me carefully. I gave Sam the OK signal, and we descended to 40 feet where the current lessened greatly. As we passed a depth of 50 feet, the current became almost unnoticeable and I started feeling as comfortable as ever, enjoying every wonder of the ocean's beauty.

Sam and I flew down into the ocean's limitless expanse of blue sparkling depths. As we continued our descent, we finned back toward the direction of the shore to make up for being pulled out to sea by the surface current. Soon the wall of the peninsula came into our visual range. At a depth of about 100 feet there seemed to be no current at all. I felt quite relieved that we hadn't overshot the peninsula. I breathed out a long exhalation and let go of all the anxiety I had just experienced. Sam signaled for me to begin the mantra meditation exercise.

Calmly, I focused on my breath. My body was relaxed and free of tension. "Om," I spoke with pristine clarity in my mind. It was extraordinarily simple. I could effortlessly feel the luminous vibratory nature of each sound element. In the silence of the fourth element I felt a profound peace that seemed to expand from my heart chakra and connect me to the whole of the ocean. My arms flowed naturally with my silent intonations of the mantra. There were no distractions, only the comfort of the ocean and the truth of the ocean mantra Om.

I repeated the exercise, but after what felt like only a few moments, Sam, tapping his dive wand on his tank, signaled me to ascend with him up the wall and toward the coral shallows. As we slowly ascended, I observed the lava rock formations of the steep, sloping, craggy, lifeless wall. As we reached 40 feet, we ascended over the edge of the drop off. From there, we swam further inland. Upon reaching the surface after our safety stop at 15 feet, we did a short swim back to the beach. Reaching the beach, we took off our SCUBA gear and rested in the sand.

"How are you feeling?" Sam asked.

"I'm fine," I answered. "I'm fine now, anyway. I don't know what happened to me out there. As soon as I saw the drop-off, I panicked. It was such a strange thing. I had so much fear that I couldn't control my reactions at first."

"Yes, similarly to when you lost your regulator the first day we met," Sam said. "What is more important than the fact that you panicked is that you used your Mystic SCUBA techniques to calm yourself. By using your mystical disciplines, you halted your limiting karmas so that you could open your awareness to see the situation in a balanced way, and save your own life. That shows a degree of mystical mastery."

I sat with no response, deeply struck by Sam's words. I did have a greater ability to see outside of my panic now. I had more control of myself. I had experienced a greater awareness of my options for life, and it had helped me deal with a tough situation in a balanced way. I also really felt that I had many more options for life, spiritually, from my experiences with Sam. *Could this Mystic SCUBA stuff really be changing me?* I wondered. I was in awe, considering the prospect that this study of enlightenment really might be, well, Real!

All of a sudden, I wanted to ask Sam a number of questions about what he had said, but he had already zipped up his gear bag and started off, up the road toward the Jeep.

Sam returned shortly in the Jeep. We loaded up our gear and then started driving to the southwest of the island. "We're going to meet Nakoa now," Sam said. "We're going to dive with dolphins." This reminder shifted me from my reflective awe into a feeling of tremendous excitement.

TOTEM DIVE

On our way across the island, we stopped off at my house. I gave Sam a tour of my house and we picked some ripe papayas for Nakoa from my trees. Then we picked up some fresh air tanks at the dive shop. Sam and Michael greeted each other warmly.

"Did you know that Michael was an oceanographer for 25 years?" Sam asked me. I was surprised. "No! Though, I should have guessed. Michael has told me more facts about the ocean than anyone I've ever met."

Michael laughed amiably.

"Michael, when was it that you started working in Hawaii?" Sam asked.

"It was 1974," Michael answered. "After my tour of duty in Vietnam, I wanted to get as far away from the things of man as I could. I moved here with my wife. I worked as an oceanographer for another 20 years and then became a farmer and dive shop operator."

"Have you shown Vanessa any of your pictures of the Habitat Aegir or Star II?" Sam asked.

"No," Michael answered, "but I have some of them at my desk." Michael quickly turned and walked inside.

"What are you talking about?" I asked Sam.

"An aqua station," Sam answered.

A moment later, Michael was back with several photographs. "Here's a picture of me SCUBA diving outside of Habitat Aegir at 520 feet over the drop-off of Oahu," Michael said, showing me a picture of what looked like an underwater space station. I was amazed. I didn't know they had aqua stations today, let alone in the 70's. In the picture Michael's body seemed to be about a quarter of the size of the length of Habitat Aegir. 520 feet deep! You can dive that deep?" I asked Michael.

"Sure," Michael said, "you can dive even deeper, as long as you have enough air to come up doing long decompression stops." Michael chuckled and then continued, "The Habitat Aegir had enough oxygen for two divers to safely dive below 500 feet and live there for a month. I was down in the Aegir at 500 feet so long that I became pressurized to that depth. I would SCUBA dive from the Aegir to over 600 feet sometimes. That would be the same pressure difference as diving to 100 feet of depth from the surface."

"You lived in there for a month?" I asked. I couldn't imagine being underwater for so long.

"A month or so at a time, 8 months of the year for a while," Michael answered.

"What was it like?"

"It was cramped and duty-intensive, but to me it was like heaven! Half of the rig was my space, the other half was my buddy's living area. I felt like I was in space, alone and free. Every morning, I would dive out into the blue waters conducting scientific experiments or just observing the underwater ecosystem."

Michael paused for a moment, and then said, "After the hell of fighting in a war for my country and then finding my countrymen so negative toward me when I returned home, I was pretty mixed up in those days. The solitude of this work was something I really needed in order to heal. Don't know what I'd have done without..." Michael paused then shook his head, "Yep, the ocean really saved my soul during a tough time." Michael's eyes became a little misty as he reflected on his past.

Sam nodded with empathy. A feeling of compassion for Michael arose within me. I suddenly saw him in a new light. Michael now seemed endearing to me, and his knowledge of the marine world, fascinating. A new recognition of the ocean's peace and healing power entered my mind.

A moment later Michael changed the subject without a hitch and handed me another picture saying, "This is Star II. It's a recovery transport I used to operate." I looked at the picture. Star II seemed to be a mini-submarine with a large glass bubble windshield. In the picture, Star II seemed to be landing on the Habitat Aegir. "I used to pilot Star II from the surface and dock on to the Habitat Aegir to begin my missions." Michael said. I looked at several more pictures of the deep underwater world.

"It's time to get going," Sam said. "We don't want to miss the boat."

We thanked Michael for showing us his pictures and telling us about his experiences living in an aqua station. Michael wished us well on our dive, reminding me in his usual manner about how to avoid seasickness while on a boat.

Sam and I climbed back into the orange Jeep and headed west to the marina. Sam took a shortcut down a steep dirt road leading through flourishing Manila palms and onomea ti foliage. After a bumpy, tank-clanging drive, we reached the harbor and parked where we had the day before. As we pulled our gear from the Jeep, I could see Nakoa and David making preparations down on the boat.

Reaching the boat, Nakoa hurried out of the captain's deck and welcomed us with a warm "Aloha!" and a cheery hug. "Are you ready for an aumakua adventure today?" Nakoa asked me, grinning.

"I can't wait," I replied.

David jumped onto the pier from the bow of the boat and jogged over to greet us. "We're going to the special site," David told me as he helped load my gear onto the boat.

"The site with 200 dolphins?"

"Yes," David said with a radiant smile.

Just as I secured my gear bag in the ship's aft, I heard the engines rumble and we began pulling away from the pier. A few minutes after exiting the narrow rocky gateway of the natural marina, Nakoa stopped the engines. Once we were adrift at sea, Nakoa fetched his wooden horn from the captain's deck. As we sat in silence at the bow of the ship, Nakoa blew the horn in the four directions. Putting his horn down, he called out a prayer to the aumakua:

I na 'aumakua kane a pau loa
Ia 'oukou pale ka po, pule ka make, pule ka pilikia
Owau nei o Nakoa ka pua keia i ke ao
Homai i mana

We all sat in silence after the prayer. A moment later Nakoa said, "Did you know that there are bottlenose dolphins just in front of us?" He turned around and pointed to an area about 100 yards out toward the horizon. David and I hurried to the edge of the bow just in time to see four large dorsal fins emerge from the gentle surface swells.

"There are bottlenose dolphins in Hawaii?" I asked amazed. "Doesn't Hawaii only have spinner dolphins?"

"Bottlenose dolphins are very, very rare in these waters," Nakoa said, "but these guys are my friends and always come to say 'hi' when they're around."

We drifted closer to the dolphins. The dolphins seemed to sense our approach. They turned and came toward us slowly. I could tell that one of them had a damaged dorsal fin.

"That one is named Happa," Nakoa said, pointing at the dolphin. "We go way back, Happa and me."

"What happened to Happa's dorsal fin?" I asked.

"He was hit by a boat several years back," Nakoa said. "The boat's propeller cut off the top of Happa's dorsal fin."

"That's awful."

"For most dolphins, an accident like that would lead to death," Nakoa said. "With a damaged dorsal fin, a dolphin cannot maneuver as well to catch fish. But not Happa, he's a smart one. He uses cunning to hunt fish. He can't dart around as well as the other dolphins, so he waits in the back while the rest of his pod begins the chase. While the fish are harried by other dolphins in the pod, Happa lines up and jets straight in."

The dolphins passed close to the boat. Nakoa held his hand out, palm down over the starboard bow in solemn greeting as they swam by. Passing us, the dolphins continued north.

"Can we dive with them?" I asked.

"No, not today," Nakoa answered. "These friends are too busy to play now. They are heading out to hunt fish. We'll move on and find some locos to swim with."

Nakoa went to the captain's deck and started the engines. Soon we were speeding south, down the coast. The sun was huge in the blue sky. Nakoa waved to the captains of passing fishing boats as we made our way.

After moving at full speed for about 40 minutes, the boat slowed. "They're gonna be here," Nakoa said. "I can feel it." He stopped the boat. Sam and I put on our dive gear and took a giant-stride into the water. David put on his mask, snorkel, and fins, and jumped in after us.

Sam and I descended about 15 feet and then stayed still, looking for the dolphins. A few moments later I heard the cheerful chatter of dolphins in the distance. Their language was so distinct—exuberant clicks and squeaks that made me grin. We kicked down in the direction where we heard the calls.

I gasped in delight as they came into view. It was a large pod. It looked as if the sea was filled with dolphins. There must have been at least 200 of them! They were swimming together in smaller groups, some very deep and others close to where we now were. A group of eight dolphins swam directly toward us. I inwardly asked them if we could join them and felt a distinct and playful "Yes!"

Keeping my arms at my sides to avoid alarming them, I joined the group of eight dolphins as they glided by. I kicked hard and sped laterally through the water with them on both sides of me. I was so close I could see the bluish color variations of their skin, the slope of their fins, and the brown-grey of their eyes. Then three of my new friends broke from the group of eight and took off for the surface at an incredible speed. I watched them from below as they exhaled bubbles from their spouts and leapt into the air spinning, an arm's length away from David.

I came to a stop to rest. The dolphins I was swimming with sped on and away. I turned and looked for Sam. He was far behind me now, swimming with another group. Huge rays of sunlight were streaming into the water, shining on Sam and the dolphins with him, and illuminating more dolphins in the deep distance.

Another group of nine or ten dolphins swam toward me. They seemed to be curious about me. Instead of swimming by, the group broke into pairs and playfully spun about me. I spiraled round and round watching the merriment of these aquatic acrobats as they banked and turned, rolled over and cut straight up to leap into the air at the surface.

Sometimes a few dolphins would pause from the fast tempo, gracefully meandering forward with simple, powerful downward fin kicks. As I hovered in stillness, watching, I felt their complete relaxation and freedom.

After a couple of more playful minutes, one of the dolphins in the group stopped just a few feet away, facing me. The other dolphins continued whizzing around us. I stopped my twirling and looked at the beautiful being hovering before me. The dolphin seemed to be examining me. I looked into its eyes and sensed a profound and ancient intelligence. I felt an undeniable connection to this marine animal. It was like a door had opened in my mind to reveal the dolphin's world of blue wonder. As the moments passed, this connection deepened.

Finally, the dolphin called jubilantly. With an upward movement of its smiling snout, it made four fast clicking sounds and then shot down toward the blue depths. The other dolphins followed the leader and were soon far beyond my sight.

As I gazed into the depths looking for that special group, another group of six came into sight. Sam was with them. They were about 30 feet below me and were hardly moving. They swam in a tight cluster with Sam in the center of the group. They kicked infrequently, yet in unison. Watching them filled me with joyful serenity.

Just then, my vision became completely encompassed by a new group of at least a dozen dolphins that had overtaken me from behind. They squeaked and clicked and spun around me. I began kicking faster to keep up with the playful group. David appeared at the front of the group 20 feet below the surface holding his breath and smiling as he swam at the head of the pack.

I spent the next forty-five minutes in total joy, playing with and observing the pod. I loved the speed, grace, and complete freedom with which they moved, racing for the surface, diving down again into the deep. It was a gorgeous underwater ballet, with the dolphin dancers gliding, spinning and jumping in an exquisite impromptu choreography.

Once we surfaced, David and I grinned giddily. "It's like they live just for the sheer delight of living!" he said. I nodded and continued smiling, feeling the dolphins' bliss as I climbed back on to the boat. Back at the harbor, as we left the ship, Nakoa gave Sam a warm embrace, "Anytime, brah. Please come back again." Sam thanked Nakoa and we departed.

The sun had not yet begun to set. Sam and I drove all the way to the Four Seasons chattering about how exciting diving with dolphins was. After our evening meditation together on the patio of Sam's hotel suite, I prepared to head home.

Sam handed me another CD and a DVD. The CD was another album by the same artist that we had listened to while meditating before. The DVD was a film by the same French director who had directed the dolphin movie we had watched the other night. Sam recommended that I watch the DVD that evening when I got home. "Both are for you to keep," Sam said. I thanked him and promised to watch the DVD as soon as I got home.

I made it home in the early evening, quite exhausted after the day's adventures. I quickly prepared a light dinner and turned on my computer to watch the film. Before starting the DVD, I checked my email. I saw a message from my friend Rebecca, who had visited me during my time in Ethiopia and had traveled with me to the town of Bahir Dar and the Blue Nile Falls. The subject of her email read, "Kiva.org – Changing a family's life with $25." In the email, Rebecca informed me about a website called Kiva.org. She explained that it was an inspiring, empowering place for an average person to help entrepreneurs in developing countries with their small businesses.

I clicked the link in her email and opened the Kiva.org home page. I immediately saw a list of entrepreneurs from all over the developing world seeking loans to finance their businesses. There was a Nigerian woman seeking $525 to launch a grocery store, a Peruvian man seeking $300 to expand his construction business, and a Vietnamese family seeking $950 to start a pig farm.

Kiva allows you to see the needs of small business entrepreneurs in poor communities and loan them money online using your credit card. The money these businesses needed was higher than the $50 to $100 needed by the mothers I knew in Ethiopia, but Kiva uses the power of the internet to network lenders. Kiva lets you loan as little as $25 toward a higher business loan request. Your money is then combined with the loan money of others, till the full loan amount is reached.

Kiva works through many NGO partners who administer the loans to the small businesses. Kiva continuously shows business progress updates on the website till the loan is repaid. Most loans are repaid within six months to a year. Individual lenders may then take their money out or reloan it to fund another small business on Kiva.org.

I thought Kiva.org was a fantastic idea. I quickly decided to do it. I became a member and loaned the Nigerian woman $25. Three people had also loaned her $25 before me that day. My contribution brought her total loan amount up to $100. It seemed like in a few more days she would have the loan to start her grocery store.

Smiling, I started watching the DVD Sam gave me. It was a beautiful artistic documentary about the sea and marine life, with no narration, only a well-matched soundtrack of diverse songs. With magnificent cinematography of the ocean world, the film featured aquatic episodes of marine animals, including playful sea lions, an ominous giant octopus, and of course, my favorite friends, dolphins. The spotted dolphins danced and glided, as if in a perfectly choreographed ballet. More than a mere film, I felt this work of art was an experience of the undersea world.

After finishing the movie, I turned my attention to my studies. *If I make a lot of money as a computer programmer*, I thought, *I'll be able to help finance many businesses all around the world!* As I read my tutorials and coded, I couldn't shake off the great excitement I felt about the loan I had just made on Kiva.org. This feeling of empowerment and possibility persisted through the night and into my dreams.

THE END OF THE BEGINNING

In the morning, I realized that Sam hadn't confirmed the location of our morning dive. After my morning meditation and a light breakfast, I drove to our regular spot, where we had originally met. The beach was crowded as usual. I parked my car in one of the few open spaces and began scanning the parking lot and the beach for a glimpse of Sam or his orange Jeep. Much to my delight, I found Sam sitting serenely in the sand near the water's edge. Hurrying over and greeting Sam, I set my SCUBA gear down. Arranging my hibiscus-patterned beach towel into a folded seat, I sat down, eager to hear about the morning's activities.

Sam acknowledged my readiness with a nod and then peered out over the ocean with his hand shading his eyes from the sun. "Do you remember when I promised you that I would take you to the greatest location for a power dive in the whole world?" Sam asked.

"Yes," I said, beaming with anticipation.

"Today we will dive at my favorite place, the greatest place of power in the world," Sam said. "So let's kit up and get ready." Sam reached over to his gear bag, unzipped it, and began pulling his dive mask from its box.

"What? Here?" I asked, doubtful. "This is the greatest dive site in the world? This place is your favorite place of power?" I looked around at the locals strumming ukuleles and the tourists playing Frisbee. "I mean, I like this place, the diving is good. But... It's just that I wouldn't think it would be your favorite place of power."

"Well," Sam said, "not right here. This is not the place," indicating the immediate vicinity by opening his arms. "Nor is it anywhere you have been before at this dive site," Sam said, gesturing toward the open water.

I squinted my eyes, perplexed, and asked, "Then where is your favorite place of power on this earth, Sam?"

Sam gave me the thumbs down descent signal and said, "130 feet below the surface."

"Oh." I had never been that deep at this or any dive site. The maximum depth limit for recreational diving is 130 feet and I had been taught that it was safer to stay well above that limit.

"As we discussed before," Sam said, "the toxic human aura of the planet completely ceases around 130 feet below the surface of the sea. On this dive, we shall dive to that depth so that you can experience what it is like to be free of that heavy auric influence. You will be able to feel what life feels like without the bombardment of the myriad energies of others."

I was intrigued, yet wary of the great depth.

Sam continued, "Diving to 130 feet is like going back in time from the Kali Yuga to the Golden Age. Your aura will immediately be cleansed and the energies of your body will come into balance. At that depth you should practice any of the Mystic SCUBA techniques that you've learned previously. Practice the ones that you are most comfortable and proficient with. At that depth your spiritual experiences will be automatic and most profound."

Fascination now overruled my trepidation. I was eager to see if there would be as significant a difference as Sam was suggesting.

We walked into the water and kicked out into the crystal blue waves. We finned out until the coral-filled bottom was no longer visible. We rested for a minute or so and then kept swimming straight out to sea. We went from the cove into larger sea swells. I was breathing hard from our extended surface swim, but kept up with Sam, who was undaunted and swift in the high seas.

After a few more minutes, Sam stopped and rested. "We're here," Sam said. "Take a couple of minutes to rest before we dive."

I nodded and relaxed on my back in the water, taking in deep breaths from my mouth. From time to time I looked into the water, seeing nothing but the sun's rays reaching far into the endless blue depths.

"Ready?" Sam asked when my breathing was again calm. I gave him the descent signal in response, and we were off. I put my regulator in my mouth and expelled all the air from my buoyancy vest. I bent my torso, gave two massive kicks, and pulled myself downward with my hands, swimming face first, flying free, falling into the blue. I couldn't see the bottom, only Sam and the blue of the immense ocean. I cleared my ears, wiggling my jaw. I felt the water rushing through my open fingers as I extended my arms like I was flying. Sam and I were free-falling as if in an infinite blue sky. My hair whirled behind me as if I had leaned my head out of the open window of a moving car. The beauty of our descent was exhilarating.

A steep, sandy slope came into view. The great expanse of sand in the darkening blue of the depths was stunningly still and picturesque. My feeling of exhilaration grew and the whole ocean seemed to glow. Sam, looking at his dive computer and slightly changing his trajectory, guided me toward a landing at the proper depth. A moment later we touched down and were sitting in the sand.

We sat facing the deep. A shining white glow hovered inches over the sandy sloping floor, merging at the horizon with the luminous blue of the ocean's depths. My body felt light and dreamlike. My eyes and mind and heart felt open and in harmony for what seemed like the first time. "Home," I felt my heart almost speak. Here at 130 feet under the sea, I felt completely happy and completely at home.

I looked over to Sam. He was sitting motionless, breathing so slowly that it seemed almost as if he were holding his breath. I looked back to the deep and began to practice the Be the Ocean exercise. I was instantly drawn into a beautifully silent connection with the ocean. I felt the ocean's heart in mine, as if I were in pure meditation on the ocean's heart chakra. Naturally, I found myself Breathing Light. With no thought, only a blissful observance, I was breathing light—the air was energy, light, life!

What felt like a second after I started my meditations, Sam signaled me with his dive wand. When I looked to him, he gave me the thumbs up hand signal for ascent. I checked my dive computer to make sure we had not exceeded our maximum allowable bottom time. It was time to ascend. We had been at 130 feet for four minutes, although it felt more like four seconds to me.

As we put air in our buoyancy vests and kicked up off of the sandy floor, Sam tapped me and pointed up toward the surface. Looking up through the lightening blue water, I saw the distant surface and the soft refracted light of the mid-day tropical sun. From 130 feet below the sea, the sun looked like a vision of enlightenment itself. Ten times larger than when viewed from the surface, the sun glistened and glittered in the undulations of the surface waves. The luminous vision filled my eyes.

Sam, signaling me again with his dive wand, reminded me to watch my dive computer for a safe ascent rate. As we carefully ascended beyond 100 feet, I noticed that the great sense of exhilaration had left me and that the ocean took on a much more familiar look and feel. Sam and I met the beginning of the coral outcroppings at a depth of about 45 feet. From there the sloping bottom became much more gradual, almost flat.

Sam and I enjoyed a long shallow dive. We did an extended safety stop, finning over the shallow corals at 20 feet. Near the end of our dive, as we were heading back up the reef, we came across a majestic manta ray. Sam pointed it out to me. The manta was ascending toward us from the deeper blue waters of the reef. I could hardly believe my eyes! The manta looked so still and serene amid the ocean backdrop. It glided motionlessly toward the northern shallows. Sam moved on ahead of me, swimming parallel to the manta. After a few moments, Sam stopped moving. I stopped too, about 20 feet behind Sam. The manta paused, turned, and glided gracefully toward Sam.

It looked like the manta was going to bump face first into Sam, until, just a couple of feet in front of Sam, the manta shifted its position, pulling up to face the surface. This was an amazing spectacle. The manta remained motionless now, two feet from Sam, exposing the whole of his underbody. From where I was behind Sam, the manta's massive white diamond-shaped body surrounded the whole of Sam's form. The manta's gills seemed to form a smiling face. To me the manta looked like an angel!

The manta just hung there in front of Sam, perfectly still. A moment later, it stirred slightly, and then moved one of its massive wings toward Sam. The wing brushed against Sam's torso. Sam then reached out and touched the manta, stroking it in a circular manner. It seemed as though they were dancing a waltz.

The manta ascended, just over Sam's head, continuing to gently touch Sam with its wing. As the manta began to clear Sam, it turned and made one final brush of its wing on his head. Sam remained motionless. The manta glided back towards the deep. Again picturesque in the blue of the ocean background, the manta swiftly raised and lowered its wings, jetting out into the blue. I watched as the massive creature shrank into the ocean void.

Sam and I ascended the shallow reef and made our way to the shore.

When we surfaced, Sam seemed bright and distant. We were just a few feet from our shore exit. Elated, I exited the water, pulled off my fins and exclaimed to Sam, "That was amazing! It was the most wondrous dive I've ever done. It felt incredible down there. And the manta ray was magnificent."

Sam nodded with a broad smile.

"I felt energized, and bright," I said, recalling my experience, "almost high."

Pausing, I tilted my head and asked Sam, "Or maybe I just felt nitrogen narcosis? I hear that nitrogen narcosis makes you feel kind of high."

I had learned about nitrogen narcosis in my dive certification course. Along with decompression illness, nitrogen narcosis is one of the most dangerous conditions that can affect SCUBA divers at depth. I was taught that nitrogen narcosis occurred because of the effects of breathing nitrogen at a depth greater than 100 feet and produced a state similar to alcohol intoxication. The benign effects of nitrogen narcosis are feelings of tranquility and euphoria. The most dangerous effects of nitrogen narcosis are the loss of coordination and manual dexterity, as well as impaired judgment and decision-making ability.

The effects of nitrogen narcosis are not themselves life-threatening, but like drinking and driving, nitrogen narcosis can be fatal, as the result of irrational behavior in a dangerous environment. I heard a story, though I wasn't sure if it was true, that a SCUBA diver who was experiencing nitrogen narcosis took off his SCUBA gear, imagining that he was a fish, and then swam around until he drowned. There is no way to predict the severity of nitrogen narcosis, and the effects can vary from dive to dive. However, there is a simple cure for nitrogen narcosis. As you ascend to shallower depths, the effects disappear almost instantly.

"Nitrogen narcosis is interesting," Sam said. "Jacques Cousteau described it as 'the rapture of the deep.' Scientists can't really determine exactly why it occurs. Scientists observe that it is caused by a greater partial pressure of nitrogen, but they don't know why it causes effects such as exhilaration, elation, and euphoria. Actually scientists and physicists can't explain it at all because what they call 'nitrogen narcosis' is an experience of consciousness that transcends the physical world and reaches into the unseen-world. Nitrogen narcosis is primarily caused by the two mystical benefits of SCUBA diving: breathing the compounded energy of air at depth, and the cessation of toxic pressures on our auras as we go deeper, due to the purifying nature of water."

"Nitrogen narcosis is just mystical?" I asked. "Why do people experience the loss of coordination? That seems so physical."

"There is a physical aspect of nitrogen narcosis as well," Sam explained. "As scientists have observed, under a higher partial pressure of nitrogen, inert gas narcosis occurs due to the direct effect of nitrogen dissolving into nerve membranes and causing temporary disruption in nerve transmissions. This causes some slight physical side effects such as interrupted coordination and manual dexterity.

"Yet the relief of anxieties, feelings of euphoria, and the slowing down of the cognitive mind are mystical factors caused by the greater energy in air and the aura-neutralizing nature of water. As your mind becomes still and your body energized, it's easy to stop thought."

Addressing me directly, Sam asked, "Were you thinking much down there?"

"No," I said, "is that normal?"

"Meditation is a common occurrence for those who dive to 130 feet.

All you need to do is get to that depth and be relatively calm for a few moments and you will most likely experience jhana, a deep meditative state. At deep depths your mind shifts into spiritual dimensions naturally.

"Many divers often report feeling high from nitrogen narcosis, but they also report feeling clear-minded and happy at the same time. Some divers note powerful concentration abilities when experiencing nitrogen narcosis. They can focus perfectly on a rock, coral, or a flashing light on their dive computers. Some divers report amazing spiritual experiences, including feelings of merging with the universe.

"Other divers report blacking out. They can remember approaching great depths, but don't remember what happened to them while they were there. They come back into their regular awareness much later, while they are ascending. Though they don't remember anything while at depth, their buddies will report that they were diving perfectly. This is a type of jhana, a profound meditative experience very similar to your meditation on the volcano when a great deal of time passed by while you were beyond thought.

"Nitrogen narcosis is really not like getting high on drugs or alcohol. A high feeling is the natural and normal condition of your free mind. If you were to get high on drugs or drunk, you would find it impossible to meditate or to practice mysticism. However when you dive to 130 feet, you have a high feeling and you are able to meditate easily."

I was enthralled by what Sam was saying. "Does everyone who dives deep feel these things?" I asked.

"Unfortunately, no," Sam answered. "First of all, many people don't dive deep because of the heightened risk of decompression sickness. Also, many of the most colorful reef attractions are not very deep.

"For those who do dive deep, many people feel very strange with more energy. Some feel dissociated by the lack of the heavy human aura. Many who dive deep are too frightened to relax. Many divers are also so psychically blocked and heavily conditioned by their habitual existence that they don't notice anything special at all when diving deep."

Sam sat down in the sand and unzipped his wetsuit. Changing the subject, he said, "Now, you've completed the primary Mystic SCUBA course of study. You have established proficiency in the basic Mystic SCUBA techniques. You've established a daily meditation practice. You've learned of the physical and energetic health benefits of air and water. You've learned deep breathing and relaxation techniques and learned many meditative SCUBA diving exercises. You've found your aumakua. You've dived below the human aura of the world, and you have learned to relax the critical tension of your mind that resulted in your breaking the first rule of SCUBA diving."

And I've learned so much more, I thought.

Reaching into his SCUBA gear bag, Sam said, "I have something for you." He retrieved a folded white cloth and handed it to me.

"Open it," Sam gestured for me to open the cloth.

I opened the protective folds to find a beautifully carved red dolphin pendant. The carving had the markings of the local Hawaiian spinner dolphins. It masterfully portrayed their perpetual playful smile. The pendant was attached to a thin, black leather necklace.

Surprised and overjoyed, I said, "This is beautiful! But you didn't have to get me a present."

"This is not a present from me. It is your ocean totem. This pendant represents the mystical connection to your aumakua, which you have learned through this study. Each of my students who completes the primary Mystic SCUBA lessons receives an aumakua pendant. This is not a present from me, but a gift from the study."

"I'm speechless," I said. Looking closely at the pendant, I asked, "Did Pono carve it?"

"Yes," Sam said, "He started carving it the day he met you." Holding his black Hawaiian gold coral manta ray pendant between his fingers, Sam said, "Pono carves the best totems."

"What's it made out of?" I asked, noticing the dark red textured depths.

"It's Hawaiian pink coral. This one has a very rich red color, but Hawaiian pink corals are usually hibiscus pink, although I've also seen them almost white. They often have a marbled quality of colorings."

Gesturing to me, Sam said, "Put it on."

I slipped the necklace on over my head and looked down at the light red dolphin totem as it rested right over my heart chakra.

"Wear the pendant whenever you want to," Sam said. "But always wear it when you go diving and perhaps when you meet with other divers, say, if you go to a dive shop or something. If you ever see another diver with a carved coral or shell pendant, they may have studied with me or another teacher from my lineage. And once you have one of these aumakua totems, chances are you will run into someone else with one.

"If you come across another Mystic SCUBA diver, it would be a good idea to chat with them. Feel free to tell them about me and your diving experiences. You may gain valuable insights from other Mystic SCUBA divers or learn how you may dive with me again, or with another teacher from my Buddhist school."

With an air of finality Sam said, "You have learned many of the major teachings of Mystic SCUBA. These lessons can forever enrich your spiritual life. And it ensures that you will never again forget the first rule of SCUBA diving!" We both chuckled.

"Now I'd better be off," Sam said. "It's funny how busy you can be when nothingness is your only goal." Sam began to stand up, looking toward his Jeep.

"Wait, what do you mean?" I asked. "This is it? Can't I learn more? I still have almost a week before I return to California. What about underwater Samadhi? I really want to experience that. Aren't I prepared?"

"Well," Sam said, "there is a lot more I can teach you in the time we have left. I am leaving just a couple of days before you." Pausing gravely, Sam said, "Yet going forward on this path takes a greater degree of courage and dedication. Continuing beyond the primary Mystic SCUBA teachings will bring you to the 130 foot depth of the self and transform your life in a profound way."

I nodded with conviction, relieved that there was a way I could learn more. I said to Sam, "I want to learn more. I'm ready and willing to work hard."

Sam continued, "Do not enter into this study unless you are very committed and open for your life to wholly change. In order for me to bring you into a state of underwater Samadhi, you will have to pass through two demanding gates of attention and take the ocean initiation."

I continued nodding and then smiled with excitement. Sam said with a growing smile, "After you take the initiation, I will gladly bring you into Samadhi. So do you want to take the plunge?"

Eager to experience underwater Samadhi, I said, "Yes. Yes, definitely!"

THE WHALE GOD

After disassembling and packing our dive gear, Sam said, "Tomorrow, we'll be diving just north of the Four Seasons. You should pick me up at my hotel lobby exactly one hour before sunrise. Don't be late. Timing is essential for this dive."

"OK," I said, quickly calculating how early to set my alarm clock.

Sam bowed and headed back to the Four Seasons. He gave me a number of errands to run before rejoining him. Following Sam's errand list, I first stopped off at the dive shop to refill our air tanks. I was looking forward to a visit with Michael again. I had a new appreciation for the information he gave me about diving and the ocean.

When I arrived at the dive shop Michael greeted me cordially. He reached into his shirt pocket to retrieve a slightly tattered photograph and said, "I found an old picture that my research buddy took back in my Habitat Aegir days." Handing it to me, he said, "I thought you might like to see it."

I looked at the picture with astonishment. It was a picture of a huge whale swimming over and dwarfing the aqua station. The majestic whale was a dark bluish grey, with long, rough-edged, mottled white flippers and barnacles under its chin. There was a SCUBA diver in the picture who appeared doll-sized compared to the whale as he floated over its head.

"What kind of whale is this?" I asked in awe.

"He's a humpback," Michael said. "You can tell by the throat grooves and long flippers more than by the dorsal fin. Humpbacks have the longest flippers of any whale. The only reason people call them humpbacks though is because of the way they bend their backs pushing their dorsal fin up out of the water when they begin to dive."

"Who is the diver?"

"It's me," Michael replied.

"The whale is so massive," I commented, still staring at the picture. "I would be afraid to be next to a humpback because of its size. Can a humpback hurt you?"

"No," Michael said laughing, "Humpbacks are filter feeders. They are gulpers. Humpbacks sieve tiny plankton and krill from the water they gulp into their massive mouths. They can eat up to 5,000 pounds of the stuff per day."

"Wow! That's a lot of food," I said. "It's so big!"

"Yes," Michael agreed, "this fellow is over 50 feet long. But humpbacks actually feel quite friendly when you encounter them. I have met this old fellow more than a dozen times over the past 30 years."

"Really?" I asked, amazed. "How do you know it's the same whale?"

"I just know when he is there," Michael said, "I can just feel it is him." Pausing reflectively for a moment, he said, "There's something about his song. He has the most imaginative of whale songs I have ever heard. He has a long, complex and beautiful song. I'm familiar with his voice. I recognize his song's melodious sequences of haunting sounds."

Michael was looking away nostalgically up to his left. He had a peaceful look in his eyes that seemed to peer into some distant invisible realm.

Michael's words warmed my heart and stirred my imagination. His words seemed to expose the same experiences and feelings that I was exploring in my Mystic SCUBA practices with Sam. I could no longer contain my curiosity. "Is the humpback whale your aumakua?" I asked, brimming with intrigue. "Do you feel a deeper, spiritual connection to whales when you're around them?"

Michael gave me a quizzical smile but said nothing. I was sure he knew what I meant, but he seemed a little uncomfortable about my questions.

"Can you help me choose a regulator?" an impatient customer called across the dive shop to Michael.

"Sure, I'll be with you in a moment," Michael answered back.

Handing me freshly filled air tanks and snapping back into his regular fact-feeding mode, Michael said, "I have also confirmed it is him by looking at his markings. Humpbacks have distinctive patches of white on the underside of their tails. No two white-patched patterns are alike. They are unique to each individual whale. It's like a fingerprint."

Pausing with an unusually warm smile, Michael said, "Now, you have a safe dive. I better go help that customer choose a good regulator. New divers often have a lot of anxiety about their regulators. After all, when you're underwater, your regulator is your interface to life's breath." I handed Michael his photograph back and thanked him.

Leaving the dive shop, I continued with my errand list. I drove down to a heavily touristed area to pick up some supplies at the hardware store. Sam wanted me to get the proper materials and assemble my own dive wand and reef-line. The store clerk was very friendly. She ended up helping me interpret Sam's construction directions, and did some of the assembly as well. I detached the dive wand and reef-line that Sam had lent me, and attached my new dive tools to my buoyancy control vest.

Next, I walked down to a nearby artisan's shop. The shop was teeming with tourists. I asked a grey-haired man working in the shop if they had any decorative bottles. He showed me to eight little potion bottles that he had in a case next to some crystals and rings. One of the potion bottles was wide and blue. It looked perfect for fulfilling Sam's request. I bought the blue potion bottle and returned to my car.

Then I went to the supermarket. Sam had said it was very important for me to get some fruit juice. He had stressed that I should make sure that it was 100% juice with no additives. I examined several containers of POG, a passion-orange-guava juice mixture. POG was my favorite Hawaiian juice. I found some all-natural POG and put it in my shopping cart. Then I picked up two containers of ahi poke, a deliciously seasoned local tuna tartar dish. I additionally picked up some provisions for home and I was done.

On my way home, to complete my final task, I drove down to the harbor where I had previously met Nakoa. When I arrived, I saw that his ship was away at sea. Locating the marine sports store next to the yacht club restaurant, I rented a two-person kayak. With some help from the shop owner, I strapped the red kayak to the roof of my car.

By the time I made it home, it was early in the evening. I did a short meditation session and ate a light dinner. Setting my alarm clock for a very early hour, I turned in to bed.

When I reached the Four Seasons the next morning, I saw Sam waiting in front of the lobby entrance, holding a beach towel and a large sunhat with his dive gear bag beside him. It was still very dark out. Sam was standing in the light of two tall flickering torches. He promptly greeted me with a bow and as I pulled up.

"Are you ready for a close encounter with a non-terrestrial intelligence?" Sam asked with a welcoming smile as I got out to help him load his gear into the car.

I was still a bit groggy from waking up so early. I thought about what Sam meant for a moment, pausing with, no doubt, a vacant facial expression.

"Today, I will introduce you to the Whale God, one of the wisest beings of the sea," Sam said, shutting the trunk with his gear loaded.

"Whale god? Non-terrestrial intelligence?" I asked. "I think it's too early in the morning for me to understand mystic riddles. What do you mean, Sam?"

"There's no time to explain now," Sam said looking to the lightening sky. "Let's get going. Time is of the essence! I know the way to where we will launch the kayak. I can get us there fastest. Do you mind if I drive?" Sam asked.

"Not at all," I said, getting into the passenger seat and checking my backpack for kayaking trip essentials.

Sam briskly hopped into the driver's seat and sped north out of the resort area. We drove for less than 15 minutes when Sam pulled off onto a well-maintained dirt road. It was still dark out, but the sky was lightening into a midnight blue. I wondered what time it was, but my car's clock was broken and I was too tired to look for my dive computer to check. We wound down the bumpy road for some time. Eventually we came to a halt at the ocean front. Sam pulled off the dirt road and parked between two palm trees facing the waves.

"Here we are," Sam said, looking at the eastern sky. "This is the place to launch. It's an easy entry and the deep waters are not too far from the shore. There you will come to the first gate of attention. Now let's get going."

Stretching and yawning as I stirred, I asked Sam curiously, "What is a gate of attention anyway?"

Sam answered, "A gate of attention is a profound transformation of awareness." He paused for a moment to load four large water bottles into his backpack, and then continued, "After you pass a gate of attention, you are forever changed. You never look at life the same way. Native Americans called the gate of attention a 'vision quest.' When you pass a gate of attention, your mind is expanded by the experience. By traversing a gate of attention, you create a profound connection to the unseen-world. You are freed from the binds of conventional consciousness.

"The first gate of attention is the gate of life. Passing this gate will bring you into a greater awareness of the unity of all things. Now we must hurry so that you don't miss the gate. Timing is of the essence!" With that, Sam hastened from the car and began untying the kayak roof straps.

I opened the door and stood up unsteadily. The cool morning sky was quickly lightening into an electric blue. Sam and I readied the kayak. As I finished assembling the paddles, I asked, "Should we get the tanks and dive gear out now?"

"We won't be SCUBA diving until later," Sam said as he finished checking the kayak seatback straps. "For now, just bring your dive mask, snorkel, and fins," Sam said, opening his gear bag. "And hurry along."

I quickly gathered my gear and stuffed my towel in my backpack. Sam picked up the front of the kayak by a handle at the bow. Grabbing the handle at the stern, I tossed my gear and backpack into the rear seat and helped Sam carry the kayak and set it to sea over the craggy lava rock shore. As I hopped into the kayak, the cool ocean water splashed my legs and face, giving me goose bumps and snapping me out of tiredness.

Sam and I began paddling, easily negotiating the morning waves at the shore. We paddled out about a quarter mile at a hurried pace. Pausing for a moment and looking to the east, Sam said, "Let's move faster." We paddled speedily, heading a bit further south at a diagonal.

"Where are we rushing to?" I asked, unable to see anything in particular at the horizon.

"To the altar of the Whale God," Sam replied.

"What is the altar of the Whale God?"

"It is where you will enter the gate of attention and receive the Whale God's message."

"What is the Whale God?" I asked. "Is it the same as aumakua?"

"While the whale can be one's aumakua," Sam explained, "the Whale God is of a more universal order. The Whale God is not a totem for one. Rather, the Whale God is a universal intelligence that can aid all. The Whale God is a living force that engenders spiritual unity. When seeking spiritual knowledge, the mystics of antiquity would seek the altar of the Whale God to hear a message of truth. The message of the Whale God reveals the truth of unity. The message of the Whale God brings you beyond dualistic awareness. The message of the Whale God helps you see the greater truth of your spirit. The message of the Whale God is the first gate of attention."

I took in Sam's words, but could only ponder their deeper meaning as I pushed on, panting and trying to keep up with his fast paddle strokes. After rapidly paddling another quarter mile or so, the sun began to peek up over the northern side of the sloping volcano. Sam's pace now became slow and gentle. As the morning sunlight cast over the bow of our red kayak, we stopped paddling. My arms were tired, but the exercise had altogether revived me out of my grogginess. We rested in silence. Sam peered into the water just beyond the bow of the kayak.

"Now what?" I asked.

"Now we wait," Sam answered.

"Wait?" I griped. "But why did we rush to get out here if it was just to get here and wait?"

"Sunrise is the only time to seek a meeting with the Whale God," Sam said. "It is the altar of the Whale God."

"Here?" I asked looking around.

"Not here," Sam said, "now!" He pointed to the sun as it completely emerged from behind the volcano.

"What do you mean?"

"Just as there are places of power, there are times of power. There are times during the day that are more powerful than other times. During times of power, there's a natural energy that aids mystical practice and meditation. So this is a time of power. During this time of power, one of the many divinities one may seek is the Whale God. During this time one can entreat the universal forces of unity. We had to rush out here to where the ocean is deep enough to entreat the Whale God at sunrise."

"Is every sunrise a time of power?" I asked.

"Yes," Sam explained, "each day's sunrise is a very powerful time. In the Far East, they say sunrise is the best time for planting seeds and the most beneficial time for meditation. Meditating early in the morning starts your day in alignment with an energy of awakening, stillness, and rejuvenation. And it is only at sunrise that you may entreat the Whale God."

"Are there other times of day that are times of power?" I asked.

"Noon is a powerful time. During the noon hour there is a beautiful shift of energy. The noon hour is a very still time, yet it is a time that is filled with life. Noon is a time that is vibrant, vivid, and clear. It's nice to meditate during the noon hour as well, when you are in nature, far from the noises of the city.

"The time of sunset is very magical. As the day fades and the night comes, a mystical energy field opens. During the sunset you can feel far beyond this world into infinity. Sunset is a time of wonder. Beautiful dimensions of life open in your mind when you meditate during sunset. Sunset is a time when you can feel charged with energy and peace."

Sunset always seemed to be a magical time of day to me. I had experienced similar feelings of wonder and peace from time to time while watching the sun set. I could certainly understand why Sam called sunset a time of power.

"Then there is the most powerful time of the day," Sam said. "The latest part of the night and the earliest part of the morning. Around 4:00 am is the most still and deep time of power. At 4:00 am it is easiest to be spiritually awake although most people with their busy minds are in their deepest slumber. At 4:00 am meditation is most profound. In Buddhism we often do special meditations at this time. Your second gate of attention will be at this magical time of power."

"That's amazing," I said. "So there are times of power every day."

"And there are other stronger times of power as well," Sam said, "besides times during the day, there are also special days during the year."

"What days are these?"

"The Summer and Winter Solstices are the most powerful times of the year. The solstices are the days when the sun reaches its northernmost and southernmost extremes. They are times associated with farming, religion, and the natural cycle of seasonal extremes. They are times where the veil between the seen and unseen worlds is thin and spiritual power is more accessible.

"During the Summer Solstice the day is at its longest duration of sunlight. The Summer Solstice is a time when ancient people harvested crops and celebrated life. Meditating around the Summer Solstice is like visiting a place of power. You can transform your mind, cultivate tremendous power, and reach new levels of stillness.

"The Winter Solstice is even more powerful. The Winter Solstice is the celebration of death and transcendence. Meditating during the Winter Solstice enables you to elevate your awareness beyond the limitation of your habitual conditioned mind."

Sam continued, "Two other powerful times of the year, two of my favorite times, are the Equinoxes. The Equinoxes are the mid-points between Solstices. They are times when the center of the sun passes directly over the center of the Earth. They are times where the day and night share perfectly equal durations. The Equinoxes are times of deep balance. The Equinox is like the blue of the deep sea: peaceful, healing, empty. Meditation during the Equinox brings your mind into stillness and your spirit into profound balance.

"Another special time of power for all beings is their own birthday. Your birthday is your personal Summer Solstice. It is the time that you came into the world. It is the time you were given life. Meditation during your birthday brings you into a greater awareness of your higher nature, your personal path to truth."

Raising his pointer finger, Sam said, "Your death day is also a very powerful time. And you only get to celebrate it once per incarnation usually." Sam laughed jovially at his own joke and then continued,

"Meditation at the time of your death is said to be the highest meditation. In Buddhism there are doctrines and teachings about how to use the power of your death for spiritual advancement. In my school we celebrate the death day of my master more enduringly than his birthday. The death of an enlightened master is often referred to as their *Maha Samadhi* or final, complete Samadhi."

We sat for a moment in solemn silence. With growing curiosity, I began to peer into the depths of the water. Seeing nothing, I looked around to the horizon. "Now what?" I asked. "If this is the right time of power and we're at the altar of the Whale God, where is the Whale God? Aren't we supposed to hear the Whale God's message or something?"

"You must first entreat the Whale God," Sam said. "Fetch the fruit juice. You'll need to call the Whale God. You're going to give *torma*."

I realized that I was getting quite thirsty. Reaching into my backpack I pulled out the passion-orange-guava juice I had bought the day before and asked, "What is torma?"

"Torma is a spiritual offering used to honor and entreat enlightened forces."

"OK," I said, as I opened the juice carton and lifted it up to my mouth to sip from.

Sam reached out and gently halted my arm before the carton could reach my lips. Clearing his throat, he said, "The fruit juice is the torma."

I lowered the carton reluctantly, but then asked, "But didn't you just say that torma is a spiritual offering for enlightenment?"

"Yes," Sam answered.

"Well what does POG have to do with that?" I asked.

"Torma is a spiritual offering," Sam answered, "because torma is given with spiritual intention. Torma is commonly a decorated cake or an orange. It is put on a meditation altar in order to acknowledge all enlightening expressions of life and entreat the transcendence of limited awareness. For the altar of the Whale God, fruit juice is a more suitable offering."

"Why do we give torma to the Whale God?"

"When you give torma to divine forces like the Whale God, you nourish the presence of awakened activity in your own experience. Torma is your spiritual offering to the Whale God that honors and petitions the Whale God to help you. The enlightening expression of the Whale God's message can then be heard. It is through the purity of your intent in giving torma that will bring the Whale God to come meet you. The message of the Whale God will open as an enlightening influence in your life."

"OK," I said, "how do I give torma?"

"Let me show you," Sam said, putting his hand out for the POG.

I handed Sam the POG. Sam held it toward the west. He closed his eyes and then slowly spilled a few ounces of juice into the ocean in a circular motion. Sam then bowed solemnly and handed the POG back to me.

"Now it's your turn," Sam said. "Offer this torma to the Whale God from your heart. Acknowledge the Whale God as a universal force of unity. Honor the Whale God as an enlightening expression of life. With humility and sincerity, call the Whale God to help you."

I closed my eyes. I followed Sam's directions, but felt that I somehow lacked sincerity. I sat quietly for a minute or two pondering the spirit of intent I felt in Sam's words and tone. A great brightness began to open in my heart. I felt that it was a giving light, that it was a light from my heart to give to the Whale God. I poured the POG into the sea as I focused on the light. "Please help me," I called out inaudibly and then bowed. The brightness subsided. I looked down and saw the cloudy yellow juice vanishing in the blue of the seas.

"You did very well," Sam said with an assuring smile.

"The Whale God is coming," Sam said looking out toward the west. "Now that you have entreated the Whale God with the purity of your torma at the proper time of power, you must quiet your mind. Quiet your mind and you will hear the Whale God's message. Only a quiet mind devoid of thoughts and impressions can hear this message."

Sam invited me to meditate with him. We sat meditating for about an hour. I didn't hear anything that sounded like a whale, but I felt a beautiful peace while gliding in the kayak over the gentle ocean waves, and meditating at that powerful early hour. After we had completed our meditation, Sam and I paddled north to reposition the kayak. We had drifted south in a peaceful current while meditating.

"Now that we have meditated and your mind is more still," Sam said. "Go into the water to see if you can hear the Whale God's message."

I looked into the water, but was unable to see anything but the fathomless blue. "What's going to happen?" I asked. I felt a little uneasy, remembering Michael's picture of the 50-foot humpback.

"The Whale God will bring you his message of unity," Sam answered, "and if you can hear it, you will have passed the gate of attention."

"What if I can't hear it?" I questioned. "Or what if I don't understand his message?"

"Then you won't pass the gate and there will be nothing more for you to learn from me for now."

"This seems very arbitrary!" I protested, fearing failure.

"Actually, it's very precise. The more still your mind, the easier it will be for you to hear his message. The Whale God's message is a communication of unity. It is a message that shows the profound connection between you and eternity. In the presence of the Whale God, when your mind is quiet and you hear his message, you will realize that connection. Realizing that connection itself is passing the gate. So go ahead. Dive down. Still your mind and seek the Whale God's message now."

I was a little bewildered, but I prepared my dive mask and fins. I looked into the water again, but saw no sign of a whale. Then I jumped in and swam around looking for a sign of a whale. The water was refreshing, but I didn't hear or see anything.

"What should I do now?" I asked Sam, finning closer to the kayak.

"Swim underwater," Sam said, "swim deep, still your mind, and listen."

I took a deep breath and began to swim underwater. I went down about 12 feet and then looked around. Still, I couldn't hear anything and didn't see anything but blue water.

I ascended and continued with my search. I swam, stilling my mind, and looking for the Whale God underwater. From time to time I would hold my breath and dive beneath the surface and listen for the Whale God, but I could hear nothing. While catching my breath at the surface, Sam invited me to take a break. Quite exhausted, I accepted.

Sam signaled me to come back toward him in the kayak. I swam back and rested holding both arms onto the edge of the kayak.

"Your mind must be still to hear the Whale God's message," he said quietly yet emphatically. "While you are in the water your mind is far too active. There is an exercise I can teach you that will help you still your mind in the water."

Pointing just ahead of the kayak's bow, Sam said, "Swim over here and I'll explain how to do the exercise." I repositioned my mask and swam out to the front of the kayak.

Sam began with his instructions, "Breathe slowly. Breathe deeply. Relax your body with your face down, breathing from your snorkel."

I slowed my breathing and loosened the tensions of my body as I floated face down, looking into the impossibly deep blue water.

"Inhale fully," Sam continued, "and exhale completely. Slow, complete, relaxed respirations."

I increased my lung volume during inhalations and pushed the air out more completely during exhalations. This slow respiration was not uncomfortable, but required my complete focus.

"Breathe to your navel chakra. As you inhale, envision an orange sphere of light in your navel center. See the orange light as about the size of a golf ball. See the orange sphere slightly expanding as you inhale.

"As you exhale the air from your navel, envision that the orange sphere of light decreases in size slightly, but intensifies in its brightness. Breathe with this focus for another 15 minutes or so."

I heard Sam's instructions and I was comfortable with the breathing exercise, but I didn't really understand how to envision an orange sphere of light in my navel. I practiced the slow, deep breathing until Sam signaled me to end. I felt relaxed and invigorated from the breathing, but I was able to hold the vision of an orange sphere of light for no more than a few seconds.

Sam helped me get back into the kayak. "I don't think I did that exercise correctly," I said. "I couldn't hold a vision of an orange sphere of light and I didn't hear the Whale God."

"Actually," Sam said, "you're making progress. It takes some practice to see the orange sphere of light. Yet didn't you feel positive energy after doing the exercise for a while? Even if you can't see the orange sphere of light consistently, your earnest effort produces very positive results."

"Yes," I said. "I did feel invigorated after the exercise. I noticed it most strongly just after I got back into the kayak. I thought it was all because I was relaxed and breathing deeply, since I couldn't see the orange sphere of light very well."

"Relaxation and deep breathing are certainly concurrent physical aspects of this exercise," Sam said, "yet I think you'll see the greater power of the orange sphere of light as you continue to practice and get better with your focus. This meditation will draw you into the stillness of mind that you need in order to hear the Whale God's message."

Pausing and looking into the sea, Sam said, "Now let's meditate again. Once you still your mind in sitting meditation, you can then take your swimming meditation to the next level."

We sat for another long meditation session. Upon finishing, I felt exceptionally still.

Sam invited me to jump into the water with a hand gesture as he put on his fins. I readied my dive mask and fins. Before I had put on my second fin, Sam had already plunged into the water. When I joined him in the cool morning water, Sam said, "Now let's breathe, slowly, deeply. Envision the orange sphere of light." With that Sam put his face down in the water and began breathing deeply through his snorkel.

I relaxed my shoulders and rested forward in the water. I was soon breathing deeply and calmly. After a few more minutes my focus on my navel center felt very strong. Although I couldn't envision the orange sphere of light very well, I had a very strong sensation of a buzzing warmth in my navel chakra.

As I continued to practice deep breathing with the orange sphere of light focus, I saw Sam dive below the water. Sam had one hand at his mask so he could pinch his nose to clear his ears. His other hand was extended far in front of him. Sam dived very deep. He kicked downward with long powerful strides. His form became very faint in my vision before he stopped his descent. He appeared to hang motionless in the water for an incredibly long time. A moment later, he expelled a mouthful of air. Sam remained motionless for another few seconds and then started for the surface. He made long curving dolphin kicks that arched his whole body as he ascended with his left arm extended. I lifted my head and watched as he breached the surface.

Breathing heavily, Sam said, "Now it's your turn. Continue with your deep breathing, relaxation, and orange sphere focus. When you feel comfortable, hold your breath and dive. No hyperventilation, just breathe how you have been practicing. Descend as I did, to a comfortable depth. At your deepest depth, expel most of your air with a strong focus on the orange sphere. Then ascend as I did."

"OK," I said. I put my face forward in the water, and continued breathing deeply through my snorkel. After a few slow respirations, I held my breath and dived just as Sam had. I dived about 20 feet below the surface, holding my breath. I looked up to see the surface. Then, remembering the exercise, I expelled most of my air while focusing on my navel chakra and the orange sphere of light. To my surprise, I was able to see the orange sphere of light clearly, as if in my mind's eye. The vision seemed somehow almost tangible. The orange sphere of light became brighter as I exhaled.

I quickly started for the surface, feeling the need for air. As I neared the surface, the clear, distant song of a whale came softly to my ears. I jolted excitedly, thinking that the Whale God was here to give me his message. I looked down, frantically searching to find the origin of the whale's song, but could not make out the form of a whale in the deep of the blue water. The whale's song faded off into the distance.

As I came up, I exclaimed, "I heard the song of a whale! Was it the Whale God's message?"

Sam shook his head and said, "Don't let excitement break the quiet of your mind. You are making good progress, but you'll have to be more still and unshaken to hear the Whale God's message. Continue your meditative breath-hold diving exercise."

I again relaxed my body and began slow, deep respirations. My focus on my navel center was strong and the vision of orange light grew in my imagination. With a full inhalation, I pulled in and dove down, clearing my ears frequently. As I floated 20 feet beneath the surface, I peered into the empty depths of the blue ocean. Exhaling through my mouth I clearly envisioned the orange light of my navel brightening. At that moment, I again heard the song of the whale. This time it was louder than before. I looked around, but still saw nothing. I needed air and kicked to the surface.

Lifting my head from the water I called to Sam, "The whale song is much louder." Suddenly, about 100 yards to the west of our red kayak, a humpback whale leaped high from the ocean! The whale breached the surface of the sea and rose more than half way out of the water before crashing down.

"Is that him?" I asked excitedly. "Is that the Whale God?"

"No," said Sam, whose eyes showed that he was nonetheless delighted, "that's a beautiful whale, but not the Whale God. But the time is nearing. Let's take a break so you can catch your breath and calm down. We'll do more of this exercise later."

Sam and I climbed into the kayak. We sat quietly as the sun rose up, high in the sky. We rested and warmed up in the tropical heat.

I wondered about Sam and his interesting life. When I first saw him, I thought he was a local diver and that I had him all figured out, but now I realized that I didn't know much about him at all except that he was a SCUBA diving Buddhist monk, who also did software.

"Where do you live?" I asked Sam.

"Here and there," Sam answered, "I move around a lot for my business."

"Like where? Where are you staying now?" I asked.

"Well, for the past month and a half, I've been staying here in Hawaii," Sam answered. "I do a lot of business in Honolulu from time to time as well. My business takes me from San Francisco to Chicago, Tokyo, and to Budapest."

"What is your race?" I asked Sam pointedly.

"Human," Sam answered.

"I mean, what nationality are you?" I asked, restating my question.

"American."

More precise with my nomenclature, I asked, "You know, I mean, what is your ethnicity?"

"Many things," Sam said. "You know how they say America is a melting pot? Well, I am the result of the melting."

Sam's vague answer only stoked my curiosity more. *Maybe he's not Tibetan, but he must also be mixed with Asian,* I thought.

"One of the few things that I'm not mixed with is Asian," Sam said answering my next question before I asked it.

"Really?" I said. "Because I always thought that you were Asian. You know, since you're a Buddhist monk and all."

Sam shook his head saying, "You must be seeing my past lives. But really, you don't have to be Asian to be a Buddhist monk. People have such narrow views of what qualifies as spiritual.

"Many people in the West associate spirituality with exotic Far Eastern traditions and cultures. They think that studying a different culture's view of spirituality is somehow more authentic than the truth of their own experience. They often find themselves getting confused between the spiritual aspects of the teachings and the cultural customs involved in the study.

"The truth of the Buddha's teachings contains principles that are universal for all beings. They worked for the Buddha in India before working in the Shaolin temple in China. As well, they worked in the Zen tradition of Japan before they came to America. And the universal principles of life are certainly applicable in our culture. The Buddha taught the truth of life. And the truth of life is as evident right here, right now, as it was in any of the cultures of the great saints and spiritual masters of the past."

Sam continued, "In the same way that you don't have to be Asian to be a monk, you don't have to be a man to attain enlightenment. Even more complicated than cultural confusions about spirituality are the misconceptions of gender and spirituality."

"Really?" I questioned. "What do you mean?"

"If there was a blond gal wearing jeans and a t-shirt meditating," Sam answered, "many would think that she's just some New Age hippie, but if they saw a grey-haired Indian man meditating in robes and a turban, many would think he's somehow special, different, and spiritual. However, the truth could be quite the opposite.

"One very detrimental aspect of culturally prejudiced spirituality occurs when women seek spirituality in traditions of the Far East. Women are often hindered in achieving their potential through these traditions. The cultures in which many of these spiritual traditions are based are very oppressive toward women. Eastern spiritual traditions have changed after the passing of their founders. They have become modified in tone and sometimes even corrupted by the male-dominated conditions of their cultures."

"Really?" I asked again. "That's hard to believe about traditions and schools that teach spiritual enlightenment."

"Is it?" Sam asked. "By the time Buddha passed away he had as many female students as male students. Yet these days there may be only 1 Buddhist nun for every 1000 monks. Spirituality of the Far East has become a boys' club. The spiritual schools of India, Tibet, and Japan by and large do not teach enlightenment for women. The traditions of the Far East often teach that a woman's greatest spiritual progress in this life is to have gained the good karma to be reborn in their next life as a man so that they can then perhaps attain enlightenment. Even Eastern teachers teaching in the West promote this view subtly, though they may have women students."

Sam paused for a moment. "Luckily, the West is much more progressive towards the possibility of rights, vocation, and liberties for women. In my lineage of spirituality, enlightenment for women is a principal concentration.

"Spirituality does not come from the clothes you wear, the gender you happen to be, or the color of your skin. Spirituality comes from meditation, stilling your mind, stopping your thoughts, and seeing the truth of your nature, the nature of life.

"In my Buddhist lineage, monks don't wear robes. I only have a shaved head because I think it looks good. And very importantly for you, in my Buddhist lineage, at least half of the monks are women. Several women in my *sangha*, or spiritual order, are enlightened. Many more of the women from my school experience Samadhi regularly."

I felt very inspired by Sam's words. But a moment later, I realized that he had never really answered my questions about his background. Determined to find answers, I asked, in a rapid burst, "What did your parents think about you becoming a monk? When did you become a monk? And how old are you? Are you really old, but you look young?"

Sam laughed and shook his head. "You know all that you need to know about me. And everything that you've told me about yourself was offered by you. This kind of respect is one of the most important qualities of Buddhist etiquette. You don't need to figure me out in order to learn from me. You should be more concerned about passing the gate of attention with the Whale God.

"The noon hour is near," Sam said. "Let's take advantage of this time of power and do another meditation session."

I gave up on learning more about Sam and consented. I put on my long-sleeved shirt, my sunhat, and more sunscreen. I felt warm and peaceful in the midday sun.

As we meditated, I felt the greatest peace. My mind felt beautifully still and tranquil. I was aware of the kayak, the ocean, and the coastal breeze, yet all things seemed to join together in a beautiful balance of being. After what felt like moments, I realized that my legs had fallen asleep. I shifted them so that the blood could circulate better. I also started to notice that I was getting hungry. I opened my eyes to check the position of the sun, and to my surprise, the sun was already heading toward the horizon. At that moment, Sam bowed.

"That was a beautifully peaceful meditation," I said after bowing.

Sam smiled serenely.

I was very hungry now. I opened my backpack to retrieve our food for a late lunch. I quickly devoured a whole container of ahi poke. My appetite had grown from all of my swimming, diving, and paddling. It seem like this was the most delicious poke I had ever had. Sam also looked satisfied after finishing his meal.

After our late lunch, Sam and I sat quietly looking out to sea. I started thinking about Buddhism and SCUBA diving. "It's kind of funny that you are a SCUBA-diving Buddhist monk," I said. "I mean, that's unusual as far as monks go, isn't it? How did this come about in your Buddhist school?

"Oops!" I said. I felt like I had just slipped. I hoped Sam wouldn't be upset by my asking another intruding question. "Sorry," I said, "I didn't mean to pry again."

Sam seemed unperturbed by my question and said, "No need for an apology. It is fine and proper that you ask questions that pertain to Buddhism, meditation, and Mystic SCUBA. How else do you expect to learn anything?"

With a supportive smile, Sam explained, "It is appropriate for your learning that you know about how the art of Mystic SCUBA has evolved into its current form.

"When my fellow monks and I had become proficient in our basic practices of meditation as intermediate students of Buddhism, my Buddhist teacher, who was an authentic *Rinpoche*, told all of us to get PADI Open Water Diver certifications as part of our spiritual practice. And that's how it began."

"What's a Rinpoche?" I asked.

"Rinpoche means 'blessed one' in Tibetan. A Rinpoche traditionally is one who has intentionally taken rebirth in this world to help people on the pathway to enlightenment. Rinpoche is a title similar to priest. My teacher was a genuine Rinpoche. He has passed away. He has entered his Maha Samadhi."

I nodded solemnly.

Sam went on, "From time to time my teacher would give odd or sometimes outlandish tasks to his students. These tasks outwardly didn't seem to be in line with traditional Buddhist teachings, yet when we engaged in these tasks, we found them to be spiritually profound teachings. SCUBA diving was one of these odd tasks. We came to appreciate our teacher's hidden methods for enlightenment.

"After a deep Solstice meditation, my teacher decided he needed to learn to SCUBA dive. From that day on, he dove quite often and became a Divemaster. He reported the many beneficial spiritual effects that he experienced during his dives to his students. Sometimes he would say, 'You can't even imagine the worlds of light I see down there!' My fellow monks and I were eager to learn to dive after hearing of our teacher's marvelous experiences.

"So I went about it much like anyone else. I found a local dive shop and signed up for classes. I did my confined water training and dive theory on the mainland, but did my Open Water Diver check-out dives in the Bahamas.

"Upon completing my certification, I was eager to do a fun exploratory dive. It was during my first SCUBA dive, directly after I became certified, when I realized why my Buddhist master gave us this spiritual exercise. Several other monks and I dived at a beautiful site the next morning. I was still a bit uncomfortable, but I was happy to explore a new spiritual activity. I remember being amazed that there were so many beautifully colored fish everywhere. I was also amazed by the splendor of the colorful coral formations. Everything under the sea looked so foreign to me.

"Everything seemed alive, though I couldn't identify much of what I saw. There were things that looked like coral but then would start swimming. There were things that resembled leaves or plants that I had seen on land, but I knew that they couldn't be down underwater. What I know now to be nudibranchs, sea apples, and sponges baffled my imagination.

"As we toured the Caribbean coral reef, I felt euphoric! Then suddenly, the scene changed. The coral reef that spread limitlessly before me came to an end. There was nothing beyond the reef. My buddy and I came to the edge of a wall. I peeked over the wall and saw coral formations reaching down as far as I could see into the deep blue. I was awed by the beauty of the terrifying drop-off.

"After some time facing this hidden, primordial fear, I eventually mustered the presence of mind to swim over the edge and descend. As I descended over the edge, I felt tremendously alive and beyond fear. I looked into the deep formless blue waters and recognized the powerful truth of my own mind.

"I then understood why my Buddhist teacher was also a Divemaster, and why he had his students learn SCUBA diving: to dive into enlightenment!"

I listened closely to Sam's words, captivated by the beauty of his story.

Sam smiled broadly. He looked toward the horizon. "The Whale God is very near. Now is the time for perfect meditation." Sam and I began meditating again as the sun drew lower towards the horizon. After a long, deep meditation, we sat quietly, looking into the darkening blue waters.

Sunset was nearing. Sam and I sat in the kayak watching the sun descend in the sky, just minutes from plunging into the sea. "The Whale God is here!" Sam said suddenly. He immediately put on his mask and fins. I followed, quickly putting on my mask and fins as well, while looking out and around for any sign of a whale. Sam and I both dropped into the water.

"Quiet your mind," Sam said. "Practice the orange sphere of light exercise."

I began deep relaxed breathing. I envisioned the luminous orange light of my navel clearly. After a few full respirations, Sam swung his fins up and dived. Completing my full inhalation, I followed Sam's lead into the deep. Sam stopped at about 30 feet and became motionless. I swam toward Sam where he floated facing the deep.

As I descended, I could hear the beginning of a beautiful, booming whale song. The song was so loud; it seemed the whale should be very close. Reaching Sam, I became still, gazing down into the ocean's blue depths. After a long quiet moment, I began to exhale. My thoughts were still and the orange sphere of light in my navel glowed in my mind like burning embers.

Low on air, I moved into position to ascend, but before my first ascending kick, Sam grabbed me by my shoulder and turned me towards him. Startled, I looked at him questioningly. Sam pointed back down in the direction that we had been originally facing. To my utter surprise, 20 feet beneath me was a massive humpback whale!

For a split-second, I felt tremendous fear and considered kicking for the surface, but after that initial feeling, I fell into an amazing awe of the majestic animal in front of me.

The whale floated in front of me. I could clearly see one of his large eyes. He just hung before me completely still and looked at me.

His presence mesmerized me. Part of it was just how enormous he was and how clearly I could see his features: the deep folds of his jaw, his huge mouth, his long back and magnificent tail. But really, what struck me was beyond his physical appearance. As we looked at one another, the whale called out in a delicate song. I felt a profound sense of peace. The whole world was perfect and blissful.

After a timeless moment of serenity and awe, the whale sank away back down toward the deep. I quickly looked back to Sam on my left. Sam bowed toward the whale. Then I looked back to the right. The whale was gone. *How could it disappear from sight so quickly?* I wondered. A moment later, I heard the beautiful whale song again, fading off into silence.

All of a sudden, I realized I needed air! I bolted up toward the surface. As I breached the waves gasping for air, I felt a tremendous joy. With exclamations of elation, I popped back into the red kayak. Sam surfaced and joined me. The sun was now just over the water.

"The Whale God was amazing!" I exclaimed.

"Congratulations," Sam said brightly, "you have passed the first gate of attention. Now look to the horizon. At this time of power we may see the miracle of the Whale God."

We sat and watched in silence as the bottom of the sun met with the ocean surface at the horizon. At that very moment, a whale jumped from the sea. It was very far off in the distance, but I could see every detail of the whale clearly. The whale breached the surface of the water and emerged directly in the line of the sun.

It looked as if the whale had jumped into the center of the sun! The whale, even its tail, had completely exited the water for a split second. The whale's body pressed high into the sky, almost perpendicular to the sea. My heart lifted as the whale seemed to fly out of the ocean. At his greatest height, I could see a flash of sunlight just below the bottom of his tail. I was astounded by the leap. The whale seemed to hang in the sky above the water for a magical moment. My heart seemed to be suspended above my being, illuminated in some magical place.

Then the whale came crashing down. There was a giant white splash of water. A golden spray filled the air, illuminated by the rays of the setting sun. I watched in wonder and amazement as the golden sun set into the sea.

"I've never seen a whale jump completely out of the water!"

"That is the miracle of the Whale God." Turning his attention back to shore, Sam said, "Now we'd better paddle to shore before dark."

As we paddled in, I was elated. I kept looking back to see any sign of the Whale God breaching the surface again. The sky glowed with a warm pink blush that faded to a radiant purple. I was tired from such a long day at sea, but seeing the Whale God face-to-face and then watching him jump into the sun was absolutely extraordinary! Upon reaching the shore, it had grown dark. Sam and I stowed the kayak and drove back to the Four Seasons.

After I helped Sam get his dive gear from my car, he handed me another DVD to take home and watch. This one had pictures of whales on the cover.

"Why do you have me watch so many movies?" I asked him.

"Films can be artistic expressions of very profound aspects of life," Sam answered. "By watching films, we can learn about many beneficial facets of existence that we don't experience normally in life. In the Buddhist tradition, as in many other spiritual traditions, stories are told to teach students to look at life in different ways. From the Indian *yantras*, to Zen *koans*, and Tibetan reenactments of the Buddha's stories, Buddhism has always used art and storytelling as an essential part of teaching. Films are the most effective modern day art form of storytelling. There are not many Buddhist movies, but mystics can learn many lessons from films or any art form that expresses and reflects the truth of life. Film is art. And art is magic! A good film can transport you to a deeper understanding of life."

I nodded thoughtfully, then yawned, covering my mouth.

Sam chuckled and said, "You must be getting tired. Please drive home safely. Get plenty of rest tonight and then come meet me here tomorrow."

I agreed and said good night to Sam. He bowed in return, and headed for his suite, pulling his dive gear bag behind him.

I was tired by the time I got home, but my curiosity about the film Sam gave me overruled my desire to sleep. I quickly washed up, changed into my pajamas, and started watching the DVD in bed. The film was about an Ocean Tribe and their Whale God. In the movie, a young Maori girl was chosen by the Whale God to be the spiritual leader of her people. I was deeply moved by the film. I felt the whale that the Maori girl rode upon in the film to be the very same Whale God I had met earlier. The plight of the girl to live up to her spiritual potential in a society that limited spirituality for women showed me something profound about my own spiritual path and about what Sam had told me about many of the old traditions of spirituality being closed to women.

When the film ended, I felt inspired. I put on one of my favorite Disney movies. It was a film that I had seen many times. I only watched one of the beginning scenes: a delightful animation featuring flying humpback whales. I felt as if I was transported back into the world of the Whale God while watching the film.

After the feature, I turned the film off, and thought about what Sam had said about the magic of movies. I had indeed learned a new perspective in which to understand women's spirituality from the first film, and the Disney movie helped me to recall the great joy of being with the Whale God.

THE SHARK CHIEF

By the time I arrived at Sam's hotel suite the next day, it was already late in the morning. Sam had left a note on his door asking me to meet him on the beach in front of his patio. I walked around the building to the beach. I found Sam playing in the waves. Actually, he was just kind of crashing up on shore like a piece of driftwood. His body was limp, but his snorkel was positioned just above the rolling waves. When I stood closer, I could see that a few feet to Sam's right were two green sea turtles feeding in the shore break. They were peacefully swaying in the waves just like Sam. Noticing me, Sam looked up and said, "Good morning. Get your mask and join us."

I retrieved my mask and snorkel and joined Sam in the shore break. I did as Sam and the turtles did; relaxed just before where the waves broke on shore. I was pushed up slightly onto the sand by the waves, but then the water would draw me back out. I was able to relax and breathe comfortably from my snorkel. Sam and I just sat there moving with the ebb and flow of the waves for over an hour. It was deeply relaxing and exceptionally fun. After some time, the turtles finished eating loose algae in the shore break and swam back out to sea.

Sam and I crawled onto shore. We lay in the sun drying off for a few minutes, and then went to one of the resort's restaurants for lunch.

"What would you do today if this were your last day alive?" Sam asked me as we ate a hearty lunch.

"Well, I don't really know," I answered. "I think I'd be quite happy spending it with you learning about the spiritual side of my life." I thought about all the amazing experiences I had had with Sam, and realized that I really would choose to spend my last day on another adventure with him.

"Are all of your affairs in order?" Sam asked. "If you were to disappear from the face of the earth tonight, would you have taken care of your accounts and left your relationships settled properly?"

"Well, I don't know," I answered. "Maybe, my accounts are OK, but if I were really going to die tonight, I'd really like to tell my friends and family how I really feel about them so that they are clear on my love for them when I'm gone."

Sam nodded, "You must live every moment of your life as if it was your last. That way you will never take things for granted, never be messy and confused about your relationships, and never miss seeing life as whole and complete in this moment.

"Passing the first gate of attention is somewhat challenging in that you must still your mind completely in order to hear the Whale God's message, but the first gate of attention is altogether easy because the Whale God is benevolent, inviting, and harmless. Tonight, you shall seek the second gate of attention, the gate of the Shark Chief. The Shark Chief has a great power, but is in no way harmless. Seeking the second gate of attention will be the most perilous of undertakings. Tonight, facing the Shark Chief you will face death directly."

I listened at the edge of my seat. In crossing the first gate of attention, I had an encounter with a humpback whale. *What is going to happen to me?* I wondered. *If I face death meeting the Shark Chief, does that mean that I will come face-to-face with one of the dreaded man-eating tiger sharks of the Hawaiian coasts?*

"Is the Shark Chief also a universal force for enlightenment like the Whale God?" I asked aloud.

"Yes," Sam answered.

I was relieved! My experience with the Whale God was a bit frightening, but immeasurably beautiful.

"After lunch," Sam said, "I'd like you to write some letters. Tell your friends and family how you really feel. Clear your mind of unfinished business. This is how a Buddhist mystic faces oblivion."

After lunch, I wrote letters to many friends and all of my immediate family. I sat in Sam's living room writing my testaments on Four Seasons post cards and stationary. It was hard telling some of my friends and family what they meant to me. Tears came to my eyes several times. Sam told me to take my time and to be complete in the communications of my heart. I ended up spending hours writing my thoughts and feelings down.

In addition to writing to my family and friends from home, I wrote a letter to Genet for her to read to my ten boys, encouraging them to work very hard in school and to pursue all of their dreams in life. I addressed envelopes and Sam gave me some stamps for them.

I also remembered a couple of accounts that needed to be settled. I used Sam's laptop to connect to the internet and pay off an outstanding bill, and wire some money to repay a small loan from a friend. Sam told me to also pay off my credit cards if I could, so I did.

Considering my finances to be strong enough, I wired another $100 to

Genet. E-mailing her, I told her that I wanted her to give the money to Mulu, a young mother of two whom I'd met through my aid work. Mulu's need for the capital to start a small business was foremost in my mind. Mulu's husband had died of tuberculosis and she was struggling to raise her three and four year old children. Mulu had learned from her mother how to weave traditional Ethiopian baskets. She wanted to work with a friend, another poor mother, to open a shop, making and selling woven items. She needed money to buy materials, tools, and a cart. She had calculated that together they could make enough money in this business to support both families.

When I was done, I felt complete. I felt as if a weight was lifted from my shoulders and that the holes in my being were now somehow knit together or filled. I closed Sam's laptop.

"Now, you are prepared," Sam said.

We meditated in Sam's living room. I felt still and awake. After our meditation, the sun was low in the horizon. Sam readied his things to leave.

Getting into Sam's Jeep, we drove south in silence. It was a long drive from the Four Seasons in the north to the southernmost point of the island. This was an area where I had never been. There was little development here and mostly dirt roads. We meandered down the rocky roads of the South Shore to a craggy beach.

"This is the just-right dive site," Sam said. "Here we will await the altar of the Shark Chief."

I nodded in acknowledgement and peered out into the twilight waters. The sun had set and the night was setting in. Sam and I assembled our SCUBA gear, pulled on our wetsuits half-way, and sat in the sand facing the darkening night.

We sat quietly for some time. Then I nervously asked, "What is our dive plan tonight?"

"At the altar of the Shark Chief," Sam said, "we'll enter the ocean from that sandy embankment by the palm trees." Sam pointed near to the right with his flashlight and continued, "Then we'll kick out a short distance to the north. There we will turn our lights off and descend. We will descend to 130 feet and you'll await the message of the Shark Chief there."

"Descend to 130 feet in the dark?" I asked nervously.

"Yes, of course," Sam said, "the light of your flashlight would surely deter the Shark Chief from approaching you. Light would ward off her power. We must descend in the dark and keep our lights off until well after we have met the Shark Chief.

"From where we descend, there is a sandy embankment below us at 130 feet, so we'll just drop until we reach the bottom. We will check our air one last time at the surface and hold our lights on our gauges so that the numbers and needles will glow slightly while we descend. We will be on the bottom for only a few minutes. In that time, you will face the Shark Chief and hear her message.

"What is the Shark Chief's message?" I asked.

"Death," Sam replied.

"Death!" I exclaimed. "That can't be good."

"Death and life," Sam said, "are two sides of the same coin. In Buddhism we face and learn about death so that we can know life more fully."

"The Shark Chief's message is the message of destruction," Sam continued. "When you descend to face the Shark Chief, you will be destroyed. The second gate of attention is the gate of death."

Death? I wondered. *Would Sam really put me in harm's way?*

"What exactly is going to happen to me when the Shark Chief appears?"

"Her wrath will destroy you," Sam explained. "You will enter into a different dimension at the altar of the Shark Chief. Things may appear differently to you down there as you descend into that primal power. But fear not, your aumakua will be with you as a force of protection. Though you will have all of the assistance and protection in the world from me and your totem, you will be destroyed without a doubt! However, it's up to you and you alone as to which 'you' will be destroyed. Or you might say it is your choice what part of you will be destroyed by the Shark Chief."

"Choice?"

"Yes. You must make a choice when you are confronted by the Shark Chief. You must choose either the bright truth of the unseen-world that you have learned while with me, or the illusion of your habitual life. You must choose the illumination of your spirit or the darkness of self-reaction and limitation.

"But in that moment choose carefully. The Shark Chief uses the power of her wrath to destroy what is not dharma. When your spirit is sided with truth, the Shark Chief will destroy and remove obstacles to enlightenment within you so that you rapidly transform and grow, forever free of the conditioned habits of mind that close your spirit from greater awareness. But if more of you sides with your limited sense of self, which is not dharma, the Shark Chief will take your life as she takes your darkness.

"Either way you learn a powerful spiritual lesson because the Shark

Chief is a great teacher of detachment from the dark. However, if you die, you won't get initiation or experience Samadhi in this life.

"If you do die, at the moment of death the Shark Chief will show you the folly of your choice and with that realization, you will be liberated from those very limitations and pass the second gate of attention into your next incarnation."

"Well, how do I choose? What if I panic?" I asked, considering the terror of coming face-to-face with a tiger shark at night in 130 feet of water.

"If you panic, you will die," Sam said. "You must side with your light, your power! You have learned mystical exercises that expand your awareness into peace, beauty, and balance. These techniques are powerful and can keep you from any harm on this dive. You must use this training. Be balanced. Have no fear. Choose light and the dharma, just as you did on the mantra dive the other day when you saved your own life in the strong current."

Mustering my courage, I said, "I can do it! I will choose the truth, the dharma!"

"That is false," Sam responded. "I am not saying that you won't choose the dharma. I am saying that you don't yet know what will happen, and how you will react. You have a false feeling of ability and control. This is your ego's reaction. You desire to win and gain, yet you greatly fear death.

"This kind of reaction will surely end your life tonight! It is quite similar to your reaction to losing your regulator, and your confidence of being safe diving alone the first day we met. Then, you didn't know what it would actually be like to lose your regulator, stuck on a reef. Tonight you don't know what it's going to be like facing the wrath of the Shark Chief. Drop this attitude at once. It will be as useful to you now as it was the day we met.

"Buddhist mystics take tremendous chances with their lives, but never recklessly. The crux of mysticism is to choose light in the face of tremendous adversity. The only truth that is certain right now is that you are ready for this opportunity."

I nodded meekly, fearful of what was going to happen.

"The ultimate fear is the fear of death," Sam said. "You fear the destruction of yourself, the end of your being. Yet this great terror arises from an even greater misconception. Death is not the end of being. Death is the doorway to greater being, new life. In Buddhism we constantly seek death in the most enlightened and constructive ways.

"Meditation is the essential practice of death. We stop our thoughts so that we can experience a greater truth, an eternity of awareness beyond the limitation of thought. Stopping thought is death. Stopping thought is the death of the self. Remember what the Buddha said, 'We are what we think. All that we are arises with our thoughts.' Meditation is the death of thoughts, that which we, the self of limited identity, arises from. We seek that death in meditation. That death leads to the end of limited awareness. That death leads to the end of suffering. That death is enlightenment. This is why meditation is the essence of all spiritual practice. Meditation is facing the death of the separate self directly, as you will face the Shark Chief tonight.

"SCUBA diving is an excellent practice for facing death. In every dive you enter an atmosphere that means death to your body. Yet, in every dive you experience life more directly because your awareness of death is in mind. The first realization you gain in SCUBA diving comes when you inhale from your regulator for the first time underwater. You realize that a place of death can be transcended. The next realization you gain in SCUBA diving comes when you do your first dive. You see the fish, coral, and the splendor of all life of the marine world. You realize that a place of death can afford new views of life.

"When people face death with fear, they are closing their awareness to the tremendous possibilities of life. When you face death with awareness and balance, unafraid, you experience life more directly. During the dive when you almost drowned, stuck on a coral overhang with your regulator free-flowing behind you, you experienced the limited awareness of fear. The other day, when you were being pulled out over the wall in the strong current, you overcame fear by focusing on your mystical techniques.

"Tonight when you face the Shark Chief, you will directly face your ultimate fear: death. Through your Mystic SCUBA disciplines, you will attempt to transcend that ultimate fear and experience the power of death in a way that forever changes your awareness of life.

"In Buddhism, we learn to face death constructively, just like we do in SCUBA diving. Side with light when you face the Shark Chief. You are learning to overcome death, the fear of death, the view of death being an end. You are coming to learn how to work with the power of death in an enlightening way that leads to limitless life and liberated awareness."

I was determined to side with light.

Sam and I sat for a long time in a deep meditation. After completing our meditation session and bowing, Sam stood up and walked to the water's edge. I stretched out my crossed legs, stood, and joined him. I felt a tingling sensation in my legs as the blood began to circulate again. "Now is the time to entreat the Shark Chief," Sam said, "Get the torma. We are at the altar of the Shark Chief."

I stepped back and retrieved the POG from where I had packed it in my dive gear bag. I handed Sam the POG carton. Sam opened it and held the POG solemnly facing the sea. Sam's eyes were closed. He slowly poured some of the juice into the ocean waves at his feet. Sam then bowed silently and handed the POG carton back to me saying, "Offer this torma to the Shark Chief. Acknowledge the Shark Chief as a universal force of destruction. Honor the Shark Chief as an enlightening expression of death. With humility and sincerity, call the Shark Chief to help you."

I closed my eyes and followed Sam's directions for giving torma to the Shark Chief. I began stilling my mind. A grave awareness of nourishing my own destruction arose in me. This feeling seemed somehow healthy, as if I was letting go of a bad habit. I poured the POG into the sea, saying inwardly, *Please help me, Shark Chief.* I bowed solemnly. I closed the juice carton and put it back in my gear bag.

"The Shark Chief is very near," Sam said looking out into the dark ocean. "Now that you have entreated the Shark Chief with your torma at the proper time of power, all you must do is confront her in the deep."

We prepared for our dive. Sam and I donned our SCUBA gear. With our flashlights on, we walked down to the rocky beach. We entered the water over worn-down lava rocks. We kicked out a short distance from shore. When we stopped, Sam spent some time checking our positioning. He shined his flashlight toward the land. We were lined up with the Jeep. Sam momentarily shined his light down into the water. We were at the edge of an underwater wall. The bottom dropped off steeply. The beam of light from Sam's flashlight faded into the deep, so I couldn't see farther than 60 feet down.

We checked our air and illumined our gauges with our flashlights. We then turned our flashlights off. The water was dark and the still night moonless. Sam spoke, "Let's descend," and then I could hear him deflating his buoyancy vest. We went down into the pitch black sea.

We descended straight down toward the sand bank at 130 feet, dropping into a black void. As I sank, I felt as if on the verge of panic. I couldn't see the bottom. I couldn't see anything at all! I lost track of which way was up and which was down. I knew, clearing the pressure from my ears, that I must be descending, but couldn't tell how fast or what position I was in. As I dropped, I tried urgently to pierce the void of darkness with my eyes. I wanted to see if there was a shark out there. I seemed to see circular shapes undulating in the deep. These unidentifiable forms added to my fear. I looked around, but was unable to see Sam. Beginning to panic, I reached desperately for my flashlight in my buoyancy control vest pocket, thinking, *OK, this is just getting too dangerous!*

Just then, I heard a dolphin's call. The sound of the dolphin jolted me out of my search for my flashlight. I then remembered to practice my mystical exercises. I realized that I was becoming tense and fearful in a tough situation. I started practicing the Holding the Ocean exercise and almost immediately became centered, calm, and relaxed.

The fear within me dissolved just as it had on the dive when I asked the ocean for healing. With no more alarm, I became aware of how intensely magical, beautiful and powerful it was to fall into the black ocean. From time to time, tiny, brilliantly blue sparks of bioluminescence trailed off from my fins and fingertips.

As I fell into the midnight sea, I could feel the turbulence of the water on my skin. The pressure on my ears forced me to clear them frequently by wiggling my jaw. I continued breathing calmly. Though I maintained the proper position for the Holding the Ocean exercise, I couldn't tell whether I was upside-down, right side up, or just tumbling into the darkness. As I continued my deep breathing, I felt a great light within my navel chakra as the darkness of the night's ocean absorbed me.

Moments later, I reached the sandy ocean floor. I saw Sam land in the marvelous bioluminescence of his descent. He must have been just a few feet above me. Resting upon the sand, Sam's movements, which had created the bioluminescence, quickly stopped and he vanished before my eyes.

I focused on deep, relaxed abdominal breathing and peered out into the impossible dark. I gazed out, seeing nothing but an occasional flash of bioluminescence from the sway of water.

A moment later, Sam grabbed my hand and began to swim forward and to the right. I had no idea why, but as soon as we stopped, I felt very different. The water seemed to take on an almost pulsing form. I looked again for Sam, but he was invisible to me again, still in the dark water.

Looking out into the silent deep, I began to make out a still, yet massive figure. It was a shark! It looked larger than any shark I could imagine. This was the Shark Chief, I was sure.

The Shark Chief hung motionless in the water for another moment, then turned and swam toward me. For some reason, I could see the Shark Chief more clearly as she approached, although there was no bioluminescence. I saw the Shark Chief as if she were a dream or a vision that defied the darkness. To my surprise the Shark Chief was not a Hawaiian tiger shark, but a massive great white!

I had faced my death two weeks ago when the lionfish had startled me, and at that time I had felt completely unready to die. This time I had chosen to come here to be judged by the most powerful predator in the ocean. As the Shark Chief approached, I asked her to help me in my quest for enlightenment.

The Shark Chief swam around me. I looked for Sam, but couldn't even see the bioluminescence caused by his bubbles. I had a feeling he wasn't even there anymore. As the Shark Chief rounded ten feet away from me, she dodged in at a sharp angle toward me with great speed! I reacted, jumping to the left and avoiding the shark's onslaught. In my leap, I bumped into what I thought was Sam next to me. I looked to Sam to see if he would give me any indication of what I should do, but it wasn't Sam that I bumped into. To my surprise, I found that I had bumped into a dolphin.

The dolphin was floating right where Sam should have been. The dolphin was as clear to my vision as if it were daylight. The dolphin called to me, making an upward nod with its smiling snout twice. My mystical lessons then became foremost in my mind. Having again remembered the importance of my training, I began practicing my chakra meditation, speaking the mantra "Om" in my mind with my breaths. I immediately felt a tremendous peace.

A moment later, I saw the Shark Chief coming in toward me opening her mouth and showing her many rows of teeth. *Surely this is the moment! She is coming in to kill me,* I thought, knowing that whether I lived or whether I died did not depend on my physical reaction.

As the Shark Chief plummeted towards me, I determined calmly and firmly, gathering my most focused attention, *I choose enlightenment!* The Shark Chief crashed into me teeth first, with a tremendous velocity. The Shark Chief bit across my shoulder and neck, yet I felt nothing and was unmoved by the attack. I saw the Shark Chief circle around and swim back to the deep, holding a dark ghostly body in her jaws.

The Shark Chief vanished. I looked to the left again, seeing the bioluminescent bubbles of Sam sitting next to me completely still. Sam stirred and began swimming toward the shore in an ascent. I followed him. At about 80 feet of depth, Sam turned on his flashlight. We slowly ascended, doing a long safety stop. Upon reaching the surface Sam said, "Congratulations, you have passed the second gate!"

I felt a great peace. I felt calm, as if the events of the evening were my own creation. I felt somewhere inside, that I had always known all of this would happen, and that this was my pathway to understanding myself.

DIVING INTO ENLIGHTENMENT

The next morning, I met Sam at his hotel suite for meditation. After a bright and peaceful meditation session, Sam bowed and said, "Today you will receive your initiation, and experience underwater Samadhi."

I smiled with excitement.

Sam and I readied our things and departed to our usual dive site in the southwest. Sam had me follow him separately in my car. After reaching the beach and parking, we assembled our dive gear.

Sitting next to me in the sandy beach area, Sam said, "First you will receive the ocean initiation. It is sometimes called the Blue Goddess initiation, because when you see the very spirit of the ocean, her true form, you see a beautiful Blue Goddess in your mind's eye.

"The initiation is a connection from your heart to the essence and spirit of the ocean. In taking initiation, you become part of this powerful spirit and learn lessons of liberation through this vehicle of the unseen-world. Initiation plunges your aura and spirit into the aura and spirit of the ocean. It creates a union through which you become a part of this blue wonder. It opens the deep, powerful nature of your own being. It washes away your past karmas and sweeps you into a greater connection of awareness, a deeper consciousness of your unity with all of being."

Sam paused to adjust his tank strap and then continued, "You have passed through the two gates of attention: the creation of the Whale God and the destruction of the Shark Chief. You have been forever transformed by the powers and divinities that live in the sea. Now, with initiation, you will become one with the whole of the sea. Are you prepared?"

"Yes," I said surely.

"Take your potion bottle with you," Sam said. "We will dive to 130 feet, below the human aura of the planet. There you will close your eyes and meditate on your heart chakra. We will descend far in the south at this dive site. We will be resting on a steep sandy slope as you meditate. During your meditation, I will conduct your initiation. With your eyes closed, look with your heart into the deep and you may see the Blue Goddess, the very spirit of the ocean herself.

"I will tap my dive wand on my tank twice when the initiation is complete. At this time, you should open your potion bottle and fill it with the water of your initiation. This water is a mystical aid to learning in meditation practice. You will find that meditating with this bottle of water on your altar or in your hands helps you still your mind."

"OK," I said.

"Then you will experience Samadhi. There is nothing in particular that you must do except be quiet and still. Just breathe deeply and enjoy your spirit's union with the ocean of being. After your underwater Samadhi, we will ascend to do a long safety stop in the shallow reef."

"Sounds perfect," I said.

Sam and I donned our SCUBA gear.

"It is time," Sam said, turning toward the ocean.

We entered the ocean and did a long surface swim to the south point of this familiar dive site. We swam far out, beyond where we had dived here before. I looked down to see that we had kicked out over the wall. As we floated at the surface of the water, I could see my favorite visitors to the cove approaching. Four dolphins split off from a pod of about a dozen and approached us. I was excited and started swimming toward them, but Sam seemed more focused on finding the proper point to descend.

Sam gave no instructions before giving the down signal. I quickly brought my attention away from playing with the dolphins and back to diving. I followed Sam and began descending. We descended down the coral reef to the sandy sloping wall.

Half-way through our descent, I could see the dolphins approaching us underwater. Two of the four dolphins excitedly joined us on our descent. We descended to about 130 feet and rested on the sandy sloping bottom. This far out from shore, the slope of the wall was very steep as we neared 130 feet. Reaching our maximum depth, I sat in the sand with my tank against the sandy wall and my feet stretched before me so that I would remain still. The dolphins whipped around us playfully. I began to meditate on my heart as Sam floated in front of me. I closed my eyes and concentrated with single-minded attention on my heart chakra.

After a minute or so, I felt a huge change! It was as if my chest had opened, as if something stuck was loosened and a doorway released its blockage. It was like a cool wave of cleansing light washed into my heart. I was awake in the waves! I felt alive, healed, and united with the light in the sea.

Though my eyes were closed, I suddenly had a clear vision. To my utter amazement, before me in the deep blue of the water appeared the Goddess! It seemed impossible, yet she was so vivid to my mind that her presence was undeniable. A beautiful, mature woman in flowing blue, white, and green robes floated not far away in the endless blue of the sea. She was dazzling to behold. She smiled with joy and her smile conveyed the spirit of the ocean's peace. Moments of this brilliant meeting passed, and then I heard the clinking sound of Sam's wand.

I didn't want the beautiful experience of the waves of light in my heart to end. The ocean Goddess began fading away from my vision into the deep. I smiled as the Blue Goddess descended into the ocean's heart. I opened my eyes, then opened my potion bottle and let the water flow into it. Sam was hovering completely motionless in front of me. The dolphins were still with us, swimming joyfully behind Sam.

Sam raised his right hand toward me and kicked closer to me. I stopped myself from following the dolphins' jetting movements. Sam rested his thumb on my dive mask, just over my third eye chakra. I closed my eyes and became immediately still.

The slight pressure of Sam's thumb on the top-center of my dive mask made my third eye buzz with a pleasant warmth. As I focused on my third eye, my thoughts slowed down, becoming distant. A peaceful feeling of quiet came over me.

My body felt light. I could feel the grains of sand beneath my hands as I shifted gently in the ocean's sway. My breathing was deep and calm. As I sat comfortably in the sand, my shoulders dropped and unwound. My neck muscles relaxed, allowing my head to naturally straighten. My stomach loosened, deepening my breathing. I could feel the tensions of a lifetime unraveling. My whole body felt the greatest relaxation and balance.

A distinct feeling of warmth started in my navel chakra, though I could still feel Sam's thumb against my third eye. The warm feeling filled my navel as I inhaled, and became foremost in my attention. The feeling expanded in my mind's eye to be a vision of the orange sphere of light. The sphere grew as I inhaled and shrank, intensifying in color and luminosity as I exhaled.

A moment later, the orange sphere of light overflowed. My visualization subsided as a surge of warm energy moved up my back. The energy moved up my neck to the top of my head, and down my front. This effortless Orbit energized my whole body.

When the warm energy had descended below my navel again, it seemed to explode upward. It shot straight up my spine to the top of my head with a tremendous velocity. As the energy ascended, it seemed to intensify, creating euphoric sensations throughout my body.

As the energy reached my head, I felt some kind of blockage, like my head was stopping the energy from flowing. This constriction seemed to close at my third eye. I could feel the intense bright energy pushing against my third eye, as if it were trying to beat down a closed door. My head started to feel full. The energy pounded within my forehead until I started to get a headache.

I felt Sam's thumb pressing harder on my third eye. A moment later, I felt my third eye open! The constriction loosened and the energy poured forward. It was as if the night had turned into day. A dark blockage gave way, revealing a bright white light before me.

My third eye buzzed with energy. With my inner vision, I peered into the light. The light was bright, white, clear, and distinct. Just gazing into the light brought me feelings of joy and peace. While I was experiencing these beautiful feelings, the light before me seemed to deepen, sparkle, and yet flow forward like clouds.

As I had a distant sense of Sam's thumb pressing my third eye, the light shifted. Before me was a dazzling ring of light. At the center of the ring shined a brilliantly bright white sphere, like a twinkling star. The shining sphere seemed to be impossibly far away.

As my attention drew directly into the sphere, I shuddered. Though the shining sphere was glorious to behold, it pulsated with a piercing light that felt as empty as death. Fear arose in me. Part of me wanted to retreat from the light, yet steadfastly gazing into the tremendous brightness, I felt something deep within me say *I choose enlightenment.*

My fear was gone. In that moment, I felt a sensation of rushing forward. I felt like I was on a rollercoaster, shooting toward the shining sphere. I moved forward through the ring of light. I transcended the great distance from the ring to the sphere with increasing velocity.

Rushing forward, the sphere of light grew before me like a sun. The light was intelligent and ancient. Looking into the shining sphere, I could see it stretch on into infinity. Entering the sphere, I had a sense of its light filling me. The deeper I drew into the light, the brighter I became. I felt transparent, like I was fading away into the light.

The light intensified. It started to pulsate with a strong vibration. I had no more sense of space. Now, there was only light, close and far. The vibration of the light took on an auditory quality. I could sense a distinct sound, formed by the pulsing light.

"Om." I could hear it distinctly. "Om." It initiated feelings of supreme bliss within my heart. All of the light was this sound. There was no separation from sound and sight. The light was Om and Om was the light. There was no separation from Om and me. I was Om, absorbed in perfection, free of all limitation.

My mind was shining, illuminated in the beautiful translucent light. Then there was only the light, a radiant unity of all being.

A moment or an eternity later, my attention drew back to the physical world. I opened my eyes, and the vision of the deep blue water reappeared before me. The words "Everything is perfect and I am completely free," glowed in my mind. I felt the greatest peace and clarity. I could hear the playful calls of the dolphins. Sam sat next to me, motionless. A dolphin whizzed by very close to us and Sam pressed his hands together and bowed.

Sam began carefully watching his dive computer. The perils of extending my no-decompression limit on a 130 foot dive suddenly came to mind. I looked to my computer. While it felt like I had only been there for moments, I now had less than one minute left at this depth. Sam gave me the ascend signal and I started filling my buoyancy vest with air.

Sam and I slowly ascended over the coral reef. I breathed in and out, observing the simple perfection of the fish, the coral, and the brilliant sunlight at the water's surface above us. I was completely relaxed, content, and at home in the ocean. I repeated to myself, *Everything is perfect and I am completely free.* The dolphins played around us as we surfaced.

At the surface, my amazement at the beauty of my experiences spilled over! As we made our way back to shore, I excitedly explained my feelings and experiences to Sam. He smiled and nodded knowingly.

"My mind," I said, struggling to find words, "...opened into... endless bliss! It was amazing! And I couldn't believe it: The ocean connected with me, and the Goddess was real. She looked as real as you and me."

"She is," Sam responded.

Sam smiled broadly as we disassembled and packed our SCUBA gear into the cars. I felt the greatest evenness and balance. I was awake and ecstatic, yet still and calm.

Sam invited me to sit with him in meditation. "Focus on your heart," Sam said softly. I sat up straight and began meditating on my heart chakra. My mind was perfectly still, calm, and bright. Meditation was automatic. I felt waves of light fill my heart and my thoughts instantly became silent. Sometime later, Sam signaled me to bow.

After sitting for a few beautifully quiet minutes, we got up and played in the water, snorkeling with the dolphins. Around noon, the pod left the cove, heading back out to sea. Sam and I returned to the beach to sit and meditate. The whole day felt completely blissful.

After our meditation, as the sun had just finished setting, Sam said, "In 18 hours I must fly home. I can do no more dives."

I nodded with equanimity at this news as I gazed at the glistening water in my potion bottle.

"Tomorrow, please come to visit me in the morning for meditation," Sam requested.

I nodded again in acknowledgement.

Sam and I departed at the beach, after which Sam bowed and headed north in his orange Jeep.

On my way home, I decided to stop by the dive shop to return my rented SCUBA tanks. While I was there, Michael looked at me with an uncommonly deep and peaceful gaze, and said, "You know, you've changed, Vanessa. Something about you reminds me of the ocean herself. Miraculous what you can experience diving into the sea."

"Yes, miraculous," I said, warmly.

When I reached home that evening, I was energized. I sat down and opened my laptop for a programming study session. My mind had never been clearer or more focused in my studies. To my surprise, some of the most difficult technical concepts that I had been struggling with now seemed clear and obvious to me.

In the late hours of the night, after making good progress in my studies, I closed my laptop. I stood and looked out into the dark night toward the distant ocean. With a feeling of accomplishment and empowerment, I looked at myself in the reflection of the window and said, "I'm ready."

I now knew what to do. Since my underwater Samadhi experience, my purpose had become clear. My uncertainty had vanished. The experience of Samadhi had given me a profound freedom from my limitations and dissatisfactions. It had given me an opportunity for life, for a better life, a fuller life, a life of happiness and endless possibility. I felt that I could share this joy and opportunity for life with so many that I had met in Ethiopia. I felt that I could offer them possibilities to bring them beyond the limitations of their circumstances. I was ready to begin giving. I would start a dedicated microfinance effort.

I will commit a percentage of my monthly income to microfinance, I resolved. *As my career grows, my giving will grow. I will get a high-paying job in the technology that I am learning. If I apply myself to my studies, I can get a high paying contract within three months.*

I carefully considered what percentage of my monthly salary to put toward microfinance. I contemplated the most generous amounts. I then deliberated over an amount that would make a difference and have the effects I wanted, but wouldn't be such a burden that my life would suffer.

Ten percent is right, I determined. I felt that many people in the United States could give 10% of their income to aid the poor without being overburdened by it. In my assessment, I would be able to live very well, have the things I need for my spiritual development, and make a significant impact on many people's lives.

As I lay down to sleep and pulled the covers to me, I smiled. Excited about my plans and finally content with my life, I was entirely happy. That night, I slept peacefully.

THANK YOU

The next morning, I made it to the Four Seasons at 8:30 am, our usual meeting time. Sam invited me to meditate with him on the patio. Though I was brimming with excitement and eager to share my new insights and resolutions with Sam, I found it quite easy to silence my thoughts.

At the end of meditating, right after bowing, I started in, telling Sam all about my realization. I excitedly explained all the details of my ideas. "After our last dive, all I could think was that I know what's right for me now and what I should do," I said. "I really want to put my microfinance plan into action."

"Very good," Sam said. "That's a fine plan."

He smiled, and said with a knowing flash in his eyes, "You are well on your way."

After a long pause, Sam said, "This financial goal to aid others will lead to your next step on the spiritual path."

"What do you mean?" I asked.

Sam continued, "It is your dharma to alleviate the suffering of others in the most powerful way possible. Following this path of service requires that you invest attention in yourself so that you can empower life-sustaining livelihoods for many families. And in the future, this path will lead to even greater possibility.

"In your resolve to hustle to get into a lucrative consulting position in the next couple of months, you will have to spend your energy and attention efficiently, and in doing so, you will have prepared yourself in terms of awareness, consciousness, and money for the next spiritual adventure.

"In the beginning and intermediate study, financial goals are a good way for you to measure your progress. The teachings are not supposed to be easy. The teachings are rare and challenging in many dimensions. In order to integrate the power and light of these mystical dives, you must apply yourself to physical life with focused attention. Money is a good measure of focused attention.

"To receive your next lesson, it is necessary for you to gain the karmic merit of giving to a spiritual cause. Your selfless giving to help others through microfinance is a spiritual cause. It is also an offering to your own spiritual evolution. The amount you give is as meaningful to the seen-world of microfinance as it is for your unseen-world of awareness, spiritual balance, and liberation. You tell yourself with every dollar that you give that both are valuable. And you're right.

"In the West, seekers often lack the etiquette of giving in a proper way. In the Far East, seekers are generous in their offerings to spiritual causes because it is commonly understood in their society that giving to a spiritual cause returns teachings, blessings, and good karma. In the West we just don't know that. So it's easier for us to challenge ourselves with goals that match our interests and that are aligned with the dharma."

Confident in my ability to succeed as a technology consultant, I recognized that it would be an honor to push myself to earn enough money to help others, and a privilege to learn such amazing spiritual lessons. *Giving people opportunities for livelihood and well-being through microfinance yields priceless returns,* I thought. *And underwater Samadhi is worth every ounce of gold on the planet.*

Sam paused for a moment, and then said, "Now, I'd like to give you some instructions for self-study for the time that we are apart, till our next meeting."

I smiled at the prospect of seeing Sam again on another Mystic SCUBA adventure.

"Continue your daily meditation practice. Meditation is the most important practice of all spiritual study. And get your PADI Rescue Diver certification. You're not really a safe diver till you learn rescue."

I agreed. I definitely planned to continue my meditation practice. Meditation had become a cherished experience in my daily routine. I also felt excited about becoming a PADI Rescue Diver. I could take the PADI Rescue Diver course on the weekends and complete it in a few weeks.

"And plan for our next meeting."

I listened eagerly.

"In eight months, you can come with me to dive with ocean dragons at the Great Barrier Reef."

"Dragons?" My imagination raced with intrigue.

"Yes," Sam said. "Dragons are the most amazing ocean creatures. They are also the most rare. Yet they are out there if you have the eyes to find them. But you'll have to learn about all of this next time."

I was delighted by the possibility of seeing dragons and diving the Great Barrier Reef.

"There, you will meet another teacher from my lineage and one of her students. She will show us the way to a very special place. She will guide us on a dive where we shall find the Dragon's Pearl."

"What's the Dragon's Pearl?" I asked.

"Have you ever seen a picture of an Eastern dragon?" Sam asked, as he picked up a spiritual book with a little hand-drawn illustration of a Chinese dragon on the back.

"Yes," I said, vaguely familiar with the image.

"Well, Eastern dragons are often depicted holding or chasing this ball," Sam said, as he pointed to the ball in the picture that the dragon was holding. It looked familiar.

"This ball is the Dragon's Pearl. It is a construct of dharma. Dragons are the symbol of enlightenment. Finding the Dragon's Pearl is a tremendous teaching of enlightenment, a powerful realization of dharma."

Sam had me write the trip information down, the date of our meeting in eight months, and the time to meet him in a restaurant at a luxury resort in Sydney for our two-week trip. Sam told me to reserve a room at the resort for two nights. "And then we'll play it by ear," Sam said. "Most of the time will be spent at sea aboard the dive boat.

"I'll be eager to hear about the progress of your microfinance plans," Sam said. "With 10% of your income as a technology consultant, you will have substantial cash to fund small businesses for the boys and women you know in Ethiopia, as well as others all over the world."

I smiled, knowing my way.

Sam bowed. I bowed in return.

Sam said, "Now if you take your leave to start your work, I will spend my last moments alone here in meditation by the beach till it is time for me to depart."

I smiled in acknowledgment and stood up. Sam closed his eyes and became completely still. I slowly withdrew back through the living room to the suite entrance. Before closing the door as I exited, I looked back and saw Sam meditating in complete serenity. Placing my hand over my heart I said, "Thank you."